THE WAY
OF THE GREEKS

THE WAY
OF THE GREEKS

by

F. R. EARP

AMS PRESS
NEW YORK

Reprinted from the edition of 1929, London

First AMS EDITION published 1971

Manufactured in the United States of America

International Standard Book Number: 0-404-02234-0

Library of Congress Catalog Number: 75-136393

AMS PRESS INC.
NEW YORK, N.Y.   10003

PREFACE

THE chief use of a preface is to warn the reader, should he chance to read it, of what he has to expect. In this case he must be told first that the title of the book is not intended as an allusion to popular fiction but refers to the Greek belief that there is a Right Way, or δίκη, of doing all things. As most of the following pages are devoted to expounding the nature of that 'Way', the word has a right to appear in the title.

Secondly, the reader must be warned that the book has two defects: it is sadly informal in style and arrangement, and, as critics will at once note, it 'falls between two stools'. It is neither a formal treatise addressed only to scholars, nor yet a handbook for the wholly ignorant. Both these defects spring from the same cause, an obstinate belief that the ancient Greeks are so interesting that others besides professed scholars must wish to know something of them. The number of popular handbooks proves in fact that such persons exist. But when the reader of such handbooks wishes to carry his studies a little further, he will find it difficult. For most serious works on the subject are equipped with a paraphernalia of notes, references, and quotations which deters any but professed students; and moreover they are often couched in a somewhat terrifying style. With the benevolent intention of making the way easier for such inquirers I have reduced this paraphernalia to a minimum, and have put what I had to say in an informal way. It is to be feared that even so these pages will be perplexing to a reader who knows nothing of the Greeks, but I have tried to produce something which will be intelligible to any one who has a smattering of such knowledge, and which a scholar may condescend to read in his easy chair. For the sake of any readers who are not Greek scholars I have usually translated and sometimes transliterated Greek words and quotations; and I hope that the presence of Greek words in the text will not intimidate them. They are not introduced from pedantry, but because most of them have no exact equivalent in English, and the Greek script helps to bring that home.

For the informality there is a second reason as well. The ground covered is wide and to treat all parts of it in due proportion would demand several volumes. I have therefore used a licence which would be improper in a formal treatise, touching lightly on familiar ground and dwelling at length on points less familiar, or where the current views seemed to need correction. These pages are therefore loosely strung, but there is a connecting thread, the attempt to distinguish the popular Greek view of things both from the modern, and from the views of individual Greeks, and to interpret the documents and monuments in the light of it.

The scholar will naturally feel this attempt to be superficial, as it is. My original intention was to give *in extenso* a number of passages illustrating the various points discussed with a commentary upon them. This would certainly have worn a more professional air, but would have infallibly repelled all but a few scholars. I have therefore chosen the present humbler course, and have perhaps failed in it. Nevertheless the conviction mentioned before is very strong. If we who teach and study the ancient Classics can only produce books for the use of our fellows, or for students under threat of examinations, we barely justify our existence. For the justification for the continuance of such studies is that they are of universal interest.

It is customary and fitting in prefaces to acknowledge

obligations to previous writers. One or two such acknowledgements are made in the text, and more are hardly
necessary. For since I projected writing on the subject I
have deliberately refrained from consulting modern writers
and drawn my conclusions from a re-reading of the Greek
authors themselves. To them I owe not only the ideas for
this work, but most of the inspiration for life. They are
beyond the reach of acknowledgements; but at least I can
acknowledge an obligation to the reader for the Press who
has detected many slips, and reformed some laxities of
grammar.

F. R. E.

CONTENTS

THE POWER OF TRADITION IN GREEK LIFE

THE history of Greece presents a paradox, which, so far as I am aware, has not commonly been remarked. That the Greeks in the space of two or three centuries, a minute fraction in the aeons of man's presence upon earth, achieved in most branches of human activity a progress wholly beyond parallel or comparison, this is the commonplace of all writers on the subject. But the way in which that progress was made has not been so clearly realized, or certainly not so often stated. It is indeed an unexpected way of progress, to our minds at any rate; and this may be the reason we have missed it, for we overlook even the obvious when we are not looking for it. We know that the Greeks were bold innovators, the rapidity of their progress proves it, but when we fix our eyes not on the results of their work, but on their method of working, we discern at first sight not boldness, but caution, even timidity, and meticulous following of tradition. This paradox deserves examination.

In the arts, especially those of which we know most, sculpture and vase-painting, this cautious following of tradition has not escaped notice. Every student of sculpture, for instance, is familiar with the 'standing male' and 'standing female type.' He can trace in them the slow and cautious modifications by which they were perfected. In vases too he observes the same slow modification in all aspects, in technique, in shape, in scheme of formal decoration, in the treatment and grouping of figures. He knows how the same little peculiarity in the treatment of eye or mouth, or of drapery, is repeated and repeated and imperceptibly modified. And more striking still, he knows how in dealing with the same theme from legend or life the vase-painter repeats again and again the same arrange-

B

ment of figures with small modifications. Greek Art, like Nature, *nihil facit per saltum*, and having found the scheme which best suits his purpose the artist is content to modify it.

In the case of Greek Art this point might be illustrated *ad infinitum*, but though its importance is not always felt, the fact is undisputed. Greek Art, especially in the Classical period, is unmistakably the child of tradition. It is in the other side of Greek life that the pre-eminence of tradition is more often overlooked. In the case of literature, for instance, no one who knows the poets well can be ignorant how often the same idea or form of expression, the same γνώμη (maxim), or the same simile, recurs. Literary histories in fact habitually point out that such repetition is not avoided by ancient taste. But the matter goes much further than that. It is not merely that the Greek poets borrow ideas or phrases from their predecessors. Nor is it even that the moulds in which their ideas are cast are traditional too; that the structure of a Greek tragedy or comedy follows a traditional form, that a Greek play compared with that of a modern playwright strikes us as strangely regular and simple and unvarying in structure; differing from it in fact much as a Greek Temple differs from a Gothic Cathedral. This is significant enough, but the influence of tradition goes deeper still. It is visible not only in isolated borrowings, or in general structure, but in the whole substance of the work.

This less obvious influence of tradition is harder to define and to illustrate. Any competent scholar can point to similarities of structure, or to echoes and borrowings of particular phrases; even elementary text-books sometimes do the latter. But only systematic study, with the clue in hand, brings home to the student how important this element is. This is no mere borrowing of an odd bit of riband or lace to set off the new garment; the new dress is made mainly of the same stuff, cunningly remodelled. No doubt there are, when the maker is a genius, strips of new stuff here and there, but the old garment is always there too. Anyone, to drop the metaphor, who sets out to trace in Greek Literature the recurrences of similar thoughts and phrases, is gradually overwhelmed by the mass of his material. He begins to feel that everything recurs; wherever he turns, he meets old friends. In fact he finds himself just in the position of the student of Greek vases, who recognizes at first glance the familiar episode, or familiar scheme, and then proceeds to note the variations.

In Literature we do not take these recurrences so much as a matter of course, but once the attention has been called to them we find them almost as common. In tragedy, for instance, the incidents may vary,—and in spite of the restricted choice of subject there is no lack of variety here—but as soon as the characters, or the poet through his choruses, begin to argue or to moralize, the same themes come inevitably to their lips. One can draw up a list of τόποι (stock themes), and safely wager that a large proportion of them will be found, in one form or another, in almost any tragedy.

Of these τόποι, the subject of ὕβρις (hubris) [1] of course comes first, but it would not be fair to argue from that alone, for ὕβρις is the proper subject of tragedy. The list includes other τόποι which are less obvious. Certain reflections on the nature of the gods, e.g. on their inscrutability, their power, and the consequent wisdom of accepting their gifts with patience; or conversely certain doubts and criticisms of their actions; these and many other topics are constantly recurring. No less constant are the τόποι which refer to human life; first and chief, of course, the injunction θνητὰ φρονεῖν (to have mortal, i.e. humble thoughts), and with it the praise of the mean, and of the mean estate, and of σωφρο-σύνη (sophrosune),[2] and a number of other reflections

---

[1] On the meaning of this word, which is very imperfectly translated 'insolence', see p. 210.

[2] Roughly 'temperance', but including sobriety of thought, and therefore often equivalent to 'good sense', or even to 'humility'.

almost as common. And more striking than these, because less expected, and more typically Greek, are some of the other τόποι; the ever-repeated antithesis of λόγος(word)and ἔργον (deed), of νόμος (custom or law) and φύσις (nature), the discussions on δίκη (justice), τυραννίς (tyranny), πλοῦτος (wealth), εὐγένεια (high birth), and their opposites, and especially the curiously expressed reflections on the difficulty of discerning a man's character.

The topics just mentioned are but a small selection from the whole list, but no mere list of topics can bring the point home fully. For with only a list before him a critic might well say that such a list, however long, does not prove that the Greeks were strongly influenced by tradition, but only that their stock of subjects for conversation was monotonously limited.

'Characters in a play', he might add, 'must talk about something, and the characters in a Greek Tragedy appear to have talked chiefly about the most obvious commonplaces. Their stock of commonplaces differs a little from ours, for they appear to have preferred nursery maxims to the weather ; no doubt a matter of climate.'

The only answer to this criticism is a careful study of these commonplaces themselves, and the use made of them; but the criticism itself reveals something. It is quite true that Greek Literature is full of commonplaces, and that the use made of them is quite frank and unashamed. For commonplaces deal with the things of permanent interest, and it is one of the marks of the Greek that he is never ashamed to use an old idea or phrase, when it is appropriate, and when the new would be less true to life. Men in similar circumstances do normally think and act and speak in similar ways; and when once the fitting expression of a thought has been found, the Greek writer no more scruples to use it because it is old, than the vase-painter scruples to use the established scheme for a pair of wrestlers, or combatants.

This use of established material is most obvious in the orators. In them, as all scholars know, we find the same τόποι repeated by different orators in almost identical words, often in a carefully elaborated and stereotyped form. They are used as frankly as a chess-player uses a recognized gambit, and are countered accordingly. The opponent sees the move, and at once knows the proper reply, or if several are possible, tries to choose the best. All this had been reduced to a system by the teachers of rhetoric, and so far is less remarkable than similar recurrences in other forms of literature; but the frankness and frequency of use are characteristic.

And when we study in detail the use made by the Greeks in various forms of art and literature of these recurrent themes, we find that they are more important than we have yet indicated. They are not only used more frequently and more frankly than by the moderns; they are not only an expedient, or, as in some inferior writers of the present, a substitute for thought; they are themselves often, and indeed most commonly, the vehicles of the writer's most serious thought. When the Greek thinks, it is usually in these forms that he thinks. And this brings us to a paradox beyond the first. Not only is the progressive Greek cautious and bound by tradition, but he seems to conduct his thinking by turning over in his mind a few commonplaces. And yet, by this curious and apparently confined process, he succeeded in covering most of the possible objects of human thought; so much so that, except in some branches of natural science, it is difficult to find a path on which the Greeks have not already blazed the trail. In thought, as in art, the Greek seems to have preferred to proceed by modifying and recombining a certain number of accepted patterns. The number of permutations and combinations, however, was so large that he was able in both cases to express himself as completely as if he had followed the modern method of inventing, or trying to invent, a new design for each new thought or subject.

The reason why the Greek preferred this method (or rather *a* reason, for only omniscience could explain the Greeks fully) is sufficiently clear, though perhaps not obvious. Greek life in all its parts rested on tradition; the presence of recurrent τόποι in Greek Literature is only one instance of a general truth. If we turn, for example, to the moral ideas of the Greeks, we find, not what we should expect in the case of a modern nation, a set of general principles from which particular duties, in theory at least, are deduced, but just the converse of this : a number of particular duties, some of them very ancient, such as the duty to suppliants and strangers, and to members of the clan or family, the observance of oaths, and others which are added later, but all resting alike on tradition. Tradition is in the first instance their only and sufficient sanction. Later on, with the birth of reflection and philosophy, general principles of justice and morality were derived from these particular duties, and these duties were then referred to the general principle; but the particular duties came first, and as late as the fourth century B.C. the average Greek still followed a set of isolated rules of conduct, of which the sanction was tradition.

And it is important to note that this sanction was to him sufficient. There are many moderns whose code of morals rests in fact on tradition, usually the tradition of a class. But if called on to justify his conduct a man would usually, in some vague way at least, endeavour to produce some general principle. He would feel that tradition or custom alone was scarcely enough. An ancient Greek would know and desire nothing higher than νόμος (custom); νόμος to him, as *mos maiorum* to the Roman, needed no higher sanction; it was the ultimate tribunal.

It is not a disproof of this statement, but rather a confirmation of it, that we find the authority of νόμος sometimes questioned in later times. For this merely illustrates the Greek method of procedure as already described. It is in fact the clearest example of it. The Greek takes the traditional maxim as his starting-point, and looks at it in the light of his experience, or, if he is a dramatist, in the light of the imagined situation, and expresses or implies his criticism, or his acceptance, accordingly. Thus Sophocles in the *Antigone* investigates the claims of traditional duties in conflict, and even those of νόμος itself. Thus the gnomic poets, and sometimes the dramatists too, tacitly or overtly correct or modify the maxims of some predecessor, these maxims themselves being usually modifications of some traditional sentiment. Thus even the philosophers habitually use these traditional maxims as a starting-point. Aristotle, in particular, does this systematically, and much of his teaching, in the *Ethics* especially, is a glorified and philosophized version of this traditional lore. In the study of philosophy the use made of traditional matter is a useful clue, for philosophers may be partly classified by their attitude towards it, and, secondly, the originality of any view can often be most conveniently tested by this standard.

This brings us to the most useful application of our study of tradition. Not only in philosophy, but elsewhere, scholars who neglect this clue at times go astray by taking as original thought what is traditional; or conversely by citing as typically Greek what is eccentric or individual. Such mistakes, as we shall see, have been the origin of much controversy and misunderstanding, especially in the region of Greek moral ideas and religion. Of such errors the most obvious is the common belief that Greek Religion was moribund by the end of the fifth century B.C. This belief, though it is not without plausibility, springs from a misapprehension of the nature of Greek Religion, and that misapprehension springs in turn from neglect of the clue provided by the study of tradition. But the nature and effect of this mistake is typical of many and therefore deserves consideration.

In all historical studies the first essential is to get the background right. Till this is done our interpretation of the facts will be grotesque. The Middle Ages, as we know, turned the heroes of Greek legend into paladins and set them in a background of chivalry, and made them act and think appropriately to the setting. No modern scholar would do this. The externals of life, furniture, dress and institutions are carefully studied. But the inside, the furniture of the mind, is harder to ascertain, and even when it is known, is sometimes disregarded. The classical studies of Walter Pater, in spite of their charm, illustrate this conspicuously. His Greeks and Romans, Marius for instance, or his young Spartans, are curiously, for all his care, un-Greek and un-Roman. They belong at the earliest to the Middle Ages, but they hardly belong to any real age. It is rather as though the light upon them were cast through stained glass. The shapes are correct, but the strange lights and colours make them seem unreal.

The mistake that many scholars have made in regard to Greek Religion is similar in kind, though less picturesque in its effect. The average Englishman, even among those who have real knowledge of external fact, usually sees Greek Religion, not indeed in the fantastic colours of stained glass, but in the colder light of a white-washed Protestant conventicle. That is to say, he conceives of religion as a matter of belief and conduct, in which rites and ceremonies, and other external forms of expression are unessential and even suspect. When the beliefs in regard to the nature of the gods are freely attacked on all sides, and abandoned by most of the educated, as they were at the date mentioned, he naturally concludes that the basis of religion has been destroyed. And he cannot set against this loss any influence of religion on conduct, for this, though not absent in Greece, is not present in the form he chiefly expects.

Other scholars, who have carried their study one stage further, escape perhaps from this error, but fall into another, and still fail to get the background right. Scholars naturally and almost inevitably form their notion of the Greek from literature, and chiefly from the poets and philosophers, and in spite of what has been said of the power of traditional ideas in Greece, poets and philosophers can never be reliable witnesses in regard to the thoughts of the average man. The philosophers inevitably, and most of the greater poets in fact, though they start from popular ideas, are critical of them, and the views they express are often not typical, but individual. Their evidence therefore must always be tested by evidence from outside.

Where this evidence is to be found is not at first obvious, for unfortunately most of Greek Literature is in this matter suspect. Nearly all the later writers, even when not professional philosophers, are touched by the influence of philosophy. Our first task is therefore to seek for evidence that is not suspect, and to decide by what tests it can be known. Till this is done we have no firm ground beneath us, and we must postpone for the present full statement or proof of our thesis.

We are in search then of the views of the ordinary Greek, but before we begin the search one objection must be met. Scholars will remind us that there were material differences between the Greeks of different states and periods, and may ask where our average or ordinary Greek is to be found. The answer to this objection is that the study of the evidence reveals a fundamental likeness in ways of thought which clearly distinguishes the Greek from the 'barbarians' of his own day, and from modern nations. This justifies us in looking for an 'ordinary' Greek and his ideas. For convenience we shall usually drop the qualifying 'ordinary'. Some of the differences mentioned will appear incidentally, but where no distinction is drawn 'the Greek' will mean the ordinary man of the classical period.

II

SOURCES OF EVIDENCE FOR THE TRADI-
TIONAL GREEK VIEW

IN our search for the views and beliefs of the ordinary
Greek it is plain that Greek Literature, for reasons
already given, must be used with caution. But this does
not mean that we must reject it wholly, or we should be
poorly off indeed. We shall find that a certain part of it
can be used almost without reserve, and much more may
be used safely, when due reserves are made.

Before we discuss the evidence of particular writers,
however, one point must be mentioned, though it is too
obvious to need elaboration. When any idea is found widespread in literature and is exemplified by all the works and
words of the Greeks, as for instance the idea of the 'mean',
it would be waste of time to search for evidence that it is
typical. In such cases we have only to notice the forms
which the idea assumes and its effects in application. Not
many ideas are quite so universal as this. Many, though
widespread, are not universal, and in such cases we have
to determine whether they are typically Greek, or
characteristic of a class or period.

For our purpose the evidence of literature is obviously
the most important. Other things, such as art and institutions, are even more trustworthy and often serve to correct
or illustrate the literary evidence, but without literature
they could not be clearly interpreted. And for our present
purpose the writers whose evidence is most valuable are
the orators. As orators in general, and the Greek orators
in particular, have no high reputation for sincerity or
truthfulness, this may seem surprising, but the reason is
plain. Poets, philosophers, even historians, naturally and
habitually express their individual opinions, and these
must often differ from those of their neighbours. They
may be, and often are, more enlightened, but for that very
reason they are not good evidence for us. The evidence

of the orator on the other hand is valuable to us, even
when he is palpably lying. For an orator, if he wishes to
persuade, must take the standpoint of his audience and
address himself to their actual beliefs and ideas; and his
audience are *ex hypothesi* average men. Very possibly
the orator does not share their beliefs himself, but that
is no matter; for if he is wise he does not make the mistake
of talking over the heads of his audience. It follows that
we can deduce from the orators more safely than from
other writers the ideas of the average Greek.

Even with the orators, however, some caution is needed,
but common sense suggests the necessary reservations and
distinctions. It is obvious, for instance, that speeches
addressed to juries in the law-courts are better evidence
than political harangues. For in the latter there is likely
to be more cant, if not more falsehood. Insincerity in
politics is not new, and the political orator often addresses
himself less to the real feelings and beliefs of his audience
than to the things they are expected to believe and feel.
This distinction, however, is not very important to us,
for what people are expected to believe is evidence of the
moral standard of the time. It is unlikely that an orator,
however much inclined to flatter, will attribute to his
hearers feelings or ideas which are quite alien to them. We
have only to remember that the standard is likely to be
pitched a little higher than the truth, and make the
necessary deductions.

The orator is likely to make his audience a little more
patriotic, a little more pious and high-principled than they
really are, but he will certainly not do the opposite. And
arguments drawn from silence are in this case specially
trustworthy. When the orator refrains from appealing to
some sentiment or belief which would strengthen his case,
and would seem natural to a modern in like case, we may
be sure that that sentiment or belief was not general. Thus
it is significant that in the funeral speeches extant none of
the orators uses the topic which would come naturally to a
modern speaker, that of immortality. It is at most men-

tioned as a possibility, but never used as a topic of con-
solation.

There are one or two other cautions necessary in the
use of the orators. Though we have seen that they
endeavour to fit their sentiments to their audience, they
do not all succeed equally in so doing, and there are other
differences.

Of all the orators Lysias is probably the most to be
trusted, for, as all his readers know, he has a unique
power of sinking himself in his subject. He puts on the
character of the man for whom he pleads, and speaks as
that man would speak to a jury of his countrymen, if only
he were a little more practised in oratory. We have
the authentic voice of the ordinary Athenian of the day.
The personal traits by which the speakers are indivi-
dualized, such as the swagger of the young cavalry officer
in ὑπὲρ Μαντιθέου, only make them more characteristic.
Thus Lysias, so far as he goes, is precious, but unfortunately his extant speeches leave many topics untouched.

Next to Lysias comes, perhaps, Andocides. That
plausible rogue, like others of his kidney, thoroughly
understood the popular mind and how to appeal to it.
He illustrates the ideas and sentiments of his countrymen
as the popular Press illustrates those of modern England.
It is a pity that we have no more of him. Isaeus, again, is
very valuable. He has not the power of identifying himself with the speaker, as Lysias has, but he is a very skilful
and practised advocate. He never forgets the jury and
what they will be thinking. Though all his extant speeches
deal with cases of disputed wills, he throws invaluable
light on Greek institutions and on some aspects of
family life.

Hyperides is another orator who appears to speak to his
brief, but the fragmentary and corrupt state of his speeches
hardly permits of a definite judgement, and in the *Epitaphios* we must make the allowances usual in funeral
orations.

The value of the other orators is less easy to estimate.

Antiphon, the earliest, is in some points unique. The curiously stiff and sententious style, the obvious tricks of rhetoric, the subtle and, to us, sophistical nature of the reasoning in some parts, the coldness even where appeals to emotion seem natural—all these give an air of unreality even to the speeches which were really delivered. It is hard to believe that they were ever addressed to a jury, for they often recall the speeches in Thucydides rather than those of the later orators. Yet some of them were addressed to juries, and we must conclude that at the date when they were delivered, in the last quarter of the fifth century, such oratory was effective; for Antiphon was a recognized master. Athens about that date had been carried away by the oratory of Gorgias, whose grotesque and luscious style of ornament would only provoke laughter in a modern audience; and other Sophists had created a taste for intellectual subtleties. Compared with them Antiphon is sober, and we cannot doubt that his speeches were meant seriously, and were so received.

Such speeches, then, were made, and the style is no proof that Antiphon is out of touch with popular feeling. Still it is possible that he was talking over the heads of his audience; he certainly has not the genius of Lysias for entering into the feelings of the common man. But, even if he misses the popular note, this does not seriously affect his value for us. For we go to Antiphon chiefly for evidence in regard to Greek ideas on the subject of murder, and the ideas which we find in him are indubitably old and primitive. These ideas he obviously has not derived from the Sophists, however they may have affected his style. In these matters he is obviously no 'intellectual'. It would be more natural to say that he is a bigoted and unintelligent conservative. But if he is that, his evidence is all the more valuable; and we may safely accept him as a guide to the ideas which are embodied in Athenian Law. Whether those ideas were still current in his day is less obvious. If we thought only of the philosophers, we should deny it, but we shall find some of the most primitive ideas about murder taken for granted by orators at a much later date. Antiphon therefore, in spite of the suspicions he rouses, may be trusted.

In the case of another orator, Lycurgus, the suspicion that he may be talking above the heads of his audience is better founded. He is a moral reformer who combines two incompatible ideals. He looks back with regret to an ideal Athens of the past which he would fain restore, and he is tinged with the philosophical ideas which helped to subvert the old order. He has something of the tone and character of a preacher, and though sincere, he, like many preachers, is sometimes a little out of touch with the real world. He must have appealed to his contemporaries in much the same way. It is pleasant sometimes to be given visions of a better world, however unattainable; and Lycurgus and his contemporaries found their Heavenly City in the glorified Athens of the past. But such visions are not good evidence of men's weekday thoughts and actions. On such things Lycurgus, though a more truthful man, is a less useful witness than Andocides, for we cannot be sure that he gives us the normal point of view.

A similar suspicion attaches to the evidence of Demosthenes, though not quite for the same reason. For all his skill, we cannot be sure that he understands the mind of the ordinary man. We know that he was personally unpopular, and that his enemies ascribed to him the character of a prig and an ungenial recluse; and his works themselves show that he lacked geniality and sense of humour. They have the narrow intensity and harshness, if not all the moral fervour, of a revivalist preacher. He delights in pointing out the sins of his auditors and in drawing grim pictures of their inevitable consequence. A man of this temper can never be entirely in sympathy with the minds of common men and with present reality; and the career of Demosthenes shows that he was not. He, like Lycurgus, had a vision of an ideal Athens which obscured his sight of the present. His public speeches therefore not only have this characteristic of much political oratory that the orator, once on the platform, speaks and even thinks in a different language from that which he uses in common life, but they are sometimes suspect on another ground. Even in his soberest moments, Demosthenes may misread the facts. He did, as we know, misread the minds of his countrymen; for though at times he carried the people with him, at others he sadly misunderstood their temper; a thing which has happened to many a well-meaning statesman since.

These weaknesses obviously belong chiefly to the public speeches of Demosthenes, and we are more concerned with what are known as the Private Orations. But even the value of the latter is impaired if Demosthenes was out of touch with common men. His success as a pleader shows that he cannot have been so altogether, and for our purposes he is in these speeches usually trustworthy. Though the ardent student of Thucydides can hardly have shared the popular view on all topics, he had skill enough to assume the popular standpoint when his vision was not obscured by his political enthusiasms. He is not a Lysias, but he succeeds well enough. We can allow for a certain characteristic bitterness and intensity.

Unfortunately many of the speeches current under his name are spurious, and each of them must be judged on its own merits. The majority seem to be, for our purpose, trustworthy enough. In one point at least they (and all speeches actually intended for delivery) are necessarily trustworthy, whatever the character of the speaker. When a speaker refers to customs or institutions which must have been familiar to the audience, we can safely accept his statements. The Greek orators could, and did, misrepresent verifiable facts, falsify quite recent history, misquote laws; but, however unscrupulous they were, and however gullible their hearers, they would not state what the dullest auditor knew to be false. And fortunately for us much of the evidence is of this unimpeachable kind.

The speech of Aeschines κατὰ Τιμάρχου is a case in

point. Whether his version of the particular facts in question is true or false, we can at least trust his account of Athenian practice in regard to one unpleasant aspect of morals. In his political speeches on the other hand he is at least as suspect as Demosthenes. He has indeed a passion for platitudes and commonplaces which should be an advantage to us in our search for the common man; but the fustian which he puts off on his audience in the guise of political and moral wisdom is such poor stuff that he can hardly have taken it seriously. It suggests the stump-orator so bemused with clap-trap that he has lost all touch with reality. Aeschines in his delivery is said to have aped the dignity and restraint of the earlier orators, but if he or his audience took such stuff seriously, it is a measure of the decline of intelligence in Athens since the days of Pericles.

The voluminous writer Isocrates hardly comes into our field; for though reckoned among the orators, he is rather an essayist or publicist, since his chief works were not intended for delivery. He is therefore not bound to keep on the plane of the common man, and in fact does not do so. Accordingly his evidence must be received with the same reserve as that of other authors, and all the more because he is by way of being a philosopher.

There is a further reservation to be made in regard to the orators. All but Antiphon belong to the fourth century, and it may seem rash to take them as evidence for the ideas of Classical Greece. This is a real difficulty, and if they stood alone, we might scruple to trust them; but comparison with other evidence seems to show that, in spite of the criticisms of philosophers, the main ideas of the multitude were not deeply changed before the time of Alexander. One advantage of concentrating the attention upon popular beliefs and usage is that it enables us to fix more precisely the date of such changes. If we think too exclusively of the great poets and philosophers, we antedate them. And this, as we shall see, has a bearing on the interpretation of literature, and especially on some stock debates. Thus Sophocles in the *Oedipus Rex* is accused by Professor Murray of 'moral obtuseness' on the ground that he believes Oedipus morally guilty, and defended by Mr. J. T. Sheppard on the ground that he does not. We have endeavoured to show elsewhere [1] that both argue from false premises and ascribe to Sophocles a moral standpoint which is not his.

Next to the orators the gnomic poets furnish good evidence. With them there is always a chance that any particular judgement may be personal and not typical—in Theognis, for instance, the cynical tone is clearly personal—but the leading ideas recur so frequently and in such similar shapes, that real doubt can seldom arise. In the rest of the early poets the individual character is more marked—there is no mistaking the personal tone of Archilochus, for instance—but the same criterion will serve in their case. And in both alike we are at least sure that their ideas have not been sophisticated by philosophy. Later on a recurrent idea may be a commonplace of the schools and not a piece of traditional Greek thought.

The value of Homer and Hesiod needs closer examination. With both poets the difficulties, for our purpose, are the same: first, to decide whether the poems are homogeneous, and secondly, what is their relation to later Greek thought. The question of date and origin does not concern us directly, but if it can be shown that the poems of Homer not only are formed from parts composed at different times and places, but contain discrepant views of life and the world, this clearly does concern us. Such discrepancies do occur, and have been pointed out by commentators, but happily few of them affect points essential to us, and those that do can be dealt with in their place. As to the second difficulty, the relation of Homer to later Greek thought, though there are obvious differences, such as the Homeric regard for women, and many others due to a different organization of society, yet careful comparison shows an unexpected continuity in essentials. The most

[1] See Chapter XII.

D

fundamental ideas of Classical Greece are already present in embryo, the idea of the mean (μέτρον) and its transgression, ὕβρις (hubris),[1] of αἰδώς (aidos), of δίκη, of νέμεσις (nemesis), and so on. Some of the ideas which we find later are naturally lacking in Homer, for they apply to things unknown to him, and some others appear only in a crude form, but the germs of the later ideas are there.

If we contrast Homer, not with later Greece, but with the literature of other races, e.g. with the Old Testament, or with the Icelandic Sagas, the fundamental unity and continuity of Greek thought stands out more clearly. All three races have a definite outlook on life, in all three there are characteristic and fundamental ideas constantly recurring, though the Hebrew does not echo the exact phrase so often as the Greek, and the Icelandic hero expresses his idea in action more often than in words. When we put the three side by side, we see that each race lives in a distinct world of thought; their ideas and the springs of their conduct are different.

It is not till we reach the age after Alexander that the Greek world changes fundamentally. Then indeed we have in many ways not development of the old Greek tradition, but subversion of it; and the Hellenistic age is more remote from the fifth century than Homer is. In that age and later the Classical Greek view of life, like the Epic dialect or the Attic, is preserved artificially, and imperfectly understood.

Homer, therefore, in spite of the differences of date and paraphernalia, may be used as evidence, and his early date is in one way an advantage. For, coming before the age of conscious philosophy, he reflects the general mind even more certainly than the gnomic poets. This statement of course cannot be proved beyond dispute, and even an attempted proof would demand a volume, but except in one point I believe that most scholars will accept it.

That point is Homer's treatment of the gods. To many

[1] The meaning of these words is discussed later, see especially Chapter XV.

modern readers, especially those of Protestant or Puritan sympathies, this treatment seems often irreverent, and at times, as in the lay of Demodocus and in the Διὸς ἀπάτη, grossly unseemly. And this unseemliness is more conspicuous in the scenes on Olympus and in the conversation of the gods themselves than in the rest of the poems. This difficulty has led to various theories. Some critics believe the more offensive episodes to be later interpolations; others hold that the society for which Homer wrote was exceptionally frivolous and sceptical, and seek for such a society in the Ionian Colonies in Asia Minor or elsewhere. If either of these theories is true, it is plain that Homer becomes a doubtful witness; but we give reasons elsewhere for thinking that both assumptions are unnecessary.[1]

It does not follow that Homer is to be used uncritically. A phrase or an idea here and there may be due to interpolation. One or two passages notoriously contain moralizing allegory or personifications more in the spirit of Hesiod than of Homer. But such things are not very important to us, for we are not concerned with the details of mythology, or the special characteristics of the Homeric Age; how much or how little conscious moralizing it achieved. It is enough for us if we can trace the leading ideas of morality and religion that run through the poems and find them to be in general consistent, and to contain the rudiments of later ideas.

Of Hesiod we may say much the same. The origin of the poems attributed to him is obscure enough, and for the student of mythology or theology they bristle with difficulties. But his poem, the *Works and Days*, the one with which we are chiefly concerned, bears on its face the character of popular and traditional wisdom, and is therefore a capital document. The points in which he differs from Homer are familiar: the more gloomy view of life, the bitterer tone, the constant moralizing and sententiousness, and so on. These things give a very distinctive flavour to Hesiod,

[1] See Chapter X.

and point to a difference of place and date and social conditions; but they do not make Hesiod less typical. The groundwork of moral ideas is the same that we find in Homer before, and in the gnomic poets after him. There are some modifications, but no radical difference. The writer of the *Works and Days* has evidently had bitter experiences, and his view of human nature and of his age reflects them, but this merely adds a personal colour without destroying the outline. Nor is he less typical because he consciously moralizes. The doctrines he preaches belong to the common stock; he is not an innovator. Even the gnomic poets and the Seven Sages after him did not often reverse, though they often developed, the common maxims, and Hesiod is less an original thinker than they.

It would be a different story if we were dealing with theology or mythology. In both these we find elements which, whether they originated from Hesiod or not, are unique and puzzling. But the only thing in Hesiod's theology that much concerns us is that he preserves unedifying legends in a cruder form than Homer. This is all the more remarkable because his theology is in some respects purer and his gods not so safely removed from moral responsibility as Homer's. This fact has an obvious bearing on the question of Homer's treatment of the gods; for few will maintain that Hesiod's offence in this particular is due to a light and frivolous spirit.

Of writers later than the beginning of the fifth century none can be used without reserve, but all furnish useful matter when used with care. The character of each writer appears plainly enough from the use he makes of the stock themes. Thus Pindar is full of such themes. He uses them critically, sometimes modifying them, sometimes giving them a deeper meaning, sometimes even rejecting them, but his thoughts as a rule run in the familiar grooves. Much the same may be said of Herodotus. Though, from the nature of his subject, his views are often presented indirectly, his comments are simple and abundant, and it is not hard to discover his attitude. Like

Pindar, he is sometimes critical, and coming later in time, is not unconscious of the earlier philosophy and sophistic, but like him, he belongs fundamentally to the stage of the gnomic poets. He is rooted in tradition and his criticisms are usually simple modifications of it. Both these writers, of course, have one or two characteristic and recurrent ideas—such as the doctrine of the φθόνος θεῶν (envy of the gods) in Herodotus—which give a personal colour to their work.

With Thucydides we are on very different ground. Though he, like the philosophers after him, inevitably thinks in the Greek fashion, he is as far as they from a naïve acceptance of traditional views. Everything with him has been deliberately weighed. He does indeed frequently make use of traditional ideas and formulae, and his history often illustrates their importance, but without evidence from outside we could not be certain with him that any idea is typical. Often, especially in the speeches, he introduces the stock phrase or idea only to criticize it or turn it upside down. That device he had learned from the Sophists, and he never tires of it, though unlike them he always uses it to express a real thought.

The Three Tragedians again cannot safely be used as a source for traditional ideas. They are indeed full of them, but they use them more in the spirit of Thucydides than of Herodotus. Frequently, of course, they put the familiar idea in the mouth of a character unchanged, but quite often it will be controverted, or its opposite asserted; and it is therefore only by comparison that we can tell which is the traditional view. Not uncommonly indeed both views may be traditional, for proverbial philosophy often embodies the opposite sides of a truth. Thus on subjects like νόμος and φύσις, wealth and poverty, high birth and low, the faith or faithlessness of friends, there are obviously two sides to the question, and proverbial philosophy expressed them both. The Tragedians often avail themselves of this either for purposes of debate or to bring out their own views. Their great value to us is not that they provide us with new elements of the tradition, but that they prove and illustrate the depth of its influence. These statements apply to all the Tragedians alike, but certain differences between them are worth noting. Euripides, contrary to expectation, furnishes us with by far the largest store of traditional maxims. Seeing that he is the furthest removed in thought from the common beliefs of his time, this is at first surprising, but the reason is quite simple. He is full of debates, as all his readers know, and these traditional γνῶμαι furnish for debate at once the favourite themes and the readiest arguments. Moreover, Euripides more than the others reproduces common life, and these stock arguments were just those used by the common man, or at least the common orator.

In Sophocles, on the other hand, though he is nearer in mind to the traditional views than either of his rivals, the use of traditional maxims is less obtrusive. They are present, but they are woven into the texture of the work, and spring so naturally from the occasion that they seem spontaneous. The wonderful lines in the *Oedipus Coloneus*[1] beginning

ὦ φίλτατ' Αἰγέως παῖ, μόνοις οὐ γίγνεται
θεοῖσι γῆρας οὐδὲ κατθανεῖν ποτε

are built up of the most familiar themes, but so aptly used and so transmuted by genius that they seem a new creation. That passage might stand beside one of the great works of fifth-century sculpture. In either we have old material, and modest innovation, and yet the work has the freshness of dawn and never fails to stir the mind with the shock of sudden beauty.

Aeschylus again differs from both. He is at once the most and the least traditional of the three dramatists. His ideas are derived from the common stock, and he makes

[1] Lines 607 ff. The lines are untranslatable, but Prof. Gilbert Murray's version preserves something of the cadence of the verse, as well as the sense.

use of the traditional γνῶμαι frankly, but to those which chiefly dominate his mind, his spirit has given an intensity and depth which makes them in essence new. In moral problems he takes us into regions which the clear-cut sanity and moderation of ordinary Greek morality cannot plumb. Though he is no hostile or captious critic of tradition, and his questions rise from the searchings of his own mind rather than from the study of philosophers, he brings home more forcibly than almost any writer of the age the incompleteness of the Greek view of life. He is more formidable to orthodoxy than Euripides, in much the same way that the Book of Job is more formidable than Voltaire. The questions he raises are prior to the belief in any particular mythology; and it is against mythology that Euripides levels most of his shafts. Aeschylus, if he can be assured that Zeus is just, is not greatly concerned with any minstrels' tales (ἀοιδῶν δύστηνοι λόγοι, as Euripides calls them). If they are wrong, he can create better. There is no need to be angry, and he is not. It makes the likeness between him and Job the greater that both of them, though so formidable in attack, believe themselves counsel for the defence.

After the tragedians it is natural to mention Aristophanes, but he furnishes less material than might at first sight be expected. It is true that in his views he is thoroughly conservative, and so far should furnish good evidence; but the burlesque turn that he gives to his characters no less than his plots distorts the image. We feel that we have before us the prejudices and extravagances of his countrymen rather than their settled convictions. No doubt the latter can sometimes be deduced, but without other evidence we should often be puzzled. Hence we get from him illustrations of familiar points more often than new matter.

Another comic writer of a different date and character, Epichármus, would, to judge by his fragments, be most instructive, if we had more of him. He is indeed more than tinged by early philosophy; but his fragments are full of matter and provocative.

The later writers of Comedy, too, are instructive. Their fragments abound in tags of popular morality and philosophy (partly no doubt because so many of them are preserved by Stobaeus, who collected such passages). But they must be used with caution because by the middle of the fourth century the influence of new ideas is creeping in. They illustrate the tradition abundantly, it is true, but their great value is that they show how far the influence of philosophy—and at a later date of foreign ideas too—had permeated. It is from them that we most clearly perceive that after 300 B.C. we are no longer in the old Greek world. It is a world still coloured by the old habits and ideas, but vitally different. The history of art confirms this belief. Hellenistic Art either turns to new paths, or where it uses the old themes treats them in a new spirit. It is dealing with a legendary past, and plays with it almost as a modern artist may play with classical themes, or as the pre-Raphaelites played with the medieval. When it most tries to recapture the spirit of the old, you feel most clearly that the old is dead, and only lives when a new spirit is breathed into it, not with its own proper life. Archaistic art owes any life it has not to what is old in it, but to what is new.

One author, however, whose works belong to the fourth century, Xenophon, is among our most useful sources. Though he has some acquaintance with philosophy, his temper, fortunately for us, is thoroughly conservative and conventional. Though relatively so late, he preserves almost unimpaired the mind of the early fifth century. His intercourse with Socrates had quickened his intelligence and purified his morality, but on every page he shows that he has no taste for philosophical speculation, and his method of defending the master whom he loved was to show that Socrates was in spite of appearances a pious Athenian of the good old type. We need not doubt that he does this honestly and that this was what he actually saw in Socrates; his odd habits and his taste for raising queer discussions were just an amiable eccentricity. So an old-fashioned country gentleman might regard a friend of university days who has somehow turned himself into a Bishop or a Professor. He knows that in spite of his weaknesses he is a good fellow and a sportsman at bottom.

The fact that Xenophon in spite of intercourse with Socrates was able to retain a mind so little tainted by new-fangled views is strong evidence that he is a fairly safe guide to the traditional Greek view. He is a little more intelligent and humane—Socrates had purged him of some of the cruder ideas of Greek morality—but allowing for this we may follow him safely, remembering of course that in some of his political and moral ideas his sympathies are rather with Sparta than with Athens. Both Socrates and his own life had influenced him in this. But when so much of our material is drawn from Athens, this bias of his helps to redress the balance and remind us that Athens is not Greece.

After Xenophon there is no witness whose evidence is generally trustworthy. Ideas were changing and we can only accept the evidence of later writers when the manner of its introduction guarantees that the idea in question is a genuine part of the traditional stock. Thus Aristotle, fortunately for us, often refers explicitly to the popular view on any topic he is discussing, and though Aristotle is late and the popular view of his day does not necessarily coincide with that of earlier ages, he often illustrates or confirms the other evidence. And apart from particular instances his whole conception of morality has its roots in traditional ideas. In that sense indeed Aristotle is the strongest of all witnesses to the strength of the tradition. His pupil Theophrastus likewise furnishes useful hints.

Three late compilations also are very useful, the *Florilegium* of Stobaeus, Diogenes Laertius, and the collections of Paroemiographi. Stobaeus, a writer of Christian times who collects passages under various heads, such as the virtues and vices, with a view to moral edification, is well worth study. Many of the passages quoted come from late authors, but he gives the source of each quotation, so that we are forewarned, and a careful comparison of the passages under each head is very instructive. For by comparing them we can descry the process described elsewhere by which a traditional view is taken up by later writers and developed or criticized, as the case may be. In fact any one who desires a short cut to the traditional ideas on many subjects will do best to turn to Stobaeus, provided he keeps his eyes carefully on the source of each passage.

Diogenes Laertius is useful in a similar way but chiefly in his first book. The ideas and sayings there attributed to the Seven Sages and to other early philosophers repeatedly confirm and illustrate the evidence gathered from other sources. It is impossible to prove the authenticity of all the maxims cited, and some are attributed to more than one author, but most of them bear the stamp of the age to which they are assigned. They show early reflection working upon traditional maxims. Some are simply terse statements of the traditional view, others modifications of it, some few are definite contradictions of it, as when Pittacus is reported to have said 'forgiveness is better than vengeance'. In that he rejects the view held by most Greeks at a far later period.

The Paroemiographi are less easy to deal with, for we cannot be sure of the date of any particular proverb unless it happens to be cited by some classical author, and many of the proverbs in our collections are manifestly late. Thus it is unsafe to draw conclusions from any particular proverb, but taken together they have a certain value. They illustrate Greek modes of thought in various ways, and they confirm our impressions on some points. They are, for instance, somewhat cynical in tone and show a mistrust of human nature which recalls Hesiod. Thus there are many proverbs about friends and friendship, but these more often warn us of the unfaithfulness of friends than praise their faith. And the maxims in general are cautionary rather than encouraging, thus recalling the prudential character of Greek morality. We must not make too much of this, for proverbs in all languages are apt to be cynical and cautious, but still this side of them is more conspicuous in Greek proverbs than in English, for instance. There is something hearty and friendly in some English proverbs and popular sayings, 'It's a poor heart that never rejoices', and the like. We find less of this in Greek.

The study of Greek proverbs brings out other characteristic traits. One of these is the love of the concrete and personal. Innumerable Greek sayings and proverbs have reference to particular places, persons, or events, historical or mythical. Sometimes the allusion is familiar, but very often the incident or person is quite unknown, or would be so, if it were not for the explanations given by our authorities. For instance, what we call 'asking for trouble' is expressed by two proverbs Οἰνόη τὴν χαράδραν and ὁ Καρπάθιος τὸν λαγωόν 'Oenoe . . . the watercourse' and 'The Carpathian . . . the hare'). We are told that the first saying refers to a time when the farmers of Oenoe in Attica damaged their farms by injudiciously tapping a watercourse for purposes of irrigation, and the second to a plague of hares in the island of Carpathos, the inhabitants of which rashly introduced hares into their island, and suffered as Australia suffered from the introduction of rabbits. In some cases the explanation appended in our collections is plainly absurd, and in others it may well be due to a late exercise of the mythopoeic faculty. But, however that may be, these sayings show once more how persistently the Greeks loved to give concrete form and substance to any idea. Such a form is much less common in our proverbs and sayings, though the instinct appears at times. It was marked in the case of Mr. Sam Weller, and he, though unusually gifted, was sufficiently typical.

The instances quoted show another feature of Greek proverbs, or rather popular sayings, for they can hardly be called proverbs. They are so elliptical that without a clue they are unintelligible, and those which appear in Classical authors often puzzle the later commentators. It is highly probable that some puzzles in our texts of Classical authors may be unsuspected scraps of such cryptic and abbreviated sayings.

The proverbs illustrate again another side of the Greek character. A large number of them contain allusions, nearly always disparaging, to the inhabitants of a particular town or district. To this we have few parallels in English proverbs, and though there are a few such sayings current, especially in the North, about the inhabitants of various towns or counties, these usually have only a local currency. Neighbouring towns or counties are sometimes jealous of one another, but they know too little of those at a distance to be jealous of them. This difference brings to light a curious fact. The Greeks, divided as they were in sympathies and in locality, seem, if we may judge from their proverbs, to have known enough about one another to create and preserve these references to local peculiarities. Doubtless it was often a neighbour who originated the unkind saying, but the saying, once uttered, had more than local currency. It would hardly have been preserved otherwise, and, more than that, several such sayings occur in literature in a way that proves them well known. Now we are accustomed to dwell, not without reason, on the divisions of the Greeks and the differences between them. These sayings are a useful reminder that, divided as they were, and much as they quarrelled, the Greeks seem somehow to have known more of one another, and to have taken more interest in one another, than the inhabitants of different parts of England at the present day. To the native of a manufacturing town in Yorkshire the towns of Devon are at most places where some people go in the summer. To an Athenian Seriphos or Thera, tiny islands both, was a known place with local characteristics, and a history. Communications were difficult, and geography was not taught in schools, but he knew that much. How he knew it is hard for us, who depend helplessly on rapid means of transit, to imagine; but that he did know it is important, and it helps to justify us in treating the Greek world, in spite of local diversities, as a living whole. It confirms our belief that there was a way of life and a way of looking at life common to most Greeks of classical times, and distinct from the ways of other times and races.

III

THE TRIBAL NATURE OF GREEK MORALITY

WE have already seen that Greek morality was based originally on a set of particular obligations, not consciously derived from any general principle. Before we examine these particular obligations in detail it will be convenient to notice one consequence which sprang from this state of things.

It is the commonplace of historians that Greece was ruined by internal dissensions, and the inability of the Greeks to form any stable union or confederacy. This inability is explained in various ways, most often by geography. Communications, the historian says, were so difficult that disunion was natural and combination hard to maintain. This is no doubt true, but the Greeks performed so many astonishing feats that, had this been the only cause, they would not have been baffled by geographical obstacles. Another and more potent cause is found in that feature of their morality which we have mentioned. The Greek acknowledged duties to those who were bound to him by special ties, but in regard to the rest of mankind, to man as man, he was under no obligation except such as were imposed by the feeling of αἰδώς; 'decency' we may provisionally translate it. Though the number of acknowledged ties gradually increased and the restraint of αἰδώς grew more effective, even the Greeks of the fifth century had not quite outgrown the stage in which men not bound by any tie are naturally hostile, and 'homo homini lupus' still holds good. That point comes out most clearly of all in the orators, but it is illustrated in countless ways, as the examination of particular duties will show. The point is too important to be treated incidentally and the chief evidence may be mentioned here.

For the Homeric age proof is hardly necessary, for it is common knowledge that while certain ties, such as those of kinship and tribe, were very strict and the duties

attached to them were clearly defined, no duty was owed
to men outside these ties, unless, like suppliants and guests,
they were under the special protection of a deity. But it
is not so often realized that a state of things not very far
removed from this persisted till much later. The evidence
is not at all recondite, but this is one of the cases in which
our prepossessions hide the obvious. The Greeks are so
civilized, in many ways so enlightened, that we unconsciously ascribe to them modern ideas of humanity, and
we are wrong in doing so. This is proved not by isolated
acts of cruelty, or by barbarous institutions such as slavery,
or even by the judicial torture (βάσανος) of slaves. If
these were proof of barbarity, we should have far to look
for a civilized nation.

The strongest proof lies not in the faults of the Greeks,
but in the character of their virtues. Among these the
Greek conception of friendship comes first. Greek Literature is full of the praise of friends and friendship, and
Greek story has noble examples of disinterested and devoted friends. Friendship called forth the deepest feelings
of the Greeks. In its highest form it was more honoured
than the love between opposite sexes; it was felt to be
more profound, and, so far as the Greeks conceived
romance, more romantic. Moreover the obligations of
friendship were very real and binding, and were normally
honoured even by those whose friendship fell far short of
romantic devotion. A man in danger could look to his
friends for defence, a man in need could look to them for
help in money; and in both cases he seems usually to have
received what he asked. The refusal conferred a stigma.

So far friendship among the Greeks seems at least as
real and as noble a thing as it is with us. It was certainly
more important, both as a motive and in its practical effects.
It was also more clearly defined, and that in two ways. The
obligations implied were determined by custom as well
as by personal feeling, which with us is the sole arbiter; and
secondly a man knew very definitely who were and who
were not his φίλοι. With us the line between friendship and

acquaintance is not sharply drawn even in our own minds, though some persons would definitely fall on one side or the other. There are very few of whom we would ask more than the small courtesies which one may expect of an acquaintance, or even of a humane stranger. Tried by this standard our friends are few, fewer perhaps than those of most Greeks; but on the other hand these acquaintances and kindly strangers are more friendly to us than the persons outside his definite circle of friends were to the Greek. The line is certainly less definite with us. Whether this is loss or gain is less clear, but the Greeks do not suffer by the comparison.

Some other aspects of the Greek φιλία are less pleasing. Friendship is praised, and sometimes very nobly, but more often than not the praise is based not on the spiritual, but on the material advantages of friendship. A friend is valued as a resource in trouble and a defence against one's enemies; the man without friends is defenceless in a hostile world. A friend in fact is an ally, and valued accordingly. As with states συμμαχία (alliance) implied φιλία (friendship), so with individuals φιλία implied συμμαχία. We shall see that this view of friendship is typical, and it implies that to the Greek even his fellow citizens, when not bound to him by the tie of φιλία, were potentially hostile.

It is the same with other ties. The Greek is surrounded, as it were, by a series of concentric fortifications against the outer world. Of these the innermost fortress includes his nearest kin and friends, the outermost wall embraces all Hellenes. In the case of an Athenian, the intermediate defences were formed successively by the bonds between φράτερες (phrateres), δημόται (demotai), φυλέται (phyletai) and πολῖται;[1] and outside the πόλις there was the weaker

---

[1] There is no precise equivalent for these bodies in English institutions. In fifth-century Athens the *polis*, or state, was divided into ten artificial *phylae*, or tribes, and these again into *demes* (originally local units or villages, but later determined by descent), and *phratries*. Of these the *phylae* were important units in the political and military system, and the *demes* too were of some political significance; the *phratry* was concerned with the private life of the Athenian citizen, and served among other things

tie with allies, Athenian colonists, and even with all Ionians. But these last ties concerned the state more than the individual, and the tie of Ionic blood was more a sentiment than a definite obligation, though at times it had political consequences. These were the natural lines of defence for an Athenian. They might be crossed by other lines, by voluntary associations such as political clubs (ἑταιρεῖαι), but at Athens at least, in normal times, these were not prominent.

Of these defences the innermost were far the strongest, and the outermost the weakest. To his friends and relatives a man could look for help in all his needs, with much more confidence than he can at the present day. He could expect sacrifices from them, and they were bound to support him on pain of dishonour. In the case of a quarrel, or a lawsuit, they were bound to support him against strangers, even if he were in the wrong. This at least appears from the evidence of the orators to have been the common and accepted view, and it illustrates very plainly the defensive nature of social ties. Naturally this primitive conception of duty did not pass unchallenged in later times.

The tie between members of the same deme or phratry figures less often in literature, but several passages in the orators show that it was real, and probably more important in Athenian life than literature suggests. It is clear that the members of a phratry looked to one another for support and sympathy, if not for such sacrifices as might be expected from friends and relatives. Even the members of a deme were bound by a far closer tie than members of the same village in modern England, and the public opinion of fellow demesmen or phrateres was evidently a powerful motive.

The tie of the πόλις, strong as it was against the outer world, had not much binding force between individuals.

to register his birth and marriage. All these bodies had a definite organization with officials of their own, and the members of each were united by the observance of religious rites proper to itself.

F

An Athenian is not restrained from injuring an Athenian by the scruple that he is a fellow citizen. If the man is a stranger there is no disgrace in injuring him; if he is personally unfriendly (ἐχθρός), there is even merit in so doing. It follows naturally that the ties outside the πόλις meant even less to the individual.

The relations to allies and colonists were based, as with us, chiefly on self-interest tinged with a sentiment of kinship, or with gratitude sometimes for past services. The most notable difference is that the tie of Hellenic blood was in one way more important than the tie of nationality now. It was not that the Greek loved his fellow Greek more than the Englishman or Frenchman loves his countrymen, but that he distinguished them more sharply from foreign nations. There were certainly things permissible in the case of foreigners, which were not permissible in the case of Greeks. To enslave a Greek city, though such things were done, was an outrage that left an indelible stain. Here again emerges the idea that obligations exist only where there are definite bonds.

This stands out even more clearly if we turn from the friendships of the Greeks to their enmities. The self-respecting Greek owed injury to an enemy as he owed service to a friend. The wish of Medea that she may be beneficent to her friends and deadly to her foes is not, as the beginner in Greek would think, the mere personal expression of her temper; it is a recognized principle of Greek morality. Not unnaturally this principle was criticized by the moral philosopher, but long after Socrates had argued that to injure another is to injure one's own soul, we find orators still appealing to the old doctrine as an accepted principle. A man avows and claims credit with the jury for his desire to injure an opponent who is his personal enemy, and, more striking still, feels it necessary to apologize for prosecuting a man who is not his personal enemy. To support a man in the law-courts was only justified, in popular sentiment, by ties of kin or friendship—then it was obligatory. To attack him was only justified by personal enmity or friendship with the opposite side. Professional advocates therefore often try to show they have some such justification for appearing. For this there is doubtless one motive which is not present now. Every litigant at Athens was anxious to show that he was not a συκοφάντης[1] or professional informer, and this helps to explain the practice. But even allowing for this it is significant. We cannot imagine a modern counsel insisting, as a special claim to the favourable opinion of the jury, that his client has a long-standing feud with the defendant, and would never have thought of bringing the case otherwise. Such a claim would prejudice him with a jury which does not think it meritorious to hate your enemy.

It is therefore quite clear that for the average Greek your duty to your enemy was not to forgive him, but to pursue him relentlessly. In fact the Athenian of the fourth century B.C. still felt with Achilles that there was a slur on his character for manliness until he had injured him in return enough to square the balance. The average Athenian, and we may safely say the average Greek, still thought so in spite of the protests of new-fangled moralists. Socrates and Euripides and others had protested, but their protests did not prevail with the multitude at first. Later, in the third century, we see from the writers of the New Comedy and others that the tide had turned. Not only is forgiveness less dishonourable, but humanitarian sentiments of various kinds creep in. The slave, for instance, is a human being, and even dares to tell his master so. But Aristotle's doctrine of the 'natural' slave (φύσει δοῦλοι) shows how bold an innovation this was even then, though Euripides had dared to voice a like sentiment. But these

---

[1] Blackmail at Athens often took the form of bringing, or threatening to bring vexatious charges in the courts, usually in the hope of being bought off by the party threatened, but sometimes for various other motives. The number of allusions in literature shows that the practice was common, for the defects of the legal system offered scope for it, and συκοφάνται (sukophantai) were a dreaded class.

changes, so far as the multitude is concerned, definitely belong to the later period, to the decline of pure Greek morality. The Stoics, cosmopolitan rather than Greek, spread such doctrines far.

In the works of Seneca we see the transformation complete. His conception of man's duty to man is modern, and sometimes, as in the *De Beneficiis*, this writer, now unfashionable and counted insincere (but who shall cast the first stone?) shows a delicacy of feeling which is rare even now. We are far indeed from that state of society in which even friendship was commonly regarded as an alliance for mutual advantage and defence. The causes of this change were many, but only one concerns us here. Political changes had broken down the old concentric circles of defence which we have described, just as changes of a different kind are breaking through similar defences now, and man, left naked, has no defence unless he can find it in his claims as man. The essence of the change in both cases is this. In the earlier stage we have strong and definite ties, of birth, locality, institutions, with real obligations attached to them, and pay for these the price of limited sympathies; in the later stage we enlarge our sympathies, and pay for this by the dissolution, or at least the slackening, of the earlier ties.

This contrast of course is not absolute. It would be absurd, and contrary to the evidence, to assume that all Greeks exactly followed the traditional scheme. Some rose above it, or fell below it, as men always will. There were disinterested friends and men of wider sympathies in Greece, as there are narrow local patriots and self-seeking friends now. But the contrast is none the less real, and owing to the strength of traditional ties and of public opinion, conformity to the standard was commoner in Greece than in modern countries.

And this standard explains some things in Greek life and history which without it would be surprising; the Athenian treatment of Melos and of Mytilene, for example, or the Corcyraean massacres, and some instances of callousness in private life especially in regard to women. Of the instances mentioned the treatment of Melos is by far the most startling; for in the other cases there had been provocation, and the fault was only the excess of an indignation justified by Greek feeling; though that excess was so shocking that it calls forth from the reserved Thucydides his excursus on the demoralization produced by the Peloponnesian war. Even that demoralization does not explain the unprovoked attack on Melos or the final treatment of it, which even Thucydides seems to feel can only be explained as an instance of the madness which the gods send on those guilty of the sin of ὕβρις. It undoubtedly shocked Greek feeling deeply.

The explanation of this, and of the other lesser outrages, is surely to be found in that feature of Greek morality which we are discussing. In the heat of anger we talk of doing outrageous things—there was ferocious talking during the war—but when it comes to the point, we do not do them. With twenty centuries of a humaner creed in our blood we cannot. The 'brotherhood of man' is an offensive phrase, most often insincere, but it has this much truth in it that we now find it almost impossible in cold blood to slaughter a human being like an ox. Brutalities due to passion and outrages by individuals occur often enough, but the nation could not coolly sanction massacre.

Bloodshed in the repression of disorder, even when necessary, is always repugnant, and is resorted to with reluctance. Even the retired Colonel of the newspapers, who suggests that strikers should be shot down, would be very slow in giving the order to shoot. Humanity with us has become an instinct, with the Greeks, even the Athenians, it was an aspiration. They aspired to be humane, and sometimes were, but passion and interest were often too strong.

This may be put in another way. Humanity was no part of the traditional morality, except so far as αἰδώς in a generous mind might stretch to cover it. ἔλεος, οἶκτος,

ἐπιείκεια (which answer roughly to 'mercy', 'compassion'
and 'sweet reasonableness'), were things on which a man
(or in the case of Athens a state), might pride himself, but
they were rather special graces or works of supererogation
than necessary duties. Their tenure therefore was precarious. How precarious it was is shown conspicuously by
the speech which Thucydides puts in the mouth of
Pericles, in which he avows that the Athenian Empire is a
'tyrannis', the thing most hateful to Greek sentiment.
There can be no serious doubt that the ascription of this
avowal to Pericles is historical, and coming from Pericles,
at Athens, it is a very clear proof how weak the respect for
the rights of men was. It is not that other states then and
in modern times have never been guilty of similar aggression; there are instances enough, especially in the history
of Renaissance Italy and modern Prussia. But they have
always been felt to outrage European morals, and not
many have ventured openly to avow or justify them. The
name of Machiavelli, their supposed defender, to quote no
more modern instance, is still a word of reproach among
men. Such things fall below our standard, and the nations
and the statesmen who practise them have an ill name.
But Athens claimed to be, and was, the most humane and
enlightened state in Greece, and Pericles her most illus-
trious statesman. The states whose rights she violated
were naturally indignant, but this does not prove that
their own standard was higher. History in fact shows that
it was not; it was clearly lower. We therefore see that in
the most enlightened state in Greece at its most glorious
hour it was possible to avow and act on principles which
now would mark out a statesman or a country for reprobation.

The conduct of Athens can be explained in various
ways. Some may prefer to say that Athens only did and
Pericles only avowed what all men do in like case; that
Athens was less hypocritical than we, and that is all: this
talk of a moral difference is moonshine, and we are making
a work about nothing.

Those who prefer this explanation are welcome to it. There always have been some who believed this of human nature and always will be, and argument will not convince them. Others will think that in the conduct of the Athenians we have merely an instance of that very sin of ὕβρις (hubris) and of its attendant infatuation which is the standing theme of Greek moralists. ὕβρις it was undoubtedly, and we need not deny the consequent infatuation. But the explanation is incomplete, for it does not tell us why ὕβρις was the besetting sin of the Greeks, or why the Athenians, with their eyes thus open, fell into it. The explanation of both is the same; that the morality of the Greeks was still in a sense tribal. The really binding ties were still very narrow. When even within the πόλις you scrupled little what you did to your enemy, and took credit for injuring him, your sense of obligation to those outside cannot have been strong. By the time of Pericles some ties of humanity were acknowledged in theory, but they had not yet become an instinct. Even when there were definite and formal obligations, as there were between Athens and her allies, these were not strong enough. In times of stress only those parts of morality which have become a rooted instinct will bear the strain. The Athenians approved and applauded humanity, but neither they, nor any of the Greeks at this time were humane by instinct. Therefore they were never proof against ὕβρις in this form, the wanton invasion of men's rights when pride or interest prompted it. The history of the Greek states and the lives of individual Greeks illustrate this abundantly, and we can now see the reason. That the reason assigned is true is all the more certain, because the Greeks were, as was natural, always on their guard against ὕβρις, and except in this form seldom gave way to it. Of ὕβρις in one conspicuous kind, defiance of the gods, the Christian sin of Pride, we find much less in Greece than in some other times and places.

It is at once a proof and a cause of this limitation in Greek morality that society in the Greek states was founded on slavery, and that Sparta, the other state which, in a different way from Athens, served as a model for Greece, showed in the case of the Helots a more marked disregard of right than Athens with her allies. For in the case of Sparta the aggression had become an institution and met with no effective protest before the time of Epaminondas.

In regard to the instances of ὕβρις on the part of Athens it is fair to say that there was a special cause besides that mentioned. In the age of the Sophists, as we know from many sources, the doctrine that might is right, and that justice is only the will of the stronger, and other paradoxes, had become fashionable, and it is clear enough that Pericles and some at least of his audience were familiar with them, and had been in part seduced by them. This certainly contributed to the aberration; but on the other hand it was an aberration, even to the Athenians themselves. Nietzsche, in founding on such aberrations his doctrine of a higher morality, which deliberately sacrifices the weaker to the stronger, and claiming the Greeks as his supporters, is inverting the truth. The Greeks were climbing out of the slough of barbarity and had not yet shaken off all the mud, and sometimes slipped back again. But they did not claim the mud as a distinction. Pericles in the speech mentioned does not claim the title τυραννίς as a new glory to Athens, but excuses it as a necessity.

IV

THE CONTENTS OF MORALITY

THERE is no point on which modern preposessions
mislead us more than when we enquire what things
are sanctioned and what are forbidden by the Greek code.
In spite of the familiar commonplace that morality varies
with the climate, the codes of all civilized nations have
much in common; and this is certainly the case when we
compare the Greek code with our own. Even if we make
the Decalogue our standard, the obvious differences are
few. The Greeks have no Sabbath, though they have
religious festivals and holidays in plenty; and they had
very clearly no scruples on the subject of graven images,
though they were aware that some foreign nations had.
But with the Greeks, as with the Jews, adultery, murder,
theft, and false witness are forbidden; duty to parents and
to God, after the Greek fashion, are enjoined; envy is
recognized as a vice, and taking the name of the Lord in
vain, as the Greeks understood that offence, was a very
grievous offence indeed.

Again, if we take the list of virtues as codified by Aristotle, we find a correspondence, in this case of course not
accidental, in the list of cardinal virtues, though the
specifically Christian virtues are naturally lacking. Even if
we take the list of the Seven Deadly Sins, there is a superficial correspondence, though the Greeks would have
interpreted most of the terms somewhat differently.

This superficial likeness conceals the real differences.
All know that differences exist, for some lie on the surface,
such as those already mentioned, and certain differences
in sexual morality, and in the obligations to various classes
of human beings. But it is more important, and less easy,
to realize that the difference runs through the whole code.
The words which designate particular acts or qualities
scarcely ever mean exactly the same to the Greeks as they
do to us; at the least they have different associations, and

often the divergence goes far deeper. And secondly, even
when the meaning of the terms is the same, the point of
view is different. The reasons for approval or disapproval
are not quite the same, and the circumstances under
which the Greek would approve or disapprove a particular
act are not the same either. He would apply Aristotle's
categories, the 'when', and the 'how', and the 'how much',
and so on, all the things that go to make up the character
of an act, very differently.

This difference is naturally least in regard to the pro-
hibition of definite acts, such as the first four mentioned
in the list given from the Decalogue. As Aristotle himself
says, no question of right degree or manner can arise in
regard to acts which are unconditionally wrong, as in the
case of adultery; and the same principle applies almost as
simply to the other three offences. Nor in these cases can
there be much ambiguity of terms; adultery, theft, and
false witness are definite and unmistakable, and though the
definition of what constitutes murder varies according
to legal codes, the act of killing at least is unambiguous.

But such unequivocal terms are few; the equivocal are
legion, and the more important of them will be dealt
with separately. A few instances will be enough to show
the difference between the Greek point of view and the
modern. The chief and greatest difference is that the
Greek is dominated everywhere by the omnipresent idea
of the 'mean' (τὸ μέτρον). Its omnipresence is familiar
enough to all students of Aristotle, but here, as elsewhere,
he reflects the general mind of Greece. The mean, according to our notions, has its proper place in certain departments of ethics; in the control of desire, for instance,
whether it be desire for physical pleasures, or external
goods, as wealth. But in things we admire and think
good in themselves a little extravagance rather pleases us
than not.[1] If it has painful results, we sympathize with
the sufferer and rather admire than condemn him.

[1] I speak, of course, of the popular view, not that of the professed
moralist.

Thus Love is accounted a good thing, and we admire the man who thinks the world well lost for love. To a Greek that same man would seem not admirable, nor even amiably foolish; he would seem foolish, indeed, but he would also seem not amiable, but mad; that is to say, wicked. To love madly, to the Greek, is not romantic, it is pernicious; its only excuse is that the power of Aphrodite, when she comes in all her strength, is hard for man to resist. This feeling of the Greeks is partly due to their conception of love, a matter to be discussed elsewhere; but the instance brings into sight, perhaps more clearly than any other, one reason why the Greeks were dominated by the idea of the mean.

The devotion to the mean springs in part from the nature of Greek theology. The gods are very powerful—from Homer on there is no question of their power—but they were not originally, and in popular belief never became moral according to human standards. Of deities like Aphrodite, who personify natural forces (whether in man or outside him), this is especially true; but even the higher gods, even Zeus himself, are not exempt. Even if we ignore his mythological failings, and affirm his justice, his dealings with man are at the best inscrutable. Even to Aeschylus it is much clearer that he punishes wrong-doing than that he protects the right. The Greek is always at the mercy of powers whose actions are in part incalculable. This was so as late as the fifth century, and much more so during the centuries in which the Greek view of life was being shaped. He had established in various ways a *modus vivendi* with the divine powers, but it was precarious.

It is customary to say that the Greeks were not oppressed by superstition. Many indeed would say that this was their chief distinction, and the chief cause why they so far outstripped the races that had come before them; that they were the first race whose mind was not in fetters. This is true in part, and it is important, but without further definition the statement is misleading. The Greeks

were not priest-ridden; that at least is a safe statement.
It is also true that the ordinary Greek was not oppressed
by fear of cruel and exacting deities, or by terror of a world
to come. The Greek race was hardly *oppressa gravi sub
religione*, as some races before and since have been.

But nevertheless things were not so easy with the Greek,
nor the world, supernal or infernal, quite so smiling, as
some of his admirers think. We cannot altogether ignore
the countless obscure cults and beliefs, many of them
barbaric and awe-inspiring enough, which the pages of
Pausanias furnish in abundance, and which modern
archaeologists have made familiar. We may indeed dis-
miss them as local or exceptional, or as limited to the less
enlightened districts and classes, but at least they lay
in the background and some of them must have been
familiar to all Greeks.

And the case is not much altered by omitting these.
We may admit, if we like, that a belief in lycanthropy was
not common outside Arcadia, or that the various ἱεροὶ
λόγοι, mysterious tales of the gods, which Pausanias
mentions but will not tell, were no part of the general
belief; but unless we fix our standard very high indeed,
we shall find such ideas and practices widespread everywhere. If there was no horse-headed Demeter at Athens,
for instance, there were Hecate and her attendants, there
were ghostly heroes, there was Zeus Meilichios and the
Διὸς κώδιον, the odd rites of the Thesmophoria, the
Diipolia, the Anthesteria, and innumerable others; and
behind them again the σεμναί (the 'awful ones', i.e. the
Furies) and the Eleusinian mysteries themselves, both of
them barely civilized and made respectable. All these
existed and were accepted, if not with undoubting faith—
faith in the modern sense, as we shall see elsewhere, is no
essential part of Greek religion—yet with acquiescence.

We see indeed from some ancient criticisms, e.g. from the
Δεισιδαίμων of Theophrastus, that excessive attention to
such things was ridiculed by the fourth century, but excess
in all things is deprecated, and Lucian's *Philopseudes*, among

other documents, shows that many of these beliefs survived till the second century A.D.; they cannot have been moribund in the fourth century B.C. Still stronger evidence is furnished by Xenophon and the orators. If in them we do not find all the more obscure or absurd superstitions, we find enough. In Xenophon, especially in the minor works, we find that life is full of little observances, omens, and precautions; life and happiness depend on observing them. Even in the *Anabasis* he and the whole army recognize as a matter of course the omen given by a sneeze.

Now we cannot have a better witness than Xenophon. Even if, with some of his commentators, we rate his intelligence as low as that of the retired Colonel, that butt of those who do not know him; still he was an Athenian of decent education, and some experience of life, and had moved in good society, even in what we should call cultured society. We cannot easily suppose him more superstitious, or less intelligent, than the average Athenian. It is a mistake to fix our minds on Euripides or the circle of Pericles, or on the great authors whom we read. Euripides satirizes superstitions, Thucydides notes oracles and omens with scientific indifference, Plato treats them with a sceptical respect; but none of these are typical. Xenophon is typical, and therefore, on this point he outweighs them all.

The Greek, then, if not superstitious, was (shall we say ?) circumspect in his religion and morality: piety, εὐσέβεια, was not far removed from prudence, εὐλάβεια. He knew more clearly what the gods forbade than what they required him to do, except in regard to forms of worship. Cheerful and beautiful as some of his rites were, they were more often an insurance against evil than an assurance of blessings. The gods did favour the pious usually, but you never could tell. Offence was easy, and if you escaped offence, still, in the common belief, gods were capricious. The idea of the φθόνος θεῶν, the envy of the gods, was

never far away. Though poets and philosophers tried to
give it a moral ground, the common man still held the
belief in its cruder form. The gods did not like to see a
man too prosperous or too successful, or above all too confident in the continuance of his success or prosperity.
Therefore the only safe course was to seek the mean and
adhere to it in his thoughts as well as in outward things.
Not to do so is a sin, and often the Greek sees sin where
we should only see a little over-confidence or rashness.
The Oedipus of the *Oedipus Rex* is an instance.

This principle of the mean is as fundamental in the
moral ideas of the common man as in those of the philosopher. We have already noticed some instances, but a few
more will help to show how far the principle reaches.
We as a rule see a vice only in the defect of a good quality;
the Greek sees it equally in the excess. To him rashness is
a vice as much as cowardice, extravagance as much a vice
as avarice. Though, as Aristotle notes, one extreme may
be nearer to the mean than the other, both are vices.
Hence the Greek often condemns definitely extremes
which we may dislike, but shrink from condemning, or even
think meritorious. Temperance in the use of wine and
other bodily pleasures, temperance in the pursuit of
honour or wealth, temperance in thought, temperance
even in religion; these are right and laudable; excess in
either direction is wrong. Thus all whom we should call
'cranks' or fanatics are not merely annoying to the common man, they are in the eyes of a Greek vicious.   More
than that their vice is serious, and may provoke the anger
of heaven, for it implies lack of σωφροσύνη (literally sound or
sane mindedness), and in some cases amounts to dementia,
ἄνοια; and ἄνοια is a very serious matter indeed.

The Greek dislike of extremes included all forms of
asceticism, and enthusiasm in the eighteenth-century
sense of the word. It was this that helped to make the
mystery cults suspect, for they were open to both charges.
And the suspicion that philosophers erred in this way contributed to their unpopularity. In the *Clouds* of Aristo-

phanes it is the pallid cheeks of the student as well as his heterodox views that come in for ridicule. Plato alludes to this when he says in the *Phaedo* that the multitude think that philosophers are 'ripe for death' or 'sick to death' (θανατῶσι); and then explains that they are indeed ripe for death, but in a sense other than the multitude understands, as seeking to free the spirit from the trammels of the body. The guarded way in which he expresses sympathy with Orphic and Pythagorean ideas shows that he felt the odium attached to them and knew that his own view was alien to ordinary Greek thought. Here above all he is in contrast with Aristotle. A philosophy like Plato's, which seeks release from the idols of common men is thoroughly incompatible with a view of life which rests on custom, νόμος, for νόμος is common opinion crystallized. This is worthy of note because Plato seems in so many ways the flower and quintessence of Greek thought that it is hard to remember that he is sometimes very far removed from the ordinary Greek.

We said just now that ἄνοια was a serious matter to the Greek, and this leads us to another point of cardinal importance. When we call a man a fool, we do not commonly mean to imply that he is wicked, though one or two passages in Scripture carry a heavier condemnation: 'The fool hath said in his heart . . .', for one. There the context leaves no room for doubt what the writer means by the word. And 'Thou fool!' at least twice in the New Testament is used as seriously. This use the Greek would readily have understood. When he called a man a fool, he implied that he was wicked; and when we should call a man utterly demoralized, he called him mad. Even natural stupidity, which in us excites pity or at worst contempt, is in his eyes not wholly blameless. At the least it is a barrier to ἀρετή. A fool cannot be virtuous.

Here we have come upon another clear division between the Greek and most modern men. When we think of St. Paul and 'the wisdom of this world' which 'is foolishness

with God', and many similar passages, we see how wide
the gulf is. For on this point most moderns, whether
Christians or not, take sides rather with St. Paul than
with the Greeks. To them wisdom, in the sense St. Paul
means, is something quite distinct from virtue.

This contrast has perplexed every reader of Plato. We
find it hard to understand why Socrates, or Plato, whichever it may be, so persistently seeks to reduce virtue to a
form of knowledge, and why he insists on the paradox that
no man does wrong willingly; that if he does wrong, it is
from ignorance. It seems to us so obvious that men do,
as we call it, 'sin against the light', and that it is a straining
of words in such cases to call their state of mind ignorance.

What philosophic justification there may be for the view
of Socrates it is not our business to inquire; but the study
of common Greek ideas helps to explain it. We have
noticed elsewhere that the Greeks at this time had no clear
conception of the Will as concerned in moral acts. That
is not only proved by the external nature of their moral
judgements, but implied still more clearly by the external
character of their morality and religion itself. One instance of it is the Athenian law of murder, which distinguishes indeed between murder and accidental homicide, but cannot escape from the idea that guilt (αἰτία) of
some kind attaches even to the latter. The act is externally
the same. This way of judging an act prevails in the
Classical period, though we find that the more modern
view has become common property by the beginning of
the third century.[1]

If we carry our minds back to Homer we shall find that
here we have once more to do with something very primitive. In Homer, when a man is wise, he is said to 'know wise
things', when he is kind or friendly, he is said to 'know kind
things'. This sounds so odd that we translate such phrases
otherwise, and disguise them. Perhaps in Homer's case we
are justified—the idea is primitive for him—but those who
first used such phrases must have meant what they said

[1] Philemon, Fragm. 94.   Kock; Stob. Fl. 9, 22.

literally. The explanation is quite simple. To the savage
or the child morality is a matter of rules. You learn the
rules, and, if you are good, you keep them. It may seem
illegitimate to extend this principle even to things like
kindness; but it is not. We say to a child: 'a kind boy does
not pull his little sister's hair'; 'a kind boy does not pull
off spiders' legs'. These are actually things which he has
to learn. Virtue for him at any rate is διδακτόν, a thing
which has to be learnt.

It is not far-fetched to see in this one explanation of
the Socratic paradox; a paradox to us, though in this case
at least Plato is in accord with common Greek thought.
It is not an easy thing at any time to decide what makes
an act right or wrong, or what parts of the mind are concerned in it. We need not be surprised that the Greeks
clung late to the notion that virtue is a matter of rules
and the knowledge of them; or that Socrates, though he
does not mean exactly that, is still influenced by this conception.

These two things, the conception of virtue as knowledge
and of right as a mean, are the two most general causes of
difference between Greek morality and ours. Some of
these differences may now be illustrated. With the Greek's
conception of duty to God we deal elsewhere, and it will
be seen there that both principles appear in it clearly
enough. We have also touched elsewhere on the duties to
parents, kinsfolk, and friends, but a little may be added
here. The reader will remember that such duties were
more clearly defined and more strictly enforced than
with us; and that this is part of the defensive organization
with which the Greek surrounds himself. How much he
gained or lost morally by this strictness it is not easy to say.
Most of our evidence for Classical times comes from
Athens, and we know that Athens was less strict in dis-
cipline than most Greek states. Aristophanes presents us
with pictures of emancipated sons, and unruly slaves, and
the like figure in the New Comedy. Nevertheless the
external marks of respect for parents and elders, as well as

actual duties, were exacted even at Athens more strictly than with us, and neglect of them remained the gravest of offences. The man who was undutiful, οὐ δίκαιος ἐς πατέρα, is placed by Polygnotus in Hades beside the man guilty of sacrilege as a type of the worst sinner. The oft-repeated story which Pausanias tells apropos of this (Paus. x. 28: Lycurgus, c. Leocratem, 95–6.) is cited by him as an instance of ancient piety with an implied contrast to his own times, but nevertheless filial piety was a virtue that was always prized and survived long in Greece. Even Aristophanes and the New Comedy, in spite of their satire, show that filial, and still more, parental affection was the rule, and the evidence of the law-courts bears this out. We find instances of family feuds, usually over property, but not more than we find now, if so many. Kinsmen usually hang together, and are ashamed if they do not, especially when the tie is close. Many of these feuds are between kinsmen so remote that we should hardly recognize a tie of kin at all.

But though the tie of kin is strong, we observe, especially in the orators, that family affection is chiefly among the male members of the house. A father almost always loves his sons and is often loved by them in return, but it is not so clear that he loves his daughters, or his wife. Daughters indeed present themselves in the law-court, chiefly in two aspects; either as persons who must be provided with a dowry, and are therefore expensive; or as heiresses attached to a property and therefore desirable objects of possession. The evidence of law-courts on such a point is naturally one-sided, but in this they may well reflect the feelings of the average Greek father.

Between mothers and daughters there was of course affection. Even without evidence (though there is some), we could be sure of this, for in some things women's ways are independent of time and clime, and defiant of νόμος. For this reason all that we shall say, or have said of the ways and thoughts of the Greeks, must be taken as applying chiefly to the Greek man. Of the other sex we can

only say that they were, not simply Greeks, but Greek
women; and where primary instincts come into play we
know that with all but a few women custom and nationality count for little, if they clash with the instinct. Thus
nature guards us against too great diversity in the
character of races by providing that the women at least
are essentially of one race.

Thanks in part to this law the wife in Greece was less
insignificant than the daughter. It is customary, and
partly true, to say that the position of women in Greece
was low, especially at Athens; that they were kept in
seclusion; that they were not educated; that the wife was
regarded not as a companion, but as a housekeeper, and a
necessary means of obtaining children. This was the case,
as is shown by the definition of female excellence which
Thucydides puts in the mouth of Pericles, that the best
woman is she of whom least is heard whether in praise or
blame. Nevertheless those writers go too far who talk
of the 'sex war' in Athens or elsewhere in Greece, and
think of Athenian women as downtrodden and rebellious.
This is to ascribe to them the feelings of our more hyster-
ical 'Suffragettes'; and even if we accept the theory that
the *Ecclesiazusae* of Aristophanes is a 'suffragette' pam-
phlet, a theory itself a little difficult, there is no evidence
for anything of the kind.

When we look at the matter quietly, we find that the
position of women in Athens was not very widely different
from that which they hold in many parts of Europe now,
except in one point, which we shall mention presently.
The Greeks believed, as others have believed, that physical
passion, which was what they understood by love, was a
transitory thing, and therefore an unsafe basis for marriage.
Therefore in making marriages they did not expect love as
a necessary preliminary. But the Greeks knew, as early
as Homer, that marriage normally begets affection, if not
love, and that, as Achilles says, 'every good and right-
minded man loves and cares for his woman' (Hom. *Il.*
9. 341.) There are many now, even in countries (such as

England) where the other view is prevalent, who believe that this less romantic view of marriage is the wiser, and leads more often to happiness. It is certainly the more ancient and widespread, and there were reasons why the Greeks, more than others, should hold it.

The Greek not only observed, like other men, that passion was transitory, but he felt that it had in itself the nature of evil, for it violated the law of the mean. To yield to passion and be dominated by it showed weakness of character, and μαλακία. That passion was usually transitory was fortunate; any attempt to prolong the madness was sheer folly. The victim of passion might plead the example of the gods and heroes, or, if he preferred, might plead that Love (whether Eros or Aphrodite) was a divinity whom a mortal could not resist—both pleas are often used;—but these were extenuations of a fault. He knew that it was a fault, and was far from glorying in it. The man who was truly σώφρων might indulge in love moderately, as he indulged in wine, but to be intoxicated with love was worse than to be drunk with wine. This view of the matter is to us a little repellent, but we cannot blame the Greeks, who held it, for preferring not to base marriage on passion.

Why the Greeks held this view is not obscure, but though the reason is familiar, it is worth mentioning. The normal Greek conceives love *either* as passion or as affection. That in fact is what it commonly is at all times. The conception of true love as something which unites passion and affection and transcends both, though there are hints of it in literature and may have been instances in life, never became common till far later. And even now, though the conception is familiar, the reality is still so rare that, as we have seen, many think it wiser not to count upon it in making marriages.

The more modern view was impossible to the Greeks, for it rests on a basis alien to their thoughts; on the idea of moral purity and the sanctity of the body, and springing from these, chivalry, the reverence for women as the embodiment of purity. These ideas are historically Christian, especially as associated with the worship of the Blessed Virgin; they are definitely mystical in essence and to the Greek would have seemed fantastic. As we shall see, his conception of purity was originally external, and when he enlarged it, his moral purity implied only such things as freedom from bloodguiltiness and other overt offences, not what we mean by purity of mind. This limitation of the idea of purity explains, among other things, how it was that the Greeks tolerated a grossness in some of their religious rites which makes them, by modern standards of decency, unfit even for mention; some of the worst being performed by women. It explains how the plays of Aristophanes could be witnessed without offence by the most respectable. It explains how the charming, and in their way bashful, boys and young men, with αἰδώς imprinted on their countenances, whom we meet in the pages of Plato or see in works of Art, could receive without a qualm jests that raise the hair of the most hardened modern. It also explains in part the grossness of mythology too. For it is obvious that the shock caused by such things as the amours of the gods is far slighter, when the idea of moral purity is removed. They then become little more than a breach of rules, not a cause of horror. The gods were hardly bound by human rules, and the idea that they could be bound by their own nature was not present till the gods themselves were conceived as holy and pure. And that idea was late in emerging and never fully established. The same thing explains why to the Greek rape seemed comparatively venial, as compared with adultery. Adultery was an invasion of important rights and implied the consent of the wife, i.e. that she had been alienated from her husband. In the other case the injury, apart from possible consequences, was 'sentimental', and with Greek ideas of purity the sentiment was less strong.

The next count against the Athenians in the matter of women is that they kept them in seclusion. This is true, and it is an evil. But the seclusion of Athenian women was

not greater than that which prevailed in Southern Italy
a few years ago, if not now; it was not a peculiarly Greek
defect.

It is usual to contrast the position of women in Homer
with that in later Greece, but the comparison, as commonly put, is scarcely fair. Undoubtedly the women in
Homer enjoy greater freedom than they did in Periclean
Athens, but the reason is not merely Athenian obliquity,
or even, as sometimes suggested, a difference of race; the
heroes of Homer as Achaeans representing the nobler
tradition of Northern races. The Achaeans may have had
these traditions, and the Achaeans may have come from
the North, but it was not so much the noble Northman
who made the difference as the conditions of the time. In
Mohammadan countries now, e. g. among the mountain
tribes in Kurdistan and Persia, where life is still at a stage
near to the Homeric, women are much less strictly
secluded than in the more settled plains. Even there seclusion is less strict in villages, where women work in the fields,
than in cities. From the nature of the case this must be so.

On the other hand, though the women in Homer enjoy
greater freedom and are more on an equality with men,
it cannot be said that they are treated with more tenderness or less brutality. The treatment of the serving-maids
at the end of the *Odyssey* shows this; and the Homeric
heroes take possession of their captive women without
scruple or ceremony. As the Trojans are not marked off
from the Greeks in Homer as barbarians, and therefore,
so to speak, lawful prey, this is notable.

In the case of Homer we must also bear in mind that
he is presenting the life of the nobles, and greater freedom
is habitually found in aristocratic circles. The same
reservation applies to the case of Lesbos, which is often
cited as an instance of similar freedom. Sappho and her
circle belonged to an aristocracy, and to one in which life,
in spite of its refinements, was still not far from the
heroic age.

The third count is that Athenian women were left

uneducated, and so could not be on an equality with
men. This also is true, but it is not a charge that would
have occurred to many Athenian women. This time it
is Sparta, not Homer, that furnishes a stick wherewith to
beat the Athenian dog. The Spartans, we are told,
managed these things better: men and women mingled
there more freely and even took part in athletics together,
and athletics were a chief part of Spartan education. But
the Athenian woman thanked her gods that she was not
as Spartan women, shameless hussies who wrestle with
men naked.

It is doubtful, too, whether the Athenian woman felt
that she was uneducated, and it cannot fairly be said that
education was deliberately denied her; and if we call her
uneducated, we can hardly call the male Athenian
educated either. Formal education even for the man was
elementary. He was taught to read and write and to play
the lyre, and by the fifth century he was expected to learn
something of Homer and the early poets. By the end of
the fifth century a favoured few derived some sort of
higher education from the lectures of the sophists, but
these were exceptions, and they were looked on with
suspicion. The higher education of the Athenian was not
formal; it was derived from life, in performing his duties as
a citizen, in the Assembly, in the law-courts, and on military service. An excellent education, but we can hardly
blame the Athenians if they did not open these activities
to women. Modern though they seem in some ways, the
Athenians could hardly anticipate the future of so many
millenniums.

Moreover the most vital part of an Athenian's education was originally his training, by athletics and other
means, to serve as a soldier. That was a man's chief duty,[1]
as it was a woman's to manage his house and perform
feminine tasks, to weave, and spin, and sew. In those
duties she was trained, just as he was trained in his; and

[1] Hyperides, *Epitaphios*, 8, shows very clearly the persistence of this
view of education.

she thought them equally honourable. Until the middle or end of the fifth century therefore there can have been no wide gulf in respect of education between the average Athenian and his wife. Even then, when an interest in philosophy and abstract studies had arisen, this cannot have affected many; for, as we have seen, such studies were not general or popular.

The opinion propagated by modern writers is commonly different. In them we read regularly that the Athenian, bored with his brainless wife, sought intellectual sympathy and stimulus with his cultured ἑταίρα or paid companion. This is moonshine. The legend appears to have arisen from the story of Pericles and his Aspasia, and from the fact that Socrates did not find Xanthippe sympathetic to his studies, and that he is recorded to have conversed innocently, on various subjects, with intelligent ἑταίραι. There were doubtless intelligent ἑταίραι—several such figure in history and literature—but we know a good deal about ἑταίραι as a class, and it is very clear that they relied usually on their physical attractions, reinforced by art, and such accomplishments as singing and dancing. In these arts and accomplishments they no doubt surpassed the ordinary wife, and it was by these that the ordinary man was attracted. In these liaisons there appears to have been at times real affection, but not often. Most ἑταίραι were, naturally, frivolous and grasping, and were treated with unpleasant callousness.[1]

There is another legend of the same kind, even less well-founded. The unpleasant vice of paederasty is known to have been common in Greece, and this too has been sometimes ascribed to the unattractiveness of women and their want of intellect. This theory is not even plausible, for the assumption that the society of a woman who lacks the higher culture is necessarily less stimulating to the mind than that of a callow boy implies a contempt for women rare even in 'feminists'. The legend of course

[1] Demosthenes, κατὰ Νεαίρας is the *locus classicus*, but the evidence is abundant.

springs from Plato's *Phaedrus*, but his picture of a sub‑
limated paederasty does not even profess to be founded on
common experience. His argument implies, and abun‑
dant evidence[1] supports him, that this commerce, like that
with ἑταῖραι, was normally founded on physical attraction.
The most that can be said is that the Greek love of beauty
cast a glamour upon it, and the admiration for a beautiful
youth must often have been disinterested. This is proved
by the multitude of their admirers, to which the καλός
inscriptions on vases, among other things, bear witness.

When we review the evidence in regard to women and
marriage, we find much what was to be expected. We
find evidence enough of domestic squabbles, and of more
serious hostility between husbands and wives; we find
infidelities on both sides; we find cynical remarks on
women in great abundance; but all these things are found
in any society and under any system of marriage. We do
not find proof that husband and wife were normally un‑
friendly; the contrary is often implied,[2] and real affection
proved, and assumed as normal. The cynical remarks do
not prove settled contempt for women, and are not
peculiar to Greece. They merely remind us that men
wrote most of its literature. Man's contempt of Woman—
if it be contempt and not disguised terror—is a feeble
thing compared with Woman's contempt of Man.

Nevertheless, though we must reject fantastic exag‑
gerations, it would be foolish to maintain that the
Athenian treatment of women was the best possible. It
was in parts unintelligent and callous, but even what
seems callous does not always proceed from injustice or
contempt. Thus the laws dealing with heiresses, which
seem to treat the woman as a chattel, and the importance
attached to the dowry, were both in part a protection to
the woman. They helped her to secure a husband, and
they made her position when married more secure. To
provide dowries was a binding duty on the kin, and when

[1] Cf. for instance, Lysias, πρὸς Σίμωνα, passim.
[2] See for instance, Isaeus, x. 19.

I

was a common act of benevolence for
ne to the rescue. The idea that a woman
led for when you had found her a husband,
ted him or not, betrays a lack of delicacy,
l contempt. Chivalrous feeling and tender-
1, as we have already seen, were not antique
virtues.

The belief that women were despised and oppressed is,
apart from the evidence derived from actual life, unlikely
on other grounds. An oppressed woman, or at least an
oppressed wife, and most Athenian women were married,
is at all times less common than a hen-pecked husband.
This rule holds good even in polygamous countries, and
Athens cannot have been an exception. It is also incredible, as many scholars have noticed, that women were
despised and abject in the country and age which created
the heroines of Greek Tragedy. These tragedies, like the
rest of literature, contain bad women, and here and there
bitter attacks upon women, but some of their heroines are
as noble and as strong as any conceived by poets or known
to history. If they fall short of later conceptions, it is
more often that they lack the Christian grace of meekness
than that they are weak or servile. Such characters cannot
have been pure products of imagination unaided by
examples of like characters in Athens. It is customary to
speak of Euripides as the great portrayer of female character, and he certainly studied women more fully, but his
women are certainly not stronger in character than those
of the other dramatists. And not only this: there are in
Aeschylus touches of tenderness and purity which, more
than anything else in Greek literature, suggest that the
later chivalrous regard for women was after all not wholly
alien to Greece.

But if it is absurd to suppose that the tragedians wrote
in a country where women were despised and insignificant, there is one thing on the other side, which they
illustrate very clearly: that customary morality allowed a
greater laxity to men than to women. This point recurs

frequently. There are protests against it even in Aeschylus and many in Euripides, but other instances show that such laxity was often accepted as natural even by self-respecting women. Deianira in the *Trachiniae* of Sophocles, and Andromache in the play of Euripides which bears her name, are the most conspicuous instances, and neither of these forfeits our respect, or is presented as contemptible.

The evidence of art is equally strong. One glance at the female figures on the Parthenon pediments and frieze makes it hard to believe that their creators thought altogether ignobly of women, but the evidence of vases, and especially of funeral lecythi is stronger still. On some vases, it is true, we meet with figures of hetaerae, but the female type in the best work of the fifth century is not only beautiful, but dignified, and neither meretricious nor sensual. The female type only begins to be sensual when women, according to the received opinion, were becoming more emancipated.

Next to the ties of birth and marriage, and inseparable from them, comes duty to country. It is a commonplace that this played a larger part in ancient life than in modern; and the chief reason why it did so is also obvious. A man's prosperity and his life depended more closely upon it. In small states a disastrous war meant ruin not for a few, but for the majority, if not all. It meant a whole land ravaged, most of its wealth destroyed or seized, and possible enslavement, if not death. And in Greece, when wars were frequent, this danger was never far away. And even in time of peace, country meant much more than it does now. The modern European, if he chooses, can emigrate without much inconvenience or risk, to another country. Unless he is naturalized there, he will not enjoy public rights, but his person and property will be secure. In Greece the thing was not so simple or so safe. The treatment of non-citizens varied in the different states, but in the most liberal their rights were restricted and the chance of naturalization remote. More-

over the Greek could not take with him to an alien city
his religion. Though the gods worshipped were the same
—and this was not so entirely—the local rites were different and unfamiliar, and there were many in which he,
as an alien, could take no part. And this meant much, for,
even if he were not devout, most of the interests and even
the diversions of the Greek were connected with religion.

These obvious and cogent reasons, to name no others,
made the safety and prosperity of his πόλις vital to a
Greek. Reasons of pride and sentiment too were probably
stronger than in most modern states. The small Greek
states were more homogeneous, as a rule, in blood, or believed themselves to be so, which comes to the same thing;
they were certainly more homogeneous in character, religion, and mode of life, and, till fairly late in Greek history,
in ideas. There were indeed differences of wealth and
bitter party feuds, but even so the citizens were not
divided so sharply as in a large modern state. In a modern
state different sections of the population are often so
remote from one another in habits, beliefs, and ways of
thought that it is hard to say what is the common quality
that binds them together; we only know that somehow it
exists. In a Greek state there could be no such doubt. The
characters of the chief states stand out clearly even to us.

So far then the Greeks had stronger motives for patriotism than we, and they had the same motives of sentiment and local affection. The face of their country was as
dear to them as ours is to us, though in a slightly different
way: particular spots were endeared to them not so much
by natural beauty as by association with legend or religion;
though that association itself implied often a recognition
of natural beauty. Thus when the later Greeks took to
painting landscapes, they would choose by preference a
spot with a rustic shrine, or a sacred tree, and offerings
suspended upon it.

The Greeks, then, had strong motives for patriotism,
and it is a commonplace of history that these motives in-
spired them at times to deeds unsurpassed by any nation.

But to say that the Greeks were patriotic, and leave the matter there, would be only to repeat what all know. The limitations of their patriotism are more instructive. Greek history furnishes not only shining examples of patriotism, but equally conspicuous instances of treason, and some of the traitors are among the most eminent of Greek statesmen. So many instances of treason in great men are hard to find elsewhere. Moreover the Greeks on many occasions, in spite of the love of their πόλις, sacrificed its prosperity or freedom to the interests, or the malice, of a party. This is even more significant than the treason of individuals.

Such things are hard to reconcile with fervent patriotism. The ancient Romans, and later contemners of the Greeks, are content to say that the Greeks were liars and traitors by nature. The more curious will demand a more convincing explanation. All writers upon Greece describe and deplore the prevalence of party-spirit, and explain it as a rule on geographical grounds: the physical structure of Greece made for isolation. But this answer covers at best the quarrels of states; it does not touch the internal quarrels, which, seeing the instant peril they involved, are harder to understand. The danger from outside should have cemented internal union, and it did not.

One explanation of this puzzle lies in a point already noticed; the curious defensive structure with which the Greek invested himself. Of this the πόλις formed only the outermost line, and the inner defences, ties of kin and associations of various kinds, were sometimes so strong that the outer defence was neglected. In other words the Greeks have not yet completely outgrown the tribal instinct, and the tribe is not entirely commensurate with the πόλις.

This assertion may seem rash to many, for the Greek state is usually taken as the type of what is called the 'city-state', and contrasted with the tribal organization of uncivilized races. Moreover it will occur to the reader that in city-states elsewhere, notably in those of Medieval Italy, the same evil of unrestrained party-spirit appears, and this suggests that the root of it must lie in the nature of the city-state itself. And this suggestion is partly true. Political life in such states is more intense than in any other form of society, and it naturally follows that party-spirit is proportionally intense.

Nevertheless the other explanation, which is less obvious and less often noticed, does apply in some measure to Greece. I have used the word 'tribal' for want of a better, not to imply that in Greek states the earlier tribes of which traces survived were actually more powerful than the πόλις, or received more of a man's conscious loyalty. In the fifth century at any rate this was plainly not the case, at any rate in the more settled and civilized states. It would be absurd to suggest that at Athens, for instance, the people cared more for the artificial ten tribes of Clisthenes than for Athens herself; though these may have been more important than the casual student would guess. By 'tribal' I mean rather that the Greek had not entirely outgrown the frame of mind that belongs to the member of a small tribe living among other tribes, all potentially, and in fact normally, hostile; where the hand of every man outside his little community is against him, and he can only look for help to that community. This feeling was present in Greece, and it was partly justified. Athenians, for instance, as we see especially from the orators, did prey upon one another with singular lack of scruple. Modern business morality, it may be said, is no less predatory and unscrupulous; but that is with us a recent degradation, and in Greece such morality was not confined to men of business.

For this reason the Greeks cherished in self-defence the narrower ties of family, phratry, and the like, and the spirit that went with them; and carried the same spirit into political associations. In England now we suffer from the opposite evil. Family and local ties are so loose that the individual becomes an irresponsible unit and therefore a worse citizen; and local patriotism is so weak that administration is often left to the incapable.

The limitations and defects so far mentioned, however, though they help to explain the excess of party-spirit, do not quite explain the treason of patriotic Greeks, especially where treason was due not to party-spirit, or even to personal spite, but to simple venality. Some instances of this are, when all is said, hard to understand, but a little light is thrown on the matter by a thing which we find often illustrated in the Greek orators. It is common there to find a man rehearsing at length the list of his services to the state with an emphasis which seems to us a little indecent. This in itself seems at first sight to conflict with the Greek dread of boasting, but it is so frequent that it was evidently permissible. The reason seems to be that Greek dislike of boasting rested less on modesty than on fear of provoking the νέμεσις of the gods, and a statement of past actions is less likely to excite their jealousy than over-confidence in one's present power or success, or rash hopes for the future. We do not touch wood—and this is the nearest parallel—when we relate our past scores, but only when we have incautiously implied that we expect equal luck to-morrow. Even this little difference, however, is significant. It already suggests, what other evidence confirms, that the Greek in his mind keeps a kind of debit and credit account with his country; that his services are not wholly disinterested. This will not surprise us when we remember that he kept a similar account against the gods. And the nature of the statements made bears this out. The speaker often avows among his motives for public service the desire for popularity and reputation, with their attendant benefits. In so doing, a cynic might say, he was only more honest than we, not less disinterested. But although such motives for public service are not rare at any time nor always to be contemned, we have sure evidence that the cynic would in this case be wrong. There are thousands perhaps who perform public services from interested motives, and they

are conspicuous, but there were millions not long ago
who performed a greater service and expected no reward,
and who rather conceal than advertise their service.   Of
the Greeks it is not only the man 'on the make' who
advertises his public services, but the ordinary citizen.
Some may say that after all the plea of service in the War
is sometimes heard now in the law-courts, but it is a plea
for mercy, rather than an argument; the Greek sometimes
uses it as an argument, a presumptive proof of his good
character.

Apart from military service, the commonest items are
matters of money expended. The speaker tells us of his
generous expenditure on liturgies, as choregus, as trierarch,
&c.; of his contributions to special levies ($\epsilon\grave{\iota}\sigma\phi o\rho a\acute{\iota}$);
of voluntary expenditure on such things as providing
dowries for the daughters of poor persons, or ransoming
captive citizens from the enemy in war.

The list reminds us incidentally how much was demanded of the Greek both by law and by public opinion,
but it reminds us of something more. There is often in
these statements an implication that the man who has
discharged these duties is not only a good citizen but a
good man. It is not of course implied that there are no
other duties, but that these come first. The point of view
in fact is the opposite of ours. If we are asked whether so-
and-so is a good man, our thoughts turn first to his private
character. Unless questioned on the point, we should
hardly mention his public character or merits, unless these
happened to be in some way conspicuous. With the Greek
this order is reversed. The public service comes first; the
other qualities are more or less an afterthought.

This point of view helps to explain a thing familiar to
all students; the Greek habit of applying moral terms to
political parties: as at Athens, for instance, the oligarchs
are $\kappa a\lambda o\grave{\iota}$ $\kappa\grave{a}\gamma a\theta o\acute{\iota}$ and their opponents $\pi o\nu\eta\rho o\acute{\iota}$. This
does not spring entirely from offensive self-righteousness
or from insolence, but partly from a genuine feeling that
the bad citizen is a bad man; and your political opponent

is a bad citizen, in that his policy will, in your eyes, injure the state. This may seem a fanciful explanation, but it coincides with what we have elsewhere learnt of Greek morality. It regards the overt act more than the moral state, and puts first the qualities that make useful citizens. Plato, as we know, placed other very different qualities before the demotic, unreasoning virtues of the common man, and Aristotle saw clearly the importance of the moral state; but these views did not permeate the multitude till a later time. In the Hellenistic age we find the change of view widespread. In this, as in other things, the decay of the free πόλις marks the transition, and chiefly causes it. Till it decays the old ideas prevail in spite of philosophers.

Thus, admirable as the Greek's patriotism was, and potent beyond other motives, there was in it as in the rest of his morality, and in his religion, something external and self-regarding. It rested, like them, on custom, on desire for honour, and ultimately on self-interest, more than on any inward principle. This makes it, if not easy, yet a little easier, to understand a Themistocles or an Alcibiades. When other strong motives come into play, when his country is, or seems ungrateful, when he is refused the honour he deserves, patriotism in a man naturally ambitious may give way to a sense of injury. A Socrates or an Aristides may refuse to forget the good he has received from his country in the evil he is now receiving, but not all Greeks can so forget. For once more comes in the Greek doctrine that a man should hate and injure his enemy. To make that enemy his country may have been a perversion of that principle, but it was very easy to a man who habitually thought in that way. This explanation is at least more satisfactory than the assumption that the Greeks were congenitally traitors. Any people that makes a principle of cherishing a grudge must often seem treacherous.

In regard to another and baser form of treason, when a man betrays his country not in resentment, but for a

3520   K

simple bribe, the case is different. Here we must admit that greed of gain, lawful or unlawful, was a besetting vice of the Greeks. The frequency of admonitions and denunciations shows that the Greeks themselves knew that it was so. There is no topic on which all Greek writers, of whatever kind, insist more frequently. It is a topic natural and necessary enough at all times, but in Greece the evil must have been unusually conspicuous. Greek history, as well as literature, furnishes proof of this not merely in particular cases, but in laws and regulations intended to deal with the evil.

Why this vice was prevalent we cannot pretend to explain in full, but it is obvious that one thing already mentioned applies here too, the want of any general principle of morality. The other familiar weakness, that moral obligation depended on the presence of particular ties might seem to apply likewise, but unfortunately in the case of this particular vice the Greeks offended against the most definite obligations. In a large proportion of cases recorded in private life the persons robbed or defrauded are kin of the offender. Perhaps the simplest explanation is the truest: that the Greeks, except at certain times and in certain favoured places, were as a whole very poor, and their incomes for various reasons precarious. The temptation therefore was obviously great.

V

RELIGION

THERE is a general impression that the Greeks did not take their religion very seriously. The scandals of mythology, the apparent irreverence with which the gods are treated in Comedy, and even in some religious rites, the way in which they are sometimes depicted in art— these, and similar obvious reasons, leave in the minds of most schoolboys and of many University students a feeling that this kind of thing is not religion. 'No doubt', they say to themselves, 'the Greeks did perform ceremonies and offer sacrifices to these gods, but either they had ceased by historical times to take them seriously, or else they had never done so.' If a doubt arises why the Greeks took so much trouble to propitiate these nugatory gods, an easy answer presents itself. These gods, whatever their short-comings, furnished excellent material for art and litera-ture, and deserved to be encouraged on that account; and the ceremonies in their honour, sacrifices, processions, dramatic performances, games, and so on, were not only excellent material for art, but beautiful in themselves and very agreeable.

This is hardly a travesty of the impression general among those who have some acquaintance at first or second hand with Greek Art and Literature. Scholars who have gone a little further would somewhat modify the picture. They remember many passages in literature, and even some incidents in Greek history, which forbid them to doubt that some Greeks at least at some times took their religion seriously. Some of these can be explained away. Aeschylus, for instance, was a person of unusual views, and his prophetic fervour cannot be taken as typical; and when the Athenians banished Alcibiades after the affair of the Hermae, and when they put Socrates to death, they were using religion as a pretext to cloak a political grudge. But the instances are too numerous for all to be explained away like these, and so the scholar as a rule is a little perplexed. He cannot deny that this very defective religion had some hold on the Greeks, but in such an intelligent nation it is surprising.

In this perplexity scholars resort to various devices, for they cannot all accept the naïve theory that the Greek gods were somehow providentially created to furnish themes for art. Some scholars, the majority I fancy, drawing on their own minds, believe that the more intelligent Greeks were monotheists, and found it useful for various reasons, such as those mentioned by Gibbon in the case of the Romans, to conform to popular beliefs. This is the most plausible, and in one sense the truest explanation. There were monotheists among the Greeks, probably as early as the sixth century B.C., if not before. Monotheism might occur to a thoughtful man in any age and place, and we know there were monotheists in Greece, and there may have been strict monotheists. But the strict monotheist, he who believes that there is One God and no other, is very different from him who believes in a supreme god with other inferior powers subject to him. And that is the form of monotheism, if it can be so called, which we commonly find in Greek writers. That form is compatible with a belief in any number of subordinate powers. And the example of Plato himself shows how natural such a belief was to the Greek.

This being so, it is misleading to assume that the more intelligent Greeks conformed, hypocritically, to beliefs they did not share. They doubtless did not believe in all the absurdities implied by those beliefs, but when they sacrificed, they were not sacrificing to nothing in order to placate the mob. There was some power, indefinable perhaps, but real enough, to which they were doing homage.

It is hardly necessary at this date to discuss another explanation fashionable some generations ago; the explanation that mythology and ceremonial were deliberately devised, whether benevolently or cynically; by cynics to amuse the multitude, or by benevolent philo-

sophers to convey salutary truths in a form apprehensible
by the vulgar. Allegory is sometimes found in poets and
philosophers, and the later Greeks often explained offensive legends as allegorical, but the popular religion certainly did not originate in any conscious fiction.

These and similar difficulties, with their attendant
growth of explanations, spring from the old root, modern
prepossessions. And the shortest way to deal with them is,
if possible, to cut that root away; and again the shortest
way to do that is to recapitulate the chief points of difference between the Greek conception of religion and
ours. The facts are quite familiar, but even accomplished
scholars find it hard to keep them in view.

To most people now, in Western Europe at least, religion means in the first place a system of doctrines con-
cerning the nature of God and man, and a system of
morality based on those doctrines. As an adjunct to these
we find prayer and the performance of ritual and ceremonies, and usually a professional priesthood marked off
in various ways from other men. We also find in most cases
some belief in a union or communion with God, whether
by the aid of ritual or other means. The stress laid upon
the last three points varies, but most Christian com-
munities and many others, as the Mohammadans, include
all five, and none would omit the first two, doctrine and
morality.

When we turn to the Greeks we find of all these five
points only one, prayer and ceremonial, as definitely established and recognized. The others, it is true, are not quite
excluded. The performance of ceremonies implies belief
in a being who can be approached by them, and who
when approached has the power and will to help; but it
implies nothing more about his nature. Morality again
is present in so far as certain gods are guardians of certain
rules of morality, and punish their breach. But the idea of
gods as more than this, as essentially the source of moral
law, and therefore its upholders always—this is no part of
religion as commonly understood by the Greek, though

poets and other moralists may inculcate it often enough.
Again the Greeks have priests, but they do not form a
separate class, and their functions do not usually go beyond
the performance of ceremonial duties. They are not, as a
rule, expected to be teachers or examples to their fellows.
The last point mentioned, the belief in a mystic union
with God, is also alien to the common religion of Greece.
It is found in certain cults, such as the Orphic rites, but
these were abnormal and suspect. Only prayer and ceremonial are universal and essential.

The modern student when he discovers this to be the
case, can hardly believe it, and most of his difficulties
spring from an endeavour to evade the horrid fact that
Greek Religion consisted of ceremonial. Most of all he is
troubled by the absence of dogma. This, if he has been
well brought up, he feels to be essential, and instinctively
tries to provide. He therefore, in some cases, invests the
statements of Homer and other early writers with something of the authority of the Bible; and he has this much
justification that the Greeks themselves treated Homer as
a moral teacher. This however leads him into difficulty.
For, having invested Homer with this sanctity, and then
observing that the Greeks as early as Xenophanes in the
sixth century B.C. began to criticize the theology of
Homer, he assumes that these attacks were as alarming to
the normal Greek as *Essays and Reviews* and later more
drastic criticisms were to a public that believed in the
verbal inspiration of Holy Scripture. Our student has
failed to notice that, though Homer was popularly treated
as a moral teacher, his claim to that position had not been
ratified by the decision of any Council, and that in fact
there was not in Greece any central authority in matters
of religion.

This point is vital, for it bears not only on this but on
many other common errors. It is obvious, though often
forgotten, that where there is no central authority, there
can be no orthodox doctrine. Delphi to the beginner
may seem the Rome of Greek Religion, but though its

influence at some periods was considerable, it was never an
authority on matters of doctrine. There was no central
authority. The Greeks derived their ideas of the gods
from Homer and the later poets, supplemented by local
traditions. These had never been either canonized or
systematized, and therefore we are in error if we think
that criticism of their statements is comparable to criticism of the Holy Scripture in the eyes of early Victorian
Englishmen or American 'Fundamentalists'. No doubt
the ordinary Greek was somewhat disturbed to hear the
current beliefs criticized, whether they were expressed by
Homer and the poets, or implied by local traditions, but
this was only because human nature always resents dis-
turbance of familiar beliefs. Such criticism was not in
itself an attack upon religion. This point is vital and calls
for fuller treatment.

In the case of religions which have a systematic theology, to attack any one of their cardinal dogmas is to assail
the foundations. But a religion like the Greek, which has
no coherent or authorized theology, is obviously not imperilled by any criticism which stops short of denying the
existence of the gods and their power to help man. It is
at once the strength and the weakness of such religions
that they are founded not on dogma, but on ritual. This
is a source of strength; for such a religion is more like a
forest tree than a building of stone. If you destroy in a
building any of its main supports, the whole collapses, but
you may lop bough after bough from the tree, and it still
lives and puts forth others. The religion of Greece is like
a very ancient tree. There are fungi and parasites growing
upon it, and some of its boughs decay, or are lopped off,
but still it lives. It does not die until vitality forsakes even
the root.

And if the root, as we maintain, be ritual, it may even
be said that in a sense ancient religion never died, for
much of the ritual survives with a new meaning in the
observances of the Christian Church. It would be perverse to make too much of this, for the new meaning

imposed on the ancient rite was often not merely different from the old, but adverse to it; but nevertheless it is not fantastic to say that the old religion did not wholly die. For if the meaning officially attached later to the rite was quite different, the spirit and ideas of the worshipper were not always so radically changed. In the most essential point of all, the feeling that rites and ceremonies in themselves are a sufficient means for procuring divine favour, paganism has not died yet.

The assertion that ritual is the foundation of Greek Religion will no doubt provoke scruples in many. First, if it is hard to understand how the more intelligent Greeks could swallow the thorns of their mythology, it is still harder to believe that they attached value to ritual not reinforced by theology or morality. Secondly Greek literature and history provide frequent instances of a higher conception of religion. Both these difficulties are serious, but not insuperable.

A religion resting chiefly upon ritual is doubtless unsatisfactory, and doubtless many Greeks felt it to be so. But the position was this. Few Greeks doubted that there were in the universe powers greater than themselves upon whom they were dependent, and who had the power and at least sometimes the will to help them. Sacrifice and ritual were the traditional method of approaching these powers and of obtaining their favour. The performance of such rites, even if the gods did not demand them as a price for favours, was at least a mark of respect and gratitude, and a proof that the worshipper acknowledged his dependence upon a higher power. And seeing that the performance of the rite implied no dogmatic statement as to the nature of the power worshipped, it could be performed in all sincerity by any one except an actual atheist. Greek Religion, in fact, from the first was compatible with a mild agnosticism. Questions and doubts in regard to the nature and ways of the gods go back as far as Homer. This being the case, the man who neglected the customary rites and sacrifices either declared himself an atheist or was

guilty of ὕβρις. To disregard any duty enforced by tradition and the custom of his fathers, came, in the eyes of a
Greek, very near to ὕβρις; to refuse to the gods the customary worship, and thus defy their power and imply
independence of it, was ὕβρις patent and unmistakable.
Therefore we need not be surprised if Greeks as enlightened as Socrates and Aristotle showed regard for
religious observances.

The second difficulty, as we saw, was the presence of
higher ideas than those implied by a religion of outward
observance. Such ideas we find, occasionally, in Homer,
and more frequently and more definitely in later writers.
It may therefore seem unfair to say that the essence of
Greek Religion is ritual; but the statement is true, if
rightly understood. It does not imply that the Greek had
no ideas of his gods higher than could be inferred from his
ritual, though that could be interpreted in a nobler way
than as a mere traffic in benefits received in return for
rites performed. The statement only implies that the
outward observance was the one thing definitely fixed and
demanded by custom, and the one which came first in
the thoughts of the Greek.

When we inquire into a man's religion, we normally ask
first what he believes, and then, if we are more exacting
and precise, we ask whether he acts in accordance with his
beliefs. We do not so naturally inquire whether he fulfils
the outward observances of his religion. We rather assume
that he does so; but even if we find that he is negligent in
this respect, we do not, when the belief is present, deny
that he has a religion at all. Though different com-
munities of Christians would regard such negligence differently, some as venial and others as very serious, the
strictest of all would hardly say that a man negligent in
observance was therefore not a Christian; they would say
rather that he was a 'bad Christian'.

With the Greek, as with most pagans, this order is
reversed. When he asks a foreigner about his religion, he
wishes to know what forms of worship he follows. The

answer will probably include mention of the gods to whom worship is offered, but this mention will usually not go beyond a statement of their names, or of those of the Greek gods whom they most resemble. If the inquirer is persistent and the informant well informed, he may even elicit one or two of the stories told by these βάρβαροι about their gods, but this is more matter of curiosity than of vital importance. That this was so appears very clearly from descriptions of foreign religions in Herodotus and other writers. Herodotus, indeed, curious about all things human and divine, does tell us not a little of the beliefs and legends of foreign races as well as of their modes of worship. But even with him these are secondary. His frame of mind is not that of a modern traveller, or at least of a modern traveller before the days of anthropology. It is not what people believe, but what they do that is his chief concern. Indeed he even outstrips the anthropologist; for the anthropologist, though trained to observe external practices, observes them to discover the underlying idea. It is this which to him makes the practices worth studying, and he devotes more pains to discovering the beliefs, or non-beliefs of the Australian Arunta than Herodotus to the theology of the ancient Egyptians.

This frame of mind, of which Herodotus is typical, is, when we come to consider it, inevitable from the nature of the case. Where there is no recognized or central authority, no court of appeal in matters of doctrine, beliefs are inevitably fluid, and it is useless to inquire into them too precisely. You will not get a definite answer, or if you do, it will not be valid for all. For when beliefs have not been defined by authority, they vary in detail from man to man. And this variation does not imply that one man is less, or more, orthodox than his neighbour. There is no orthodoxy; there is only piety; and piety is shown by a willing and reverent observance of the customary rites and ceremonies. These are definite and can be known and studied, and therefore it is these to which the ancient

Greek looks when he is investigating the religion of a nation or an individual.

But rites and ceremonies, an obstinate questioner may say, are after all but 'beggarly elements'. If we cannot reasonably look for definite theology, surely we may look for morality. Unless these rites have at least some moral meaning they are obviously worthless, and no rational and reflecting man could take them seriously. The answer to this objection is that the rites undoubtedly have a moral meaning, or at least a moral value, but it is not of the kind which the questioner, if he be a normal modern European, expects at first sight. The average modern takes it for granted that a religion, if worthy of the name, must teach and inspire morality in its adherents. It must itself declare, with authority, in the name of God and as proceeding from him, what the laws of morality are; and must in various ways exact from its followers obedience to those laws, and must furnish incentives thereto, and it must make such obedience a condition and a test of sincere belief. Now Greek Religion does none of these things, or at least does not do them explicitly and directly. We have seen that it does not teach theology, and for the same reason it cannot teach morality. There is no authority to decide the laws of morality any more than the principles of theology. And having no recognized doctrine it cannot furnish clear and definite incentives to moral conduct. Moreover the rites which it employs are in many cases derived from a time of barbarism, and contain elements, and imply ideas, which seem to a civilized man immoral.

In spite of all this however, Greek Religion, even if outward observance is its essence, is far from being morally worthless. To begin with, the rules of the temple, or cult, exact of the worshipper at least ceremonial purity. And if this purity is originally only external, the transition from this to deeper things was easy, and comes early. Even in Homer we feel at times a perception that the gods demand not only clean hands but a pure heart (or at least the Greek equivalent for that, for their conception of

moral purity was different). The germ of this belief is
latent even in such a phrase as ὅς κε θεοῖς ἐπιπείθηται,
μάλα τ' ἔκλυον αὐτοῦ, 'the gods hear best the prayer of
him that obeys them'; and it appears more clearly elsewhere. In Hesiod the idea grows plainer, and it is reiterated in later literature. That the sacrifice of the
righteous man is alone acceptable to the gods is a familiar
idea, and it does not concern us here that the righteousness meant is itself somewhat external. So far as this,
then, ritual is associated with morality, but it remains
true that the essential thing is the ritual. For it alone
is stable and definite; its connexion with morality is
precarious.

It may well seem that we exaggerate in this the difference between the Greeks and the followers of later religions. Many men at all times, and nearly all men at
some time, slip into the sin of regarding worship as a
machinery for procuring divine favour. If only the nobler
Greeks escaped this error, they were not, it may be said,
so much unlike ourselves. But the difference is essential.
The Christian and the Mohammadan, and the Jew
after the time of the prophets, is explicitly and em-
phatically taught that a right spirit is more pleasing to
God than sacrifice, though that is necessary too. If he
fails to bring a right spirit to his sacrifice, it is not from
ignorance. But to all but the more thoughtful and intelligent of the Greeks performance of the outward act is
the essential. The ordinary pious rustic, sacrificing to
Hermes or Pan and the Nymphs, would go away with a
quiet mind, if he had decently and reverently offered sacrifice according to his power. He would not examine his
conscience to discover whether his frame of mind and his
conduct were such as to recommend him to the divine
favour. This is clearly an important difference.

It is a difference still more important that, although he
had some inkling that the gods required of him a right
spirit, the Greek was never taught by his traditional religion that they required of him also 'a broken and contrite

RELIGION 77

heart'. But that most vital difference cannot be dealt with incidentally.

There is however yet another connexion between ritual and morality. Outward observances, even though they do not teach morality, may contribute to its growth. Dr. Warde Fowler[1] has pointed out with great acumen and judgement how the Roman religion, more formal and external than the Greek, helped to form the Roman character. Their religion performed the same service for the Greeks, but this point again cannot be dealt with in small compass, and must be treated separately. Two things, however, are simple. The devout observance of rites was, as already noticed, a useful safeguard against ὕβρις (hubris)— this itself was enough to justify them in the eyes of any Greek—and it was also a safeguard against superstition. The Greek, having duly performed the rites required by the custom of his fathers, felt himself at peace with the gods, and entitled to their protection. He was no longer subject to that paralysing terror of unknown and hostile powers which is the deadliest part of superstition. If he had bought his peace with heaven a little too cheaply, he did not discover it till later.

Whether, or how far, the ordinary Greek believed the gods to be the source of the moral law as well as its guardians need not be discussed here. The question obviously concerns the philosopher rather than the common man, and even the philosopher does not find it easy. The famous speech of Antigone on the ἄγραπτα κἀσφαλῆ θεῶν νόμιμα, the unwritten laws of the gods, and other passages, show that the idea was familiar, and it was enough for the common man to feel that certain νόμοι had the divine sanction. Exactly how or why did not greatly trouble him. The more thoughtful were sometimes troubled by observing that the gods, according to mythology, did not always obey the laws which they imposed on mankind, but this did not disturb the multitude. They accepted the stories rather in the spirit of the pious and simple-minded

[1] *The Religious Experience of the Roman People*, Macmillan, 1911.

farmer in a story by Mr. Eden Phillpotts, who modelled
his conduct strictly upon that of Abraham, even to the
point of seeking an equivalent for Hagar. There were
dangers in this frame of mind, as Greek experience also
showed, but in spite of it the ordinary Greek still con-
trived to believe that the gods expected of him obedience
to certain rules of morality. The gods were gods and for
a mortal man to scan their ways too narrowly was verging
too nearly upon ὕβρις. Dangerous persons like Euripides
did it.

We have endeavoured to make good the proposition
that the essence of Greek Religion was worship, and not
belief or morality, and to show that in spite of this it
received and deserved serious respect even from the more
intelligent Greeks. If this proposition is true, the consequences are important, but can only be briefly indicated
here. One consequence we have already noted. Criticisms
of mythology, and even criticisms of particular beliefs
about the nature of the gods, are not of necessity attacks
upon religion or expressions of general disbelief. When
they occur in writers like Pindar and Aeschylus, who are
essentially reverent and friendly, such criticisms are rather
a proof of belief than of unbelief. They desire to clear the
gods of unworthy imputations. This does not imply that
the friendly critic accepts as true and edifying those parts
of mythology and traditional belief that he does not
criticize. It means rather that, theology being fluid, and
mythology not subject to any canon, every man is free to
take or reject, and to interpret, the tradition according
to his ideas of right and probability. The traditions con-
cerning the gods are in fact in the position of the Apocrypha as defined by the Thirty-nine Articles. They may
be read for edification, but not to establish doctrine.

Even when we come to a writer like Euripides, whose
tone is not always friendly, it is easy to mistake his attitude,
and scholars with modern, or perhaps one should say, with
eighteenth-century prepossessions, have sometimes done
so, and have been misled thereby into discovering various

mare's nests. Some of these we hope to point out elsewhere; it will suffice here to mention the chief sources of
error.

Euripides, in certain of his plays, does unmistakably attack certain legends and beliefs as immoral or absurd. We
may further grant that for many reasons it is probable that
he disbelieved most of the current ideas about the gods,
and *a fortiori* the tales of the poets, ἀοιδῶν δύστηνοι λόγοι.
Therefore to the modern, with whom belief is the test,
Euripides is an unbeliever. And being an unbeliever he
naturally makes a mock of the gods; and when he does not
do so, but appears to treat them with respect, he does it
with his tongue in his cheek. That is the inference drawn
by the late Dr. Verrall and by some other scholars; and
accordingly they take pains to show that when the gods
appear to play a dignified and respectable part, this part
is not to be taken seriously. The gods are still being
mocked, though more covertly. What appears on the
stage is not what really happened. The characters on the
stage are themselves deceived as to the true course of
events; they are led to believe that a god has really intervened. Only an initiated few, enlightened by sundry
hints, see through the delusion and know that no god was
there. Thus a modern dramatist might make play with
a ghost in which all his characters believe, while a natural
explanation is covertly suggested to the audience.

Such a play as this is conceivable, and as an exceptional
device might be entertaining, but it would grow mono-
tonous on repetition, and it is somewhat hard to combine
with serious tragedy. We are fortunately not compelled
to believe that Euripides, in order to save at once his skin
and his self-respect was under the awkward necessity of
never admitting divine intervention into his plays except
as make-believe. He is doubtless critical, but he is a Greek
of the fifth century B.C. and his spirit is not quite that of
'écrasez l'infâme'. He may fall foul of ἀοιδῶν δύστηνοι
λόγοι, he may be indignant enough at the immorality of
some myths and some popular conceptions of the gods,

but he is not thrown into a fury by every mention of the
miraculous, and by every suggestion that unseen powers
may intervene in human life. That curious state of mind
is already somewhat obsolete and it never prevailed in
Greece before the days of Epicurus.

Such hostility to religion would have been in Classical
Greece irrational. The modern dislike of miracles proceeded chiefly from the injudicious use of them by
Christian apologists; the dislike of established religion
proceeded from a belief that the dogmas of the Church
fettered the minds of men, and that the priesthood was
tyrannous and grasping. But in fifth-century Greece
apologetics were hardly born as yet, and miracle in itself
was no stumbling-block; for the conception of natural law,
as we understand it, was hardly born either. At most it
was one theory among many. The priesthood was not
powerful enough to be tyrannous, and it had not in any
case the sway over the minds of men which is conferred by
a definite dogma. One class of sacred functionaries, the
μάντεις, or professional interpreters of omens, is often
accused of venality, and this imputation is sometimes extended to the oracles at Delphi and elsewhere. But this
is an exception that proves the rule, for against the μάντις
many Greeks, not Euripides only, betray some *animus*,
though by so doing they do not always imply disbelief
in the honest μάντις, or in all omens. There is no such
animus against priests in general. Against the received
theology, if the word can be used, it would have been
puerile to tilt or to cherish hatred; it was too much like
fighting the air. It is true there are persons now who can
work themselves into a frenzy at the mention of a fairy
tale, but Greece bred few cranks. When the stories were
harmless, the most critical were content to let them be,
or used them as they found convenient.

This is just what Euripides does. He attacks immoral
tales, but he has no scruple in using others for his own
purposes. In the *Alcestis*, for instance, Dr. Verrall assumes that he cannot seriously mean us to believe that

Heracles rescues Alcestis by wrestling with Death, and he invents a theory of a trance in order to clear Euripides of any such degrading concession to popular superstition. But to make of death a personal power is a thing very natural and innocent; only a theological pedant could object to it. And if he is personal, he can be wrestled with; and Euripides makes Heracles wrestle with him. That does not prove that he believes, or even expects his audience to believe, in a personal and tangible Death. Shakespeare does not compel us to believe, except for the moment, in the ghost of Hamlet's father, or in Macbeth's witches; and whether he himself believes he does not tell us.

It is not a difficult assumption that Euripides, when it pleased him, treated the supernatural part of the received legends in somewhat the same spirit. It is only on some such assumption that he becomes intelligible. He is certainly more of a propagandist than Shakespeare or most great dramatists, but we do violence to the facts, if we try to find propaganda everywhere. Nothing is more obvious than that his plays are conceived in very different spirits. In the *Ion*, for instance, propaganda is unmistakable, and for once something of *animus* against Apollo, a reason for which we shall suggest presently. In the *Helena*, at the other extreme, it is difficult to see anything but a burlesque, or if not that, a treatment of the legend in the spirit of light comedy. There is scarcely a pretence of seriousness, or if there is, it is only just sufficient to allay the scruples of the more orthodox. It comes in fact near to the character which Dr. Verrall would impose on so many of the plays. It may be noted that such treatment was all the easier because the legend on which the play is based was not itself quite firmly established. There were mythologists who denied that Helen had ever been to Egypt. The legend in fact belongs to the Apocrypha, if for the moment we may count the better attested legends as canonical.

Between these extremes there are plays of various types. In the most there is incidental propaganda, sometimes more, sometimes less; but as a rule the legends are treated seriously and their miraculous elements used as is convenient. Sometimes a naturalistic explanation of the legend serves the dramatic purpose best, and is used accordingly. Thus in the *Orestes* the Erinyes become the hallucination of Orestes, and are not actually presented; a very natural and effective use of the story. In other cases no such explanation is suggested and the story appears to be accepted as it stands. In several plays the treatment of the divine personages (especially in the θεοφάνεια) is a little perfunctory, but this is no proof of deliberate travesty. Euripides was more interested in his human characters.

Two of the plays, the *Hippolytus* and the *Bacchae*, stand out as apparent exceptions, for in them the divine personages are treated more seriously, and almost sympathetically. In the *Bacchae* indeed this difference is so manifest that some critics have seen in it a recantation. Euripides in his old age, they think, has come to see that there is something in those divine powers which he once derided. On the common assumption that Euripides, as a sceptic, must never be allowed to present a divine legend sympathetically—though Mr. Shaw's *St. Joan* must now give pause to such critics—this theory is plausible enough; more plausible at least than Dr. Verrall's transformation of Dionysus into a mesmerist. But once we allow that Euripides, though sceptical, is not morally bound to be always poking fun at the popular divinities, the problem grows simpler; and it is not difficult to see why in these two plays his treatment is more sympathetic than in others.

The divine figures in these plays, Dionysus in the *Bacchae*, Aphrodite and Artemis in the *Hippolytus*, all stand for something real; Dionysus for the force, whatever it be, that inspires the ecstasy of the mystic; Aphrodite for Love; and Artemis for that fierce passion for an ascetic purity which is found in some young minds. These passions, whether they proceed from an inward impulse or not, seem to those possessed by them to come from a power outside themselves. The belief that they do is natural, and Euripides would probably not have denied it outright. The distinction between 'personal' and 'impersonal', 'conscious' and 'unconscious' was not yet clearly drawn. Even Anaxagoras postulates νοῦς (mind) in the ordering of the universe, and Socrates's complaint that in practice Anaxagoras left νοῦς in the cold and only made use of mechanical causation indicates how vague such distinctions still were. Anaxagoras himself had clearly not worked out the implications of his νοῦς. If that was so, Euripides, his admirer, would have little scruple, even as a philosopher, in personifying the powers in question. Here he was not merely accepting a popular belief for dramatic purposes, but dealing with something he felt to be real. He therefore treats them with more sympathy and power than the more rarefied Olympians. Yet of the latter there is in fact only one, Apollo, against whom he declares open war. And we notice that the god whom he attacks is not so much Apollo, as the Apollo of Delphi. Now Delphi was pro-Spartan, and Athens, especially during the Peloponnesian War, would view an attack on the Delphian Apollo with some indulgence, if not with satisfaction. There are signs elsewhere, most notably in his attacks upon Sparta, and his treatment of Menelaus, a Spartan hero, that Euripides either shared or indulged the prejudices of his countrymen.

I have dealt with Euripides at some length because this is a crucial instance, and one often debated. His case sufficiently shows that the Greeks, even when sceptical, approached the received religion in a spirit quite different from that of some modern sceptics. To multiply instances would be superfluous, and the attitude of different writers naturally varies; but whatever author we read, it is always well to remember that apparent acquiescence does not imply a grounded belief, nor particular criticisms, however strongly worded, a general disbelief in the received religion.

The predominance of ritual and absence of dogma in Greek Religion throw some light on another debated point. Much labour has been spent by students of religion and by anthropologists upon discovering the origin of its various rites. So long as such inquirers limit themselves strictly to the formal origin, and say that such and such a rite resembles an early form of rite found elsewhere, and may be derived from it, or from something similar, such inquiry is legitimate and reasonable. But the inquirer is seldom content with this. More often he thinks that in suggesting an origin for the form of a rite he has explained its meaning; and here a whole crop of fallacies raise their heads.

First of all it is scarcely legitimate to speak without reserve of the meaning of a rite even in the case of historical Greek Religion; it is still less legitimate in the case of the rites from which the Greek may have been derived; and thirdly it is wholly illegitimate to assume that the meaning has passed unchanged from one to the other. It is scarcely legitimate to talk of the meaning of a Greek rite, and to argue from one instance to another, because, in the absence of central authority or dogma, we can never be sure that the same rite bears precisely the same meaning in different places. We know quite certainly that all the gods, not even Zeus excepted, appear in different places with very different attributes and functions. Some of the functions they perform locally are the last we should expect of that particular god or goddess; and it is plain that except in name the local deity has not much to do with the corresponding Olympian. This being so, it is rash to assume that the meaning of similar rites did not vary likewise. There is evidence that it did, particularly in the case of those rites of which the Eleusinian Mysteries are the typical instance. Exactly what deities were worshipped;

who they were, deities of the underworld, or merely givers of fertility in this world; what doctrines, if any, were taught to the initiated; all this is obscure even at Eleusis. The thing most certain is that the answer given would have been different at different periods. And if this was so at Eleusis we may be sure that there was at least as much uncertainty and instability in similar cases elsewhere. The utmost it is safe to say generally is that this or that rite appears to belong to the type of the Spring or Harvest Festival, or whatever it may be. Unless we have in the case before us more direct evidence than the form of rite, we cannot pretend to know more of the meaning. Such evidence is sometimes forthcoming, but not very often.

It is still less legitimate to assume a fixed and definite meaning in the primitive rites from which the Greek are supposed to be derived, first because rites indistinguishable to the outsider may be used for very different purposes. This is the case, for instance, in some of the ceremonial dances of the Australian aborigines. This is natural enough, for the powers of invention are limited even in the civilized man, and much more in the savage.

But beside this, and more important, when we look in every primitive rite for a meaning that can be expressed in definite words, we may sometimes be looking for what is not there. To look for such a meaning is natural to us with habits of definition and analysis, but we have to do here with a very different state of mind. An analogy, not, I hope, too remote, may help to describe it. Some kinds of birds have their courting ceremonies, as elaborate and definite as many primitive rites. What purpose they serve and why they are performed we cannot ask the birds, and the ornithologist does not know. A generation back he would have explained them glibly by sex-selection, but now he admits that explanation to be unsatisfying. There is evidently something in the avian mind, instinct or whatever name we choose, which tells the bird that in the mating season this is the proper thing to do, and it does it.

Primitive man is doubtless nearer than a bird to a consciousness of his motives in acting, but we have not far to go for proof that his consciousness is dim. Children, as all know, are ritualists and like to reduce their acts, their games especially, to a set form; but it would be unkind and silly to press a young child for the meaning of its ritual. It is not much more useful to ask the savage. When questioned on such points he often gives, as inquirers have discovered, different answers to different persons; and this is not always from reticence or deceit, it is sometimes because he does not clearly know. The act itself is the important thing, it is definite and fixed and obligatory; what it means is secondary.

Indeed, if we reflect a little, we shall find that even the civilized and intelligent man cannot always give us in words the whole meaning of his ritual actions. Their distinctive quality and value is that they enable him to express in act what he cannot so well express in words.

Most of this is familiar ground to all students of religion, but they sometimes forget their knowledge. And they certainly do so when they invest a primitive rite with a definite and elaborate meaning. They err still more, when from resemblance in a particular rite, or point of belief, they infer a whole set of ideas with which that rite or belief is connected in some other case. This error was conspicuous in some theories, once fashionable, on the subject of totemism; but in that instance it has been sufficiently exposed by many writers already.

It is hardly necessary now to prove at length that it is illegitimate to infer the meaning of a later rite from a primitive one which it outwardly resembles. For when the meaning of the primitive rite is so vague, and that even of the later rite so fluctuating and ill-defined, it is scarcely likely that any clearly defined idea has survived the passage from one to the other; and it is always possible that the meaning has been entirely changed in transit. That it has been changed to some extent is certain, for a civilized Greek could not, if he would, think the same thoughts as a savage. In the case of a religion which, like the Greek, has no fixed dogma, the only meaning we can safely ascribe to a rite is that which was assigned to it by those who performed it. This meaning we can ascertain from contemporary evidence, if we are lucky enough to find it. We cannot discover it from possible origins. Many years ago I remember hearing Miss Jane Harrison say in triumph, after tracing the origin of some local cult of Zeus: 'There! I knew that Zeus was only that old snake.' The whole fallacy of this method lies in that word 'only'.

It would be irrelevant to pursue the point further. Its chief value is that it brings out more clearly the importance and the function of ritual in Greek Religion. To the savage the thing done is the essence of the rite, and to the Greek piety and religion mean first and foremost the performance of rites, not belief or morality.

Therefore Xenophon[1] without absurdity can ascribe to Socrates the sentiment that piety lies in worshipping the gods νόμῳ πόλεως, according to the rites of one's country, and that those who do otherwise are foolish busybodies, περίεργοι and μάταιοι. The word περίεργοι is characteristic. To the Greek it is waste of time to be too curious in these ¡matters. Custom prescribes the rite to be performed and he performs it; its theological implications are hardly his affair. He is sincerely pious, but, if not exactly sceptical, at least a little agnostic. He does not expect to know all about the gods or their wishes, but he does know that they demand worship. The theologian will also note that he is not an advocate of the right of 'Private Judgement', for he accepts the νόμος πόλεως.

We have called Greek religion and morality 'external'; and such from our point of view they undoubtedly were; but there is another side of the matter which is easy to overlook, and by no means insignificant. To the Greek himself neither of them was 'external', and he would hardly have accepted the word as a fair description. For he did not distinguish between the two things, form and

[1] *Memorabilia*, i. 3. 1.

spirit, external and internal, in the same way as we. We habitually contrast them, and indeed in religion some sects regard them as mutually hostile: to the Greek they were inseparable, though distinct. This does not mean that he could not distinguish between soul and body, or between the outward act and its motive; he did so, of course, frequently. But to him the presence of the one implied the other: a beautiful form was the expression of a beautiful spirit, the ugly of an ugly.

We do not assert that the ordinary Greek, especially in early times, expressed this conviction to himself in abstract terms, but he held it implicitly and acted upon it from the first. This indeed is generally admitted. If this is true, the alleged externality of his religion, for instance, assumes another aspect. If the gods themselves were conceived and represented as beautiful; if the temples raised in their honour, and many of the rites by which they were worshipped, were beautiful too, the presence of that beauty was in itself an evidence of a spirit which informed it. The one could not exist without the other. The unphilosophic Greek would not have put it in these words, but it is beyond controversy that he felt it.

Without raising difficult questions of metaphysics we may allow that in this the Greek was in one plain sense right. The men who created those statues and temples, or who took part in those rites with an appreciation of their beauty, were honouring the gods in the noblest way they knew and ascribing to them the noblest quality. For, though it is rash to say, as some would, that beauty was the religion of the Greeks, it is quite certain that they placed nothing higher than beauty.

This is a subject on which it is only too easy to grow cloudy and fantastical; but it will be safe to say this. Most moderns (not all of course) are apt to think of beauty as something superadded, as a final embellishment to goodness, except of course in works of art, if even they are excepted. The Greek began at the other end. When he called a thing good, he meant first of all that it was beautiful; to that other qualities might be added; they might even be essential; but they did not come first.

These two convictions of the Greeks, of which there can be no serious doubt, that form and spirit (or idea) imply one another, and that beauty is an essential part of goodness, illustrate Greek Religion in other respects also. First, though it may shock some minds to say so, the Greeks, in making the gods beautiful, were from their point of view making them good too. For whatever qualities they lacked, they possessed the first requisite of goodness, and the lack of those other qualities was less keenly felt by the Greek, who put them after beauty, than by us, who put them first. Thus, when we deny, as we have done, that the gods, at any rate in the beginning, were moral, it must be with the reservation that they were beautiful, and therefore, to the Greek, good, if our scruples still refuse them the title 'moral'.

This attribute of beauty they possessed securely as early as Homer, and we cannot doubt that to him beauty meant as much as to any later Greek. The lines[1] in which the Elders of Troy exclaim, on the sight of Helen's beauty, that it was worth the sufferings of nine years' war:

οὐ νέμεσις Τρῶας καὶ ἐϋκνήμιδας Ἀχαιοὺς
τοιῇδ᾽ ἀμφὶ γυναικὶ πολὺν χρόνον ἄλγεα πάσχειν·

are a compliment to woman's beauty which the three thousand years since have never bettered. It is from Homer too, if further evidence were needed, that Tyrtaeus derives the idea, which he so oddly elaborates, that the death of the old in battle is more to be deplored than that of the young, because an old man looks less comely in his death. That reason, put forward soberly and earnestly to professional soldiers, the young men of Sparta, as a reason for courage in defence of their elders, is more conclusive proof than any work of art that the Greeks thought much of beauty. Conceive a modern general saying to a

[1] *Iliad*, iii. 156–7.

corps of young men : 'Die in defence of these veterans;
for they will not look so well when they are dead as you!'
Tyrtaeus says it seriously, and we feel it grotesque. Perhaps it is, or else magnificent: significant it certainly is.

The second point illustrated is this. Many moderns
complain that Greek art is cold;[1] others praise it for the
same quality. Doubtless Classical Greek Art is governed
by σωφροσύνη, and those who in Art prefer ἀκολασία (in-
temperance), as many now do, must find it cold and dull.
But the reason why many of those who admire Greek Art
still find it cold is that they are not fully sensitive to the
significance of form. There is no need of emphatic gesture
or facial contortion, of dramatic themes, of moving ad-
juncts and pathetic elaborations, when the mere lines and
shapes themselves can tell all that you have to say. There
is no thought or emotion, no dream even, but has its
proper form, and can be expressed in line and contour.
The meaning or emotion may be elusive, as it is in great
music, but that such art can stir the feeling as deeply as
any art can is quite certain. In music Bach is cold to
some modern tastes; and the reason is just the same. The
feeling is so completely transmuted into the form appropriate to the art, that those who must have emotion raw
and labelled before they can see it, deny its presence.
Those who are sensitive to form prefer the older method,
because they find its appeal more permanent. It may
seem too fanciful to suggest that such work is imperishable
because in it the form has been wedded to the eternal idea;
but it is certain that it has an eternal youth. The art that
transmutes thought and emotion into pure form is always
fresh; that which merely depicts them palls.

Greek Religion, like Greek Art, seems to us cold. It is
fashionable to assume that the worship of the Olympian
gods did not evoke any deep feeling or religious fervour.
If intense feeling was evoked at all, it was, so we are told,
in the mystic cult of Dionysus and kindred rites. In them

[1] See Chapter XIV.

only we must look for real religion, if religion implies emotion. The Olympians were too remote and abstract to stir emotion in the ordinary man.

If we admit that religion cannot be real until it is orgiastic, this statement of the case is doubtless true; but if we are content with a lower degree of fervour, a mild and genial warmth such as the eighteenth century might commend; then even the Olympian religion cannot be altogether contemned. A Greek hymn, it is true, strikes oddly on our ears. Praise and thanksgiving, ascription and prayer are usually restricted and apparently perfunctory; the main theme is often a narrative of some episode in the myths of the god addressed, and not always an edifying episode. Edification and the expression of personal emotion, we feel, are less important to the singer and his audience than beauty of form. Our feeling is true, but beauty of form, as we have just seen, is to the Greek in itself religious, or essential to religion, and he does not look for edification. If he is truly pious, he goes to church, so to speak, in order to pay honour to the gods; if he is less truly pious, in order to obtain benefits from them; he does not go in order to obtain instruction.

Hence the secular-sounding hymn, and similar things, do not prove levity or lack of real feeling. And if we remember the nature of his art, we shall not expect the Greek to obtrude emotion in his worship, even if he feels it. And if the emotion is not obvious at first sight, we shall not hastily deny that it is present.

Emotion, we may admit, is not intense. We have already seen how the Greek distrusted intense emotion; but there is evidence enough that the Olympians were not to the common man mere abstractions, or their worship mere formality. The evidence is too abundant to need citation. Even if we neglect as doubtful evidence the more striking utterances of the great poets, we find not only that the Greek everywhere is punctual in outward observances, but that his thoughts are full of the gods at all times. To them he habitually ascribes his prosperity or misfortune, to them he turns for protection in danger, for relief in distress, for counsel in perplexity. It is not to be conceived that the man who did this felt no emotion in respect to the beings whom he addressed in his worship. Such an idea could only occur to a mind possessed by the notion that a decently ordered ritual is a proof of insincerity and lukewarmness.

And the scholar will remember that in the cases mentioned the deities to whom the Greek most naturally turns are usually the despised Olympians; Zeus first, and then the other Great Gods. There might be local preferences among these; at Athens the name of Athena, at Argos that of Hera would perhaps come first to the lips, and so on; but the other gods were not excluded. Apollo, Artemis, Poseidon, especially, might be invoked almost anywhere according to circumstances.

On the other hand the deities specially associated with mystic cults, Dionysus and Demeter, in whom some students see the vital religion of Greece, were not so often invoked except in special localities, or in connexion with their special functions. And though the rustic might devote his worship chiefly to the rustic deities, Hermes, and the Nymphs, or some more local and peculiar cult, this again is no proof that the Olympians were felt as unreal or unimportant. It rather illustrates a familiar weakness of the human mind. The ignorant, or perhaps it is safer to say, the simple, in Catholic countries, often find it more comforting to address their prayers to a local or familiar saint than to the throne of the Eternal. They feel that the saint has more leisure to attend to their humble needs. This may be bad theology, but it does not prove that the peasant of ancient Arcadia, or of modern Brittany or Sicily, doubts the reality of the higher powers whom he is shy of approaching.

Greek Religion then, in spite of appearances, was a thing serious enough to the Greek, and not without influence on his life. This is proved even more forcibly by a thing which we have so far only noticed incidentally. Of all the precepts of Greek morality none is repeated so often and so unanimously as the maxim that men must bear with patience the gifts of the gods. This maxim is found first in Homer and the idea in one form or another is ubiquitous in Greek literature. It is the theme of every moralist and there is hardly a play, and one might almost say, hardly a chorus in any play, where it is not touched. This precept may be thought wise or foolish, pious or cowardly, but it is certainly fundamental in the minds of nearly all Greeks. This point is too familiar to need elaboration, but it is too vital to be ignored. To many Greeks no doubt it meant little more than what we mean when we say that we must 'make the best of things' or 'face the facts'; it is not always a proof of pious submission to the divine will. But it implies at least that man is dependent upon the gods and that it is unwise and useless to cavil at the gifts they send him. And no man who holds this belief can regard his relation to the gods as unimportant, or fail to be influenced by the belief in his conduct.

VI

SIN

WHETHER the Greeks had the conception of sin has often been debated, and both sides of the question may be maintained without absurdity. The answer will depend partly on the definition of sin and partly on the period we consider, for here the development of ideas is more marked than in most parts of Greek morality. If any act which offends a god is to be called a sin, then the idea of sin is present as early as Homer. For in Homer there are certain definite offences which the gods punish, although they are quite indifferent to other actions which modern morality condemns.

But if the idea of sin is taken to imply not only an act offensive to the gods, but a wrong state of mind, and still more if that state of mind must be felt as estranging the offender from God—and all this is implied in the later conception of sin—then the case is not so simple. And still less simple is it, if sin is evil not because it is the breach of an arbitrary rule, but because it is in necessary conflict with the holiness of God; and that also is implied in the later doctrine. For if ideas such as these were present at all, they are not to be found upon the surface of Greek life at any time, and certainly not in Homer. Homer's heroes break the rules, and are punished, but the rules are arbitrary, or at least they are determined, so far as they go, by human needs. The sanctity of oaths, the rules of hospitality, and the rest, were necessary for the preservation of society. Such rules plainly did not proceed inevitably from the holiness of the gods, for the gods were not holy. Nor was the Homeric hero oppressed by consciousness of sin. He frequently had to consult a prophet before he discovered that he had sinned. When he discovered it, he performed the external act of atonement prescribed by custom, or in special cases by a prophet, and so made his peace with the offended god; and only the particular

god concerned was offended, the others did not mind. This
atonement made, the account was squared. There was no
disturbing sense of sin left.

Indeed Homeric theology leaves no place for a sense of
sin, for when a man does wrong conspicuously, we are
usually told that some god had blinded him, or taken away
his wits. Believing this he could not well be oppressed
with a sense of sin. In all Homer the person who comes
nearest to expressing a sense of sin is, oddly enough,
Helen, in the lines (*Il.* vi. 344), where she calls herself
κυνὸς κακομηχάνου ὀκρυοέσσης, shameless and mischievous.
This indeed sounds like a troubled conscience, but it is
more in accord with Homeric ideas to suppose that Helen
is tactfully expressing regret for the painful result of her
unwise action, and such regret is not a sense of sin.
Monro's translation of ὀκρυοέσσης (or κρυοέσσης) as 'a thing
of horror' goes too far, if it is meant to imply moral
repugnance. Even by modern standards Helen's conduct,
if reprehensible, was not revolting.

At a later stage than Homer we find some things which
approach nearer to the modern conception. It is commonly said that the practice of purification for homicide is
post-Homeric. Whether it is really later in date is doubtful ; it is more probable that it, and some other religious
practices not mentioned by him, already existed, but
not in the particular society for which he wrote. Whatever its origin, it is *prima facie* an evidence of a sense of sin.
Further evidence is furnished by the mystery cults which
became prominent in the seventh and sixth centuries.
In all of these, rites of purification were a central part ;
and to our minds rites of purification naturally suggest
a sense of guilt or sin to be purged away. But the inference is not necessarily valid. These rites appear to have
been of very primitive origin, closely resembling the rites
of initiation of which anthropologists find many instances
among primitive peoples the world over. We must not
make the mistake of assuming, with some recent students

of the subject, that a rite which has primitive features
retains its primitive meaning for all who practise it.
Ritual is conservative and rites sometimes acquire wholly
new meanings. This fact is admitted by orthodox writers
in the case of the Catholic Church, and is too familiar to
need proof. But in the case of the Greek mysteries the
primitive origin is clear; the *onus probandi* lies with those
who wish to show that they had in fact acquired a higher
meaning. For the initiation rite in itself implies no idea
of sin; it merely symbolizes the passage from one stage of
life and of knowledge to another. That is the meaning of
its 'new birth', when that, or some such term, is used.

In the case of the Greeks there is some evidence to
show that both these rites, that of purification from
homicide and from other forms of pollution, and that of
initiation, did in time acquire an ethical meaning, but
we shall only understand the process by which this meaning was acquired, if we grasp that it was not originally
present.

Here, however, one observation may be useful. To
some minds it will seem that rites of this kind, however
primitive, and even offensive, in their form and in their
conscious object, do in some dim way bear witness to
a sense of sin and a desire for purification. Such feelings,
they would say, are universal in mankind, however dimly
conceived, and such rites, however grotesque, are an
expression of these feelings. This belief I am not concerned to dispute; but at present we are dealing only
with the ideas which the Greeks consciously attached to
these rites, and there is no clear evidence that they
originally connected them with any sense of sin.

The rites of purification undoubtedly suggest at first
sight a sense of guilt, but when we look closer it is doubtful if they really imply it; and pretty clear that in the first
instance they did not. When we find that the guilt of the
homicide is thought of as resembling a physical infection,
an infection which is incurred even when the killing is

accidental, and that this was the popular view as late as the fourth century, it is hard to suppose that any moral idea was originally present. It is not even clear that homicide in itself was originally an offence against the gods; for the punishment of homicide devolved not on the Olympians, but on the obscure powers of the world below, and these again are apparently, at least in some conceptions, the spirits of the dead. In that case the pollution, μίασμα, αἰτία, or whatever it be called, is in essence but a prolongation of the blood-feud into another world.

Again, and perhaps more important, we find that the effects of the αἰτία against which purification and expiation are intended to guard are originally material. The αἰτία is a danger, not a disease of the soul. It is an infection which, if not removed, may spread to the community, but the evils it produces are still material: damage to crops and herds, and the like. Material penalties have often been made the symbols of the spiritual; but that was not the case here. This was not 'the worm that dieth not', it was just an unpleasant consequence of homicide, a prolongation of the blood-feud. It does not in itself imply remorse on the part of the offender.

That in later times the idea of remorse was present need not be denied, but the gradual and difficult way in which this idea enters the scene, is evidence that it is not original. When we think of sin, Aeschylus, of all the Greeks, comes most naturally to the mind. Every one in reading Aeschylus is inevitably and rightly reminded of the Hebrew prophets, with their recurrent theme of sin and repentance. What else but sin is it that hangs over the house of Tantalus in the Oresteia? What else but sin can he have in mind as he repeats his themes of the inevitable penalty of wrongdoing; of the blood that, once shed, no man can recall; of the evil deed that begets evil deeds for its children; of the infatuation that seizes on the wrongdoer, προβούλου παῖς ἄφερτος ἄτας; in his δράσαντι παθεῖν, and a thousand other memorable phrases? The assumption that in all this the thought of Aeschylus is, if not the same,

at least near akin to that of the prophets whom he recalls
in phraseology, is almost irresistible. But a phrase of his
own warns us that the assumption is hasty : τριγέρων μῦθος
τάδε φωνεῖ, 'my doctrine is world-old', he says in reference to the maxim δράσαντι παθεῖν. Aeschylus, as all
serious students know, takes certain of the traditional
ideas and develops them in his own way, making them
more profound and more moral. Thus (in *Agamemnon*,
750 ff.) he takes another world-old doctrine (this time
called παλαίφατος) and deliberately corrects it. The traditional idea was that great prosperity of itself brought
ruin on the prosperous man and his house; a version of
the familiar idea of the envy of the gods, which persisted
at least as a half-belief as late as the time of Horace, and
is still latent in the minds of those who 'touch wood' even
now. Aeschylus corrects this to the more rational and
moral doctrine already mentioned, that it is the evil deed
that produces evil and perpetuates it; implying of course
what is elsewhere stated explicitly by him and by other
moralists(e. g. Theognis, 153-4) that great prosperity is apt
to breed the wicked deed.

This doctrine, however, sound though it be, is not,
strictly taken, a doctrine of sin. It is in itself merely an
assertion that one evil deed leads to another and that the
consequences extend from generation to generation. This
is a fact proved by experience, and may be admitted
without acknowledging the existence of sin. It is in fact
admitted at the present day by men who regard sin as a
figment of theologians. It is therefore at least possible
that Aeschylus regarded the matter in the same way, and
it is important to decide whether he did or not, for the
conclusion we reach will affect our judgement of Greek
ideas in other cases.

To give and discuss all the evidence in Aeschylus would
demand a volume, and we must be content here to point
out the conclusion to which it leads. Taking all the
evidence together it is impossible to deny that a conception of sin is present, but it is present in a peculiar and

limited form. Aeschylus believes the infection, the μύσος, to be moral, not merely physical. It affects the mind of the offender, and does not merely produce unpleasant external consequences. But on the other hand the sin, or whatever we are to call it, comes in a sense from outside. It is laid on a man by an evil inheritance from which he cannot escape. Though it infects him, it is rather fate than anything in his own nature that is responsible. And because this is so, because the evil does not spring originally from a moral imperfection, a wrong state of mind, but rather causes it, it cannot be removed by repentance, by returning to a right state of mind, but must work on till the debt is paid.

And how difficult, under this conception, the payment is we see from the *Eumenides*. The truth is that logically the debt on these principles can never be paid. There are ceremonies of purification, but Aeschylus feels that though the common conscience is satisfied by them, these do not suffice. Though the ceremonies are performed, justice in the form of the Erinyes is not satisfied. To appease them it needs the intervention of the gods, and the solemn inauguration of a new court to satisfy them, and even then they are reluctant to be appeased; and Aeschylus by making the votes of the jurors equal and thus constraining Athena to give her casting vote shows that he too feels how close the issue is.

It may be said that parricide is abnormal, and that in a normal case the normal procedure would be enough; but the truth is that, so far as we can see, there is in the scheme of Aeschylus no proper place for forgiveness. The sin, coming as it does from outside, not from the corruption of the sinner's heart, cannot be removed by repentance, for repentance does not deflect the forces that set the evil in motion. Though Aeschylus used this play to give a divine sanction to the Court of the Areopagus, all that that court could do was to ensure, by punishing the guilty, that the ἄγος did not fall on the community, but on the criminal. But fall somewhere it must, and Aeschy-

lus feels that in letting Orestes escape he is acting in a way
not justified by his premises. Hence the elaborate devices
and the special pleading by which he secures acquittal.

It is impossible, in discussing Aeschylus, to avoid theology entirely, if we wish to make clear the difference between his conception of sin and that most general, though
not universal, at the present day. Aeschylus, and the
traditional morality of Greece, has no doctrine of a Fall,
or of original sin. To him and to the Greeks in general sin,
if we call it so, is not a corruption of man's proper nature,
a fall from a state of goodness to which he can be restored
by repentance and divine grace. Such ideas are alien to
ordinary Greek thought, and Sin therefore remains to
them an unfortunate accident. There is a remote suggestion, perhaps, of a doctrine of the Fall of Man in the
Hesiodic story of the Golden Age and the successive
decline of men in the ages that follow. But the suggestion
is very remote, for the story in no way implies that men
of the later age have themselves fallen from a higher state
or have any power of returning to it. They are by nature
and inherently inferior to their ancestors, and have no
power of becoming better. The story is merely an expression of the idea that men are not what they used to be;
a belief common in all ages.

The Greeks, therefore, lacking the idea of a fall from
grace to which restoration is possible, were logically in the
same position as those modern moralists, who, whether
they call themselves Determinists or not, believe that a
man's actions are determined by causes which he cannot
control, whether these causes are the effects of heredity or
of environment. Such a belief, taken strictly, leaves no
room for moral responsibility and for anything that can
properly be called sin. Aeschylus, we cannot doubt, does
somehow believe that a man is morally responsible, at
least in part, but he cannot and does not explain how, for
with his premises there is no explanation; and still less
can he tell us how the sin once committed can be redeemed.

For if the cause of the act is outside the man's control, repentance is irrelevant. This in fact is the opinion of the modern writers whose position is logically similar. Aeschylus is less consistent, for in reading many a passage we feel that the evil deeds whose effects he traces are to him sins of which the burden is intolerable. But having no logical basis for his feeling he cannot tell us of any escape from the burden. All that he can do is to reiterate the ancient doctrine that a man should shun the ὕβρις which sets in motion the fatal train of evils.

In the idea of ὕβρις there is perhaps the germ of an explanation of the origin of sin. But discussion of ὕβρις must be reserved for another place.[1] For a doctrine which attempts a deeper explanation than Aeschylus can give, we must go outside traditional morality and ideas based on it. Such a doctrine we find in Plato, for in this as in other points he follows a line of thought which is distinct from and often opposed to the traditional beliefs. He is the most conspicuous exception to the rule that the Greeks proceed by modifying traditional material. But even he does not start in a vacuum; he also modifies earlier ideas, but he takes them from a different source, chiefly from the Orphics and Pythagoras. Whether the ideas he so took were Greek in origin or not, does not concern us. They were certainly not part of the traditional stock. The Orphic sect and other mystic cults stood apart from the general religion of Greece as a kind of Dissent. That they were always counted as alien is proved by many things; by the legends of Orpheus, by such historical events as the suppression of the Pythagoreans, and by the guarded way in which Plato himself alludes to Orphic and similar doctrines, and the contempt with which he speaks of some of their degenerate professors. Being alien to tradition, therefore this doctrine lies a little outside our scope, but must be shortly considered, for the traditional view becomes clearer by the contrast.

[1] See Chapter XV.

In Plato the rites of purification and rebirth, which, as we saw, were probably ceremonies of initiation in origin, have assumed a new meaning. The transformation, though the evidence is scanty, had doubtless begun before Plato. It is at least clear that a moral meaning had been attached to the ceremonial purification and that the purified worshipper was believed to be in some way identified with the god. The last belief indeed was primitive, though its moral implications were probably much later than the belief. The same is true of the myths like that of Zagreus which in a very barbaric way give mankind a kinship with the divine. In that myth man was formed of the ashes of the Titans who had first eaten the heart of Dionysus; man therefore contains so much of the divine. The grotesque nature of the myth suggests an early origin.

Plato (it is convenient to use his name, even if with Burnet we believe the doctrine to be derived from Socrates himself) adopted these doctrines, especially the last, in his own system. The soul, according to him, is in its own nature divine and immortal and pure, but in man is infected and defiled by the body in which it is imprisoned; for matter is evil. Even this idea may not be entirely new, but the way it was developed by Plato is characteristic. Man's aim is, or should be, to release himself, or rather his soul, from the pollution caused by contact with his material body; and this process can only be accomplished in a series of reincarnations. So far Plato may still be developing an earlier doctrine, but the method of purification, at least, is his own. Purification can only be accomplished by righteousness, and—here we come to veritable Plato—by wisdom and knowledge of the truth, and this knowledge again can only be attained by the study of philosophy; and philosophy here means metaphysics; the other branches are ancillary and propaedeutic.

In this last and most characteristic doctrine we return to Greece. To make virtue, happiness, and final salvation

dependent upon knowledge, and that the knowledge of
metaphysics, is peculiarly and indubitably Greek. From
Homer onwards we find knowledge playing a part in
regions we should think quite foreign to it. The Greek
naturally conceives knowledge as an essential part of any
kind of human excellence. This is his instinct and his
rooted habit, and Plato's doctrine is only intelligible in the
light of it. But the history of this idea must be treated
separately.

   That Plato's doctrine has a bearing on the problem of
sin is apparent. Here at last we have a conception of sin
which makes it inherent in man's nature, and not an
accident; and so opens a door to redemption by the road
of purification. In this Plato, by departing from the
traditional view, is able to carry us further than Aeschylus.
On the other hand, by making knowledge the essential, he
comes near to making wickedness not sin, but error;
though he does recognize that the ignorance which causes
wickedness has in part a moral origin. Thus in Plato sin is
not so much the intolerable burden as an impediment and
an imperfection. He kindles a passion for knowledge,
virtue, purity, but, in spite of the terrors of his myths of
underworlds and eternal damnation, he does not awaken
the same awe as Aeschylus. Sin, which is a mistake, is less
terrific. This defect, if it is a defect, in Plato comes from
defective psychology. Neither he nor any of the Greeks
had any clear idea of the will as a factor in moral actions,
and therefore ascribed to knowledge functions it cannot
perform. In this point Aristotle was more clear-sighted,
though none of the Greeks carried the subject far. In
this, as in other things, they may have showed their good
sense, in restricting themselves to the knowable.
   The subject of sin might be illustrated further, but little
would be gained by doing so; for neither popular belief
nor philosophy progressed beyond the stage reached by
Plato. Later philosophy indeed rather turned aside
from the idea of sin than developed it further. Sin, in any

natural sense of the word, is manifestly excluded from the
Epicurean universe in which the gods take no thought of
human affairs, and the Stoics, though in a different way,
excluded it almost as thoroughly. Though their doctrine
of Πρόνοια (Providence) leaves a loop-hole for divine intervention, their attitude to life is scarcely compatible with a
sense of sin. With them man works out his own salvation,
and in so doing relies on his own strength. It is this, if
anything, which sets him free from vice and weakness and
enables him to defy the assaults of the world and fortune.
Indeed the typical Stoic in his defiance of fortune comes
close to what the earlier Greeks would have called defiance
of the gods, and appears to be guilty of the great offence
μὴ κατ᾽ ἄνθρωπον φρονεῖν. To accept the gifts of the gods
with patience was the Greek principle ; to treat them with
contempt savoured of impiety. The truth is that by the
time of the Stoics men had begun to feel that the dis-
ordered world in which they lived was governed by τύχη
(chance or fortune), not by the old gods, and though
worship of τύχη had become common, defiance of τύχη
was less shocking. The older gods, partly for their credit's
sake, had been removed to dignified distance, and even
when their interest in human affairs was not actually
denied, and the Stoics did not deny it, men did not—at
least where the tincture of philosophy had spread—attribute their daily fortunes to the gods so simply as the
Homeric heroes had done. On the other hand the same
feeling that the world was out of joint, which in the
downfall of Greece gave rise to the worship of τύχη,
fostered in other minds the desire for means of release from
this distempered world, and exotic cults came in to
revive or replace the earlier mystic cults. There is no
need to dwell on this familiar chapter in Greek history,
for though these new cults kept in view the idea of sin,
and of purifications or redemption, there is no sign that
they added any new idea of moment, and they seem
often to have been lower and more purely ceremonial
than the cults they replaced. In the minds of those not

touched by such cults the idea of sin, if it can be so called, seems, in spite of the various influences mentioned, to have progressed little since the days of Homer. There were certain things of which the gods disapproved, and if you did them, you had to make atonement; by sacrifice, if you could; if not, by suffering the penalty. Beyond that their thoughts did not travel. It was a crude conception, but substantially the same as that held in all ages by the majority of those who believe in sin. Scholars of an earlier generation would have pleaded that higher ideas were to be found in the Eleusinian Mysteries. But though these appear in their later stages, and possibly as early as the fifth century, to have contained some moral ideas, the evidence suggests that these were borrowed from other cults, and it is waste of time to look to them for higher teaching than is found elsewhere. Their function was rather to popularize and make respectable the ideas formed in the suspect mystic cults.

VII

FUTURE LIFE

SOME readers of the chapter on Religion may feel surprised to find so few allusions to what is, to them, the most vital point of all, the Greek beliefs in reference to a future life. The reason for this omission is that the subject has been very fully discussed by many writers, notably by Rohde,[1] and in this case the popular view has been generally studied and is familiar to most students. It would therefore be waste of time to discuss it fully; but it may be useful to state and emphasize certain points.

The first and most important of these is the extreme vagueness and inconsistency of the popular beliefs on this subject at all times. We find this inconsistency already in Homer, and it persists till the end of the Classical period, and indeed later. Definite doctrines in regard to the future life were to be found in certain sects, for example in the Orphic rites, and as literature shows, they were not without influence, but such doctrines never became part of the general belief. On all the points we regard as most vital, whether there was a future life at all, what its nature was, and whether in it the good were rewarded and the bad punished, the average Greek had never quite made up his mind. On the first point we may perhaps say that he did most commonly believe in some sort of existence after death, but he was not free from doubt, and he most certainly was not sure whether this existence was more than the persistence of an unsubstantial phantom devoid of consciousness. 'If there be any consciousness in Hades', is the typical way of introducing a reference to the subject among the orators, and elsewhere. It is regularly mentioned and discussed as an open question.

This conception of the after-life as the existence of a powerless phantom the Greeks inherited from Homer, and it seems always to have been the view most prevalent

---

[1] *Psyche*, of which an English translation is now available.

among all but those who were strongly imbued with mystic teaching. But even in Homer this view is not consistently held. Even if the eleventh book of the *Odyssey* be disregarded, there is evidence elsewhere of a quite different view of the after-life. The phantom of the common Homeric belief goes down, when the man is killed, to Hades. But the custom of sacrifice at a tomb, which we find established in Homer, belongs to another and quite different conception. It implies that the spirit of the dead man is present in or near the tomb. More than that, it implies that the dead are not powerless phantoms, but potent to help or hurt, and therefore are to be propitiated. This aspect of the belief is not prominent in Homer, but analogy, and many rites of later Greece, prove that it lies behind the sacrifice to the dead.

We therefore have in Homer two incompatible beliefs in regard both to the nature of the after-life, and the local abode of the dead. It is commonly assumed that these beliefs were originally derived from two separate races, but whatever their origin, both were present simultaneously in the mind of the historical Greek. While in general he seems to have adhered to the Homeric view of the nature of the dead, and certainly conceived them as dwelling in a Hades under the earth, not in the tomb, he nevertheless performed with great regularity those rites at the tomb, which implied their presence there. In the case of the actual rites of burial he patched up a kind of reconciliation between the two beliefs by saying that burial was necessary to obtain for the dead man his due admission into Hades; but the recurrent annual rites, whether public or private cannot be so explained. Some of them imply not only that the spirits of the dead are present, but that they have power to help, for in both classes of rites they are invoked to send blessings to the living. This belief appears even more clearly in the worship of heroes.

Thus the Greek had always present in his mind at least two incompatible beliefs; though of the two one or the other would be the stronger in different minds. But the

confusion goes much farther than this. In Homer, as is
well known, Odysseus seeks the world of the dead not, like
Heracles or Orpheus, by descending into the earth by
some great cavern, but by sailing to the bounds of Ocean
to a land of dreadful night, where the Cimmerians dwell,
wherever that may be. This points to yet a third belief as
to the position of the world of the dead. It is true that
having arrived there Odysseus calls the spirits to him by
pouring the blood of his sacrifice into a pit which he has
dug, a proceeding which recalls the ordinary ritual at the
tomb; and it is also true that in the latter part of the book
he appears to be no longer standing by the pit, but by
some unexplained process has been transported into the
Underworld; but these discrepancies cannot change the
fact that this world of the dead is definitely set in a new
locality. The first discrepancy rather shows that Homer,
in following this different legend, wherever he derived it
from, adapted it unconsciously to the familiar ritual; the
second shows that the author who added the latter part
of Book xi—in this case there can be little doubt that it is
a later addition—was either so possessed by the more
usual belief that he overlooked the inconsistency, as a
careless reader does now, or did not trouble to effect a
more plausible transition.

This belief, that the land of the dead is situated not
underground but somewhere at the world's end, must
have been familiar to readers of Homer, but does not
seem to have been general. On the other hand a similar
idea, the story of the Islands of the Blessed, did establish
itself in popular belief. And this introduces yet another
inconsistency; for the same heroes who are preserved in
the Islands of the Blessed are also represented as being in
Hades. Homer, indeed, is not explicit and appears not
to know the belief in this form, but the contradiction is
plain enough in later times. In the well-known *scolion*
addressed to Harmodius and Aristogiton Achilles and
Diomedes are expressly said to be in the Islands of the
Blessed, and not so long after the date when the *scolion*

was written Polygnotus was depicting these and the other
heroes of the Trojan War in his painting of the Underworld at Delphi.

One more problem, one more discrepancy, goes back
as far as Homer. Though the dead in Homer are usually
shadows without intelligence or consciousness ('consciousness' is what we should probably say, when Homer writes
οἴῳ πεπνῦσθαι· τοὶ δὲ σκιαὶ ἀΐσσουσιν (*Od.* x. 495)), this
conception is not carried through consistently. The
words of Achilles to Odysseus, that he would rather be
the poorest of serfs on earth than the king among the
dead, imply at least a consciousness of pain; and similar
inconsistencies occur elsewhere. The most important and
most obvious of these is that, whatever be the fate of the
other shades, certain conspicuous sinners at least are being
punished and tortured in the Underworld, and their
punishment definitely implies not only consciousness but
at least the rudiments of a belief in rewards and punishments after death.

It has been maintained, not without ground, that this
description of these punishments is another late addition
to the original Homer, and that it was inserted when the
mystery religions had spread the doctrine of rewards and
punishments in the after life. This is possible, though
figures such as Sisyphus and Tantalus seem to belong to
folk-lore rather than to any particular doctrine, and may
therefore be very early; but in any case the date is not
important. The passage shows that by the sixth century
at latest, and probably much earlier, the idea of punishment after death was not unknown. But—and this is the
important point—the punishment in Homer is reserved
for some conspicuous sinners of legend, just as the Islands
of the Blessed are reserved for some favoured heroes.

And this belief, or something like it, was always the
most general. It might well be, men felt, that in the after
life some conspicuous offenders were punished, some
special favourites of the gods rewarded. The poets affirmed it and it might be so. But these things belonged

to ancient days when the world was different, and the heroes of that age were not so far removed from the gods. Many strange things had happened then, but it did not follow that such things happened now. One did not expect the gods nowadays to appear in visible form as they used to do habitually; though they did so perhaps still, as to Philippides, such things were very rare at best. And so, if the gods in earlier days had carried their loves and hates in some cases beyond death, it by no means followed that they were so much concerned with the fate of the common man. Belief in the story of Tantalus did not presuppose any general system of posthumous retribution.

We are now so familiar with the idea of a judgement in the Lower World, with the figures of Minos and Rhadamanthus, and the rest, that we find it hard to remember that no such definite picture was present in the mind of the average Greek of the fifth century. He might know that stories of this kind were told, but unless he were the devout initiate of some mystic cult, they were just stories, not part of his belief. When Pindar, or another poet, gave utterance to such ideas, he would recognize it as an esoteric doctrine, not as the expression of a general belief.

The evidence that it was not a general belief is quite conclusive, and whatever poets or other writers may say, and however eloquently they may voice a personal conviction, they cannot shake this evidence. Whenever Greeks talk seriously of death, not voicing a personal conviction, but appealing to the common man, they never assume in him any belief in a system of rewards and punishments after death. Even existence after death, in any shape, is mentioned guardedly and as a possibility, not as a certainty. The topic most obvious, and most natural to a speaker who is consoling the bereaved, as in the various Funeral Speeches, the hope of a glorious immortality, is never used at all. Had it been part of the common belief, this is inexplicable.

And, on the other side, the corresponding topic, the threat of posthumous punishment for the evil-doer, is also

lacking in the places where we naturally look for it. As we
note elsewhere, the Greeks believed, if somewhat vaguely,
that the gods did punish wrong-doing; but such punishment, according to the common belief, fell on the sinner
in this life, or on his descendants. The belief that the sins
of the fathers are visited on the children is prominent in
the gnomic poets, and pervades the thought of Aeschylus.
It is illustrated by many stories of all periods. Moreover,
when the Greeks, as they often do, express a doubt of the
divine justice, it is to this belief in inherited guilt and
punishment that they look for a solution of the problem,
not to a readjustment of the balance in another world.
The eagerness with which even in late times they report
stories of inherited punishment is in itself proof that the
thought of future retribution was not firmly rooted in
their minds. If the wicked prospered, as they did, it was at
least some comfort to feel that their descendants would pay
for it, even if they themselves had no Hell awaiting them.

Such, I believe, were the common ideas in regard to the
future life. That they were from first to last vague and
contradictory is not surprising. For the lack of definite
doctrine is characteristic of Greek Religion, and on a subject so obscure as this their ideas were naturally even less
definite than elsewhere. They always were indefinite, but
the cause and nature of the difficulty were not quite the
same at all times. The original uncertainty arose from the
vagueness of primitive thought and from the presence of
beliefs of different origin and mutually incompatible.
Then, as men grew more mature in mind, we have such
simple speculations as we find in Hesiod, or the more
elaborate systems of the Orphic teaching. But since these
were not systematic, and in the case of the Orphica were
rather rival systems than harmonizations of the old, and
since they were not generally accepted, these more definite
doctrines merely increased the confusion. When systematic philosophy arose, the confusion increased again,
for of these new teachers some rejected the old beliefs

altogether, and all modified them drastically or reinterpreted them.

Thus in the early stages of Greek history the common man is vague in his beliefs because of the nature of his own mind, and because definite doctrine is not yet born, and cannot be till men are more mature. The mixture of incompatible beliefs adds no doubt to his perplexity, but logical incompatibility of ideas would hardly trouble him as it troubled the philosophers later. In earlier days the Greek, like other men at the same stage, was not so much sceptical as simply vague. He believed what there was to believe; but it was not much. Later on there were more definite doctrines which he could believe if he liked, but they were various and incompatible, and he was now more conscious of incompatibility. Moreover before the beginning of the fifth century all these doctrines, the new and the old alike, had been challenged, and to the doubt which of them was true was added the more serious doubt whether any of them was true. To mere vagueness and perplexity was added scepticism, and the uncertainty of his belief was not quite of the same kind as in earlier centuries. Nevertheless he seems to have clung in this last stage to the vague beliefs we find in Homer more often than to the more definite teaching of later times; a fresh proof that the former were always predominant.

This review of the case exposes one error which, though quite groundless, is often found. There was no Age of Faith in Greece. We are apt, when we come to the period of philosophical questioning, to contrast it almost unconsciously with an earlier period of unquestioning belief. We have seen already that such impressions are misleading, but the present topic makes the fallacy more apparent. In the earlier time men's views of the after life were so indeterminate and contradictory that, though they may have doubted less, they had little definite to believe. In later times, from the end of the sixth century on, though doubt had become explicit, the beliefs attacked were at least more substantial. The mystic sects had filled in the picture of the Underworld and developed the doctrine of future retribution. And, even if these new doctrines were not accepted definitely by the majority of men, they were held by many in some parts of Greece, and were not wholly unknown to the rest. Thus the later Greek, whatever his personal views, had in his mind a fuller and deeper, if not a more definite picture of the after life. The idea that it was a real life, and perhaps a life of definite happiness or misery, was at least present to him as a possibility. And when such ideas had penetrated the Eleusinian Mysteries, their influence must have been widespread.

The influence of beliefs in the future life on conduct and moral ideas, if not on ritual, was therefore probably greater and not less in the later period. In spite of sceptical teachings, and in spite of the fact that few held the newer beliefs firmly, it was something that men were at least conscious of their existence. That there may be a Heaven and a Hell is a thought which, once admitted to the mind, has a restraining force on all but the stoutest sceptics. Such a thought was present in the fifth century, and it did not die. Epicurus is one evidence of this. His singular conviction that human misery was chiefly due to the terror of a future life implies at least that such fears were not unknown. The conception is singular, for literature gives little sign that the Greeks in general were afflicted by such terrors, and the stress laid upon it by Epicurus suggests either some exceptional experience or some personal idiosyncrasy. Still it may well be that in his day, the early third century, such fears were more rife than formerly. That age saw both a recrudescence of old superstitions and the introduction of Oriental cults. The barbarism which the Olympian religion had submerged came to the surface again when the disasters of Greece had thrown doubt on the power or the will of the national gods to help their worshippers. For, as we have seen, it was that, more than philosophic scepticism, which discredited them. (Of that the ithyphallics addressed to

Demetrius Poliorcetes are a cardinal piece of evidence;
Bergk, 1314.)

These later developments of the Hellenistic and Roman
period, though in part of foreign origin, were nevertheless,
in respect to the prominence of doctrines relating to a
future life, in line with the earlier course of Greek Religion. For the subject, as we have seen, had been growing
more prominent in the classical period; and held a larger
place in men's thoughts as time went on. The strongest
proof of this is that the traditional morality is wholly independent of the belief in a future life. Had that belief
been strong or important in early times, its influence
would have been visible in morality. Instead of that it is
left for the mystics and then the philosophers—or some of
them—to develop this motive. In traditional morality, as
all know, the strongest motive for right conduct and
ἀρετή was not the thought of a future life, nor even, as
a general principle, a desire to stand well with the gods;
it was the desire of fame, the desire to leave an honoured
name among generations to come. That motive was not
admitted on sufferance, as 'the last infirmity of noble
minds'; it was regarded, till philosophy advanced other
teaching, as the highest and purest. Pericles, as reported
by Thucydides, not only assumes glory as the object of
individual endeavour, but uses it as the justification of his
policy. The hardships of war and siege, and the unpopularity which Athens has incurred by her aggressions, are
justified and compensated, not by the advantages gained,
or the hope that her Empire will endure for ever—for it
is the nature of all things to decay—but by the thought
that the memory of her achievements will live for ever.
(Thuc. ii. 64.)

This utterance of Pericles is notable not so much because it illustrates the potency of this motive to the Greek
mind, for that hardly needs proving, as because it shows
at once the purity and the intensity to which it could rise.
It was doubtless a dangerous motive, if it could be used
to justify tyranny, but it was not ignoble. And if we

compare it with the motives which sway nations and statesmen now, we cannot say with confidence that they are purer or higher than this. The modern statesman as a rule appeals only to the desire for material advantages. Even when he is moved sincerely by humane motives and the desire for justice, his plea for justice and humanity means in effect that all men have an equal right to be comfortable. He would be very coldly received, if he called on his countrymen to sacrifice their comfort and their lives for anything so remote and insubstantial as the hope of undying fame.

This comparison is doubtless unjust. Men are sometimes better than their avowed principles, or than they know themselves. Men, as we know, are still ready to die and to suffer for their country without thought of material advantage, and often without desire for glory. So far, it may well be said, they are not worse but better than the ancient Greeks. But nevertheless it is still true that the good they seek for themselves and for their country is normally material, and they would regard as fantastic, if not criminal, the suggestion that a country's policy should be directed by the thought of future fame, when such policy implies serious peril in the present. Pericles, it is true, argues that the safety as well as the honour of Athens now demand persistence in the policy once begun, but it was desire of honour that impelled her to begin it. A less ambitious policy, he admits, would have been safer; but it would have been less honourable.

The truth is that for the Greeks the hope of an immortality of fame was not simply a substitute for the hope of personal immortality, but it had something of the same character. As it has seemed reasonable to the devout Christian and Mohammadan to sacrifice life or happiness in this world to the attainment of eternal happiness hereafter, so the noblest of the Greeks thought it reasonable to sacrifice theirs for an eternity of fame. It was for them, so to speak, an 'other-worldly' motive, and appealed to the same human instinct that makes men desire sometimes to sacrifice all for the highest that they know. And the desire, it may be noted, is expressly for posthumous fame. Honour in one's lifetime is prized, but far more an honoured name hereafter. The idea is as old as Homer, and a pathetic turn is given to it in the lines where Helen avows the belief that Zeus has laid an evil fate on herself and Paris in order that they may be a theme of minstrelsy among men to come (*Il.* vi. 357–8). Thus we see that man in coveting fame is perhaps fulfilling the purpose of the gods. This life is transitory and sad, but glory is not transitory, and to seek eternal glory was the Greek way of laying up treasure in Heaven.

VIII

RELIGION AND INSTITUTIONS

On nearly every page we have implied or illustrated the fact that Greek thought and institutions were intimately connected with religion; but our picture of Greek life will still remain imperfect, if we think of this connexion in modern terms. Modern life, or at least the life of modern England, provides no analogy to the state of things in ancient Greece. When we have stated that the Greeks had rites and ceremonies connected with every occasion in life, public or private, and that all their institutions had some form of religious sanction and consecration; even when we have shown that they performed these rites assiduously and that their performance had, in the modern phrase, 'an influence for good', we have still not reached the heart of the matter. Nor have we reached it when we show that religion in some points furnished rules of conduct, and enforced them; though to many this will seem the most vital point of all. When we say all this we are still looking at the matter from the modern English point of view. It is like saying that the Greeks went to church very frequently and regularly, and that they were duly edified by doing so.

To the ancient Greek all these things looked very different. For him religion and secular life were not separable. Though he recognized the distinction between sacred and secular, he would hardly have said that religion provided a sanction for his institutions or for his morality. That statement implies that institutions and morality are things separate and independent, and that religion is something superadded; and to the Greek they were inseparable. They were inseparable in their origin, and remained so in the thoughts of men until the times of philosophical scepticism. How far any given institution was shaped by practical needs and how far by religious beliefs it is impossible to say; the two motives were not distinguished in

the mind. Men did not say: 'it is expedient that our
separate *phratries* should be combined in a tribe; therefore
let us combine, and let us strengthen the bond by estab-
lishing a common worship for all the members of the
tribe.' On the contrary a tribe was a thing which had a
common worship; you could not have a tribe without
common worship any more than you could have a family
without common worship and common ancestors. Even
in the later times when tribes combined in city-states,
each state or πόλις must have its common worship, distinct from that of the bodies which formed it. Without
that it was not a πόλις. A πόλις was not a secular institution established for human convenience, it was a community united by the worship of common gods, and by
particular rites.

The same principle holds generally in all institutions,
as for instance in the great games of Greece. These, as is
well known, are not athletic contests which have been
established to attract competitors and have then been
placed, as an additional dignity, under the patronage of
some god. They spring from ritual and are an integral
part of it. This is so much the case that even the act of
training for athletics in palaestra or gymnasium is under
divine patronage, and a statue of the patron god stands in
the practice ground. The history of the drama provides
another familiar instance, and other examples lie ready on
every side. Life and religion are inseparable.

This principle, once grasped, gives a deeper insight into
various sides of Greek life already discussed. Among these
is the Greek view of women and of marriage. When the
modern student reads that marriage was regarded simply
as a necessary means of obtaining legitimate children, and
the wife was regarded accordingly, he concludes that the
Greeks had low views of the nature of women and of
marriage. We have already seen that this conclusion is
only partly true; we can now see that from the Greek
standpoint it is grotesque. To raise up children who
should perpetuate his family and so ensure due perform-

ance of the rites in honour of himself and of his ancestors after death was originally the most binding and sacred of all duties; and though the belief that the future happiness of the dead depended on these rites grew less definite with time, and though other duties of later origin, such as patriotism, began to rival the claims of family, yet the sense of this obligation never died while paganism endured. Marriage therefore was a religious obligation. A man did not marry to suit his inclination, though it might happen to do so, but because it was a duty to his family. If he derived pleasure or advantage from it, so much the better, but that was not the prime object of the institution.

It follows from this that, when a woman married, she too was playing her part in the performance of a binding duty. If she married expressly to raise up children (ἐπὶ παίδων ἀρότῳ γνησίων) this was no degradation and no sign of contempt for women. It cannot be degrading or contemptible to discharge an obvious duty. And if her inclination was scarcely consulted, much the same applied to the man. Marriage was much like any other social duty to family or to state. A man served the state as a soldier, whether he liked it or not; and he served the family by marrying, whether he liked it or not. No doubt he derived as a rule some advantage from marriage, as he did from other social services, otherwise they would not have survived, but the personal advantage was secondary.

Such was the original conception of marriage. It appears defective to those, now the majority, who think of marriage as a thing instituted only for the pleasure or advantage of the two parties. Once this conception becomes established, the disregard of the feelings of bride and bridegroom alike appears brutal, but there was originally no thought that their feelings should be considered. The later Greeks themselves found the old conception of marriage defective, when they too began to think of marriage not simply as a social duty but as an institution for the benefit of the persons concerned. But that view of marriage, as of other institutions, is late, and did not become general till after the Classical period. And the other view, as we have already seen, never quite died, but still prevails in a softened form in the countries most deeply imbued with classical culture.

In judging the Greek views of marriage, therefore, whatever our private convictions may be, we must realize that it is not a degraded form of something higher, as if the Greeks had declined from the standard natural to man, but an institution in accord with their whole scheme of life. Thus only can we understand it rightly. It dates from a time when conduct is prescribed by custom, and personal feelings hardly count. To have pleaded in such times that one did not wish to marry, or to marry this or that person, would not have seemed, as it seems to us, natural and right; it would have seemed unnatural and wrong: the selfish preference of a private whim to a public duty.

This same clue will help us elsewhere. We have called the morality of the Greeks 'tribal', and have pointed out how narrowly restricted their sense of duty was; that they owned no obligation to men with whom they had no definite tie of kin or community of rights. This appeared to be, as it is, a defect in ancient Greek morality, that it recognized no duty to man as man. But just as it is a mistake to suppose that the Greek view of marriage implies contempt for women, so we shall be mistaken here if we think the limitation of duties implies a special callousness towards mankind. The limitation is rather a condition necessary to the structure of society as it exists, or as it existed when the Greek code grew up. It is rooted too in religion. Religion, custom, and duty—here almost indistinguishable—all prescribe that a man shall help his friend and injure his enemy. It is his duty to society to do so, for in primitive society, where the stranger is potentially, if not actually hostile, this is the only means of safety. The society, whether it be family, or clan, or larger unit, must present a solid front to the world. Every member must help the rest as a matter of course. As in the case of marriage, it is not a matter of feeling, but of duty. Tribesman must help tribesman whether he likes him personally or not. The very use of the Greek words φιλῶ and φίλος, especially in early times, illustrates this, especially their use in Homer. φιλῶ means not 'to love', but to show kindness in act, and φίλοι are often not what we call friends, but persons to whom help is due, whether as kinsmen or for some other reason. Personal affection, though doubtless often present, is not implied.

The duty to 'hate' one's enemy is the converse of this. It is not a matter of feeling, but a social duty. A man who does not hate his enemy, and if he can, injure him, or at least inspire fear in him, is not doing his duty to the community, or to religion. For the enemies' gods too are potentially hostile to his own.

This may seem a primitive state of mind, and the state of society in which it originated was more primitive than what we actually find in most parts of Greece in the fifth or sixth century B.C.; for by then the bounds had been extended. The outer line of defence was now the πόλις, and the inner lines of hostility and suspicion between the parts of the state might profitably have been allowed to fall into decay. But the old feeling, as we have seen, still persisted, and its persistence now becomes more intelligible. The Greek in fulfilling the maxim that he should hate his enemy did not feel that he was indulging a private grudge, but that he was discharging a public duty. That feeling survived, as such things do, even when the true ground for it had partly ceased.

This explains what before looked puzzling, why an orator in the humane Athens of the fourth century so often goes out of his way to show that he has a personal quarrel with the man he is prosecuting. It is not merely that he is rebutting the suspicion that he is a συκοφάντης or blackmailer, though that motive in Athens was strong; it is that he feels himself to be performing a duty. To injure an enemy was not simply a gratification of his enmity, though it doubtless was that, but a meritorious act. He avows it and takes credit for it accordingly. That he did so as late as the fourth century merely shows that the feelings natural, and in some sort even right, when the code was formed, outlived their origin and their justification. Such survivals are common everywhere, but they are more conspicuous in Greece because the transition from primitive society to full civilization was in many ways so rapid and complete.

The same clue helps us again to the understanding of religion. When a modern audience is told that the essence of Greek Religion was ritual, it goes away with the impression that Greek Religion, whatever one may say, did not amount to much. Religion to that audience means belief and conduct, with ritual added as a means of strengthening the belief and of stimulating right conduct. We often hear it said without surprise that so and so is a very good man, 'but of course he has no religion'; or conversely that 'he is very religious, but his religion does not seem to do him much good'. To the Greek both statements would have seemed strange. To the Greek of early times they would barely have been intelligible; to the later Greeks, to Plato, and even to Aristotle, they would have seemed odd and perverse. For here again the things were barely separable in thought, and in practice inseparable. Custom, νόμος, told you that there were certain things you should do, certain things you must not do, in respect to gods and in respect to men. Some of these we should call moral duties, as for instance fidelity to oaths; others, such as sacrifice, we should call ritual observances. The Greek did not separate them. All alike were prescribed by his code and all were binding. The good man was he who performed them all to the best of his power. No doubt there were degrees of importance—to omit a libation was less serious than to break an oath—but this was not because the one thing was an inward feeling or act and the other an outward observance. That was not the essential distinction. If you were a good man, you did what custom required, and if you could not comply in all respects, you came as near as circumstances allowed. You did not say 'I will be moral, but have not time, or means, to be very devout'. Still less did you say that external observance did not matter, if your conduct was good. You might, and did plead on occasion, that from a poor man the gods would accept a humble sacrifice, a cake or a pig of dough, if you could not afford the living victim. Such a plea was legitimate, for it did not imply any contempt for the observance enjoined by custom.

In all cases it is the breach of custom, of the νόμος πόλεως, which is the essence of the offence. And in matters of religion the law of the state is likewise the law of the gods. There were cases in which the two might conflict, as they do in the *Antigone* of Sophocles, but not here. Here they coincided, and any act which suggested contempt for the νόμος πόλεως was an offence against the gods, and *vice versa*. And it was severely regarded. In the indictment of Socrates, the onus of the charge is that he does not believe in the gods of the state (οὓς ἡ πόλις νομίζει). It is not that he holds wrong or even pernicious views, though the words suggest that to us, but that he offends against the code (νόμος). This jealousy for the strict observance of the code is distinct from fanaticism, but the instance of Socrates shows that it could be as narrow and as dangerous.

This jealousy for the code is deeply rooted. It springs in part from the belief that the right way of life (δίκη) is that prescribed by custom, and that it is all of a piece. If you touch any part of it, you imperil the whole. More than that, you imperil, not your own soul, but the safety of the state. Religion, as we have seen, is not a private, but a public, or at least a social duty. The rites of the family are necessary to the safety of the family, the rites of the state to the safety of the state. This feeling was as strong in Rome as in Greece, and the most striking of all instances is furnished there by the Emperor Augustus. He, as all know, took great pains in all sorts of ways to revive the decaying religion of Rome. In this, though he was what we should call a sceptic, he was quite sincere. For religion and its observances were part of the old Roman way of life (the *mos maiorum* which corresponds to the Greek νόμος); and he believed, and those who supported him, such as the poets Horace and Virgil, believed too, that the greatness of Rome depended on the revival and preservation of that old way of life. And being Romans they felt not only that it was humanly expedient, but that it was in some sort required by divine powers. The *instituta maiorum* had a sanctity which expediency could not give.

Another, and less serious difficulty is removed by the same line of thought. We have noticed that the Greeks often treat as serious what we regard as small matters of deportment, or etiquette, or even of fashion. This becomes intelligible when we remember that the right way of doing all things, even the smallest, is originally prescribed by custom. The original sanction, as we see from the curious precepts in the latter part of Hesiod's *Works and Days*, was a taboo. It was unlucky to do things otherwise. Later on this was replaced by custom, but custom was a serious thing, and, as we have just seen, it did not sharply distinguish between the trivial and the important. The hold of custom in small matters grew less strong with time, but even in the fourth century B.C. it still regulated things which we regard as matters of personal taste.[1] Moreover it is pertinent to recall that the external and internal were not contrasted as with us. To wear your cloak in a decent and becoming way was not an 'external' trifle. Doubtless the line between custom and mere fashion was often faintly drawn in such matters, but the Greek point of view is perhaps as reasonable as our own.

[1] e. g. Demosthenes, 1122 and 1124.

IX

THE RELATION OF GREECE TO THE SAVAGE

THE last century has seen many theories of the origin
of religion. Corrupted Revelation, Ancestor worship,
Sun myth and Nature myth, Animism, Totemism, Magic,
Phallic worship, Vegetation Spirits and Dying Gods, all
have been invoked in turn and all had some vogue. None
has proved in the end so convenient a key to all the locks
as its bolder supporters hoped, but nearly all have added
something to our knowledge, and several have been supported with admirable learning. Yet even the best of
these investigators, whatever their services, have one
serious defect: they leave out the most interesting part
of the story. They show us the primitive rites or beliefs
from which some later religion sprang; they do not show
us the process of change. We see at one end a savage, often
a very crude and unpleasant savage, and at the other a
civilized man, a Greek for instance, both performing
similar rites, and, as they sometimes leave us to infer,
holding similar beliefs. This is like giving us the first and
the last chapter of a novel, and leaving us to bridge the
gap for ourselves. It is even worse than that, for the last
chapter, if not the first, is incomplete. We cannot seriously suppose that the civilized man attaches quite the
same ideas to the rites he performs as the lowest savage.

This defect is on the face of it somewhat serious. An
anthropologist who only concerns himself with the beliefs
and rites of primitive races has the right, if he chooses, to
stop there; but the student of religion who uses primitive
rites and ideas to explain those of civilized men is logically
bound to show how the one passed into the other and
what change they suffered in the process. Neither of these
is often done, or even seriously attempted. We cannot
perhaps complain so much that we are not shown the
process of change, for the necessary information is lacking.
Our primitive savage we can construct from modern

analogies and a few hints supplied by archaeology, and we know something more definite about the later Greeks; but milleniums lie between them, and to those milleniums archaeology furnishes but the faintest clues. We are reduced here to guess-work and analogy, but even so we must make shift to explain the process as reasonably as we can. To jump from one end of the story to the other without attempting to connect them intelligibly is ludicrous.

To make no attempt to define the attitude of the civilized man to the primitive rites and beliefs that he preserves is still worse, and leads to manifold errors. No scholar, if questioned on the point, would deny that the civilized man and the savage cannot see things with the same eyes; yet some writers on the subject often speak as if they did, and assume, or seem to do so, that a rite is explained when a parallel to it is adduced from Australia or Central Africa. And those who avoid this error sometimes fall into the worse one of assuming that to the civilized Greek these primitive rites looked much the same as they would to themselves. It would be invidious to mention names, but any one who has read a little in modern writers on this subject will easily remember instances of both errors.

Where great men and women fail it is not likely that a mere amateur will succeed, and I have no new light to cast on the subject; but it is fair to the reader to offer him such a rush-light of assistance as I can in his dark journey from the savage to the Greek. It may save him a stumble here and there, and at the worst it will remind him that the road is dangerous.

There are many ways in which the rites of an earlier religion may pass into the service of a later. The simplest is when the process is conscious and deliberate. Thus the Catholic Church preserves various ceremonies of which the form is derived from paganism. This is admitted by orthodox historians. In this case the form is found convenient and retained, but the meaning attached to it is definitely changed. If we would know this meaning, we must consult the theologian or ecclesiologist; we cannot infer it from the pagan use of the same rite. There are of course some writers who maintain that the Catholic Church derived many of its ideas as well as its rites, and those not the least essential, from paganism; but there is no question that the Church has now a definite system of theology, and that its rites must be interpreted in the light of it.

In such a case as this all is clear; both the process and its result are on record. The Reformation is a similar instance. Protestantism retained many of the rites of the Catholic Church, but attached a different meaning to some of the most important. Mohammadanism again borrowed from the Catholic Church, from Judaism, and from paganism, but put its own interpretation upon the things borrowed. Unfortunately the case is not so plain with the history of ancient paganism. Here the change seldom comes about at a definite moment, or if it did, we seldom have the record of it; the causes of change are various, and the process is often unconscious. The change may be due to conquest, to the later interaction of different strata in the population, to borrowings from neighbouring tribes or from foreign nations, to natural development of ideas, to the speculations of prophets or of philosophy, primitive or developed.

All these causes were present in Greece, and they are blended inextricably. There was conquest. Nearly all scholars are agreed that Greece was invaded from the North by the Achaeans some time in the second millenium B.c., probably about the middle of it, and that they established themselves as a dominant aristocracy, if no more, in some parts of the country, and brought their religion with them. What the earlier population was, whether homogeneous in race or beliefs, we hardly know. Nor do we know definitely what each race contributed to the later religion. Most scholars believe that the Achaeans introduced the Olympian hierarchy, or at least a religion in which Zeus was the supreme god. Some would maintain that they substituted a patriarchal for a matriarchal system of society, and in accord with this enthroned Zeus in place of female deities who had been supreme in the earlier religion.

Both these conjectures may be true, but they do not enable us with any certainty to separate the new elements from the old. Zeus, if any of the gods, belongs to the Olympian system; yet his worship is often associated with rites and ideas as primitive as any in Greece; in Crete, for instance, where, according to legend, he was born and even had a grave; in Arcadia, on Mount Lycaeus, where he was worshipped with rites that suggest human sacrifice; in Athens, where he is associated with the very primitive rites of the Diipolia. These instances alone are enough to show how hard it is to disentangle the two elements. Even in the case of Zeus we cannot always be sure whether a particular rite belongs to him, or to some more primitive being masquerading under his name.

Still without rashness we may conjecture roughly what has happened. The Achaeans, we must suppose, brought their gods with them and established them in the strongholds of their power. This, by all analogy, they were bound to do. But this was probably all, and it is less than we are apt to think. They did not apparently proselytize or persecute; paganism seldom did either. The subject population in the towns they ruled would continue to follow their ancient rites; still more the inhabitants of the countryside. This is proved not only by probability, but by the state of things later. In every Greek city we find many primitive rites surviving beside the official religion, or absorbed into it. In some cases in fact the earlier deities seem to have entered into and transformed the later comer. We have noticed how this happened to Zeus himself in some cases; and his consort Hera fared no better. The Hera of Argos in some respects looks so like a primitive deity of the matriarchal stage as to suggest that her connexion with Zeus and Olympus is late. If so, she shows that the ancient local deities sometimes succeeded not only in transforming but in completely swallowing the intruder. For Argos is a seat of Achaean power, and Hera is its chief deity.

This leads to a fresh point. The Achaeans, if they brought their gods, did not bring with them any coherent religious system; or, if so, they did not establish it. We do not find in the states once held by Achaeans, or in those held later by the Dorians who followed them, any such system: we do not even find that Zeus, or any other god, consistently stands first in actual worship with other deities grouped round him. We find there, as elsewhere, one god or goddess locally predominant, and one or two others less prominent: the rest of the Olympian hierarchy in the background only. In Argos Hera receives the chief place, in Sparta Apollo; in Messene alone, Zeus. This state of things suggests that the worship of the Dorians was tribal rather than national, that though they may all have acknowledged some common deities, each tribe paid special honour to one. Either that, or else the older powers again asserted themselves here too, and that god of the invaders became most prominent who could best be associated with an earlier local worship. Apollo Karneios at Sparta, and the neighbouring Apollo of Amyclae, like Hera at Argos, both have primitive traits, and Zeus Ithomatas in Messene may well have ousted an earlier deity of the hill-tops; for the worship on Mount Lycaeus and other hills makes this probable. Even if none of these conjectures is true, even if the belief that the gods mentioned were Dorian and not original is false, this only renders it the more certain that the Dorian conquest brought no sort of system even to the districts conquered.

After the conquest, as doubtless before it, there was the interaction of local worships and ideas both inside and outside each city, state, or tribe. This is a story too complicated to tell even in summary, but instances are familiar. Delphi and the other oracles, the Olympic games and others, the mysteries at Eleusis, these, and countless less important instances, illustrate such interaction of religious observances outside the boundaries of the state. Inside it was doubtless even more frequent, though less conspicuous. The extension of mystery religions in the sixth century and later, the re-emergence of ideas relating to the dead different from those which prevail in Homer, with the attendant cults of heroes and of the Eumenides, all seem in part to be due to the intrusion of old ideas submerged for a time but surviving in the subject population, and afterwards coming to the surface again. In Athens we have a curious instance of internal interaction in the elevation of Athena at the expense of Poseidon, with its parallel on a lower plane in the glorification of Theseus in place of the earlier Heracles. Here we have apparently a deliberate political object in the change, for Athena and Theseus were both associated with Athenian democracy, while Poseidon was the champion of the aristocratic families. Here, then, as in some measures of the tyrant Cleisthenes of Sicyon, after whom his namesake in Athens was called, we find religion used in the way assumed by the sceptics of the eighteenth century, as a political tool; but in Greece such instances are not very common.

This interaction of local cults continued throughout Greek history. By the fifth century, it is true, the Olympian hierarchy was pretty well established, if never wholly fixed—the list of the twelve great gods, who were worshipped at a common altar, varies slightly in different cities. We may assume that some notion of such a hierarchy had penetrated to the remotest parts of Greece. But primeval local cults survived in plenty as late as the time of Pausanias, who wrote under the Antonine Emperors. The ideas attached to these cults by their adherents must have been modified unconsciously by the more advanced religion round them; but on the other hand they sometimes emerged from obscurity and were made the vehicle of new ideas, which in turn influenced the official religion. This happened at Eleusis, and in the worship of the σεμναί transformed into the Eumenides at Athens;

and in general the powers of Earth and of the Lower World seem to belong to a primeval stratum which re-emerged after the age of Homer. This is generally recognized by archaeologists now, but in other cases we cannot always be sure whether a seeming new development in religion is not really a revival. We cannot assume without further evidence that a thing is late in origin because we only find it prominent at a late period. In some cases there is such further evidence. The worship of τύχη (Fortune) which is typical of Hellenistic Religion may fairly be called a late development; for if the idea of τύχη is not new, the widespread worship of Fortune is characteristic of an age when faith in the old gods was shaken.

Foreign influences are less continuous, but not negligible. They are stronger early and late than in the central period. Aphrodite, if not actually imported, owes much to the East, as is shown for instance by some parts of her worship at Corinth and elsewhere, and by her alternative name of the 'Cyprian'. Dionysus, if not actually imported from Thrace, derived from there some important characteristics, probably in the age between Homer and the Classical period. Even Apollo of Delos has some mysterious connexion with the North of Europe, and his sister Artemis was not immune from foreign influences. Even if her legendary connexion with the Tauric Chersonese means no more than that the Greeks found there a goddess whose rites in some points resembled hers, the kindred Bendis was introduced from Thrace in the fifth century, and Ephesus before that had identified her with the Nature-Goddess worshipped so widely in Asia Minor and Syria. That goddess appears under many names and forms, of which Cybele is the most familiar. In one of those forms she brought with her to Greece her attendant Adonis. It is very possible that this Eastern goddess merely replaced or modified a similar deity of the pre-Achaean population, but the influence of the East is undeniable.

These instances might be multiplied, but they suffice to show that foreign influences were present, and to some

extent the nature of them. They contributed something
to the common stock of ideas and rites and modified the
character of particular deities, but they do not seem to
have changed the character of religion essentially. The
mysticism associated with some rites of Dionysus is perhaps an exception, but Dionysus in most parts of Greece
was early reduced to something like a respectable Olympian, and purged of disturbing savagery. He became an
authorized outlet for certain feelings and emotions. It
was only in the Hellenistic period that foreign influence
affected the essence of Greek religious ideas. The ancients
themselves, when they speculated on the origins of their
religion, were fond of finding foreign influence, especially
Egyptian, in all kinds of places, but their conjectures are
usually quite fanciful.

The foreign influences of which we have real evidence
were not powerful enough to subvert the fundamental
ideas of the Greeks about the nature of the gods. Foreign
cults did not enter Greece in classical times by force of
conquest or any process of popular enthusiasm and conversion; unless we count the Dionysiac cult, here too, as
a partial exception. Nor were they as a rule officially
introduced by the state, as happened in the case of Cybele
at Rome. Except Aphrodite, whose Oriental traits are
usually ascribed to Phoenician influence, and Dionysus,
who, as we saw, was civilized before admission, none of the
definitely foreign gods figured *in propria persona* in the
religion of the state, at least in Greece Proper, unless they
could disguise themselves in the shape of some native god.
In other cases their votaries were found chiefly among
aliens and resident foreigners, and their worship was usually
little accounted of. The contemptuous use of the word
μητραγύρτης illustrates this.

Having reached this point the reader may well feel that
he knows little more than when he started of the process
by which Greek Religion developed from its primitive
originals. Nevertheless he has gained something, if he
sees more clearly than before that the development was

gradual, unsystematic, and in great part unconscious; still more, if he perceives that it was quite different from the process that modern analogies suggest. In Greece we have no general and conscious conversion, and no imposition of new rites or tenets by the state or by a priesthood. There are indeed partial exceptions; we have noticed that the ruling powers sometimes favoured a particular cult, and Delphi, for instance, sometimes ordained or authorized a new rite; but neither ever attempted a general revolution in religion. The state organized and in part supervised existing cults, but it did not normally initiate new ones; or if on the advice of Delphi it did so, such new cults were of a familiar type and brought no radical change.

Yet, the reader well may say, all this only renders the matter more obscure. The religion of Greece as we find it in the Athens of the fifth century is very different from the primitive cults from which it sprang. If those cults were not altered radically by conquest, or by authority, or by foreign influence, how comes the change? To this question no one can give a complete and satisfactory answer; but here again a distinction may help. How the primitive rite was preserved and acquired a new meaning is not very difficult to conjecture, even if we cannot trace the process in detail. The point more difficult to explain is how from a multiplicity of local worships, each centred round one god or goddess, or at most a small group of deities, there developed something like an ordered hierarchy, or such an approach to that as we find even in Homer. Here again modern prepossessions mislead us, and we are apt to overlook the real difficulty. In matters of religion we are so accustomed to a central authority of some kind that we forget that there was nothing corresponding to this in Greece. We have already seen that the Olympian system cannot have been imposed full-fledged by Achaean or Dorian conquerors. Who then did impose it? for they were our best card. If they did not, it is hard to see who did.

Here we cannot take refuge in Delphi, for, though it may have contained an oracle of some sort from very early times, it was clearly not of national importance in Homer's day. Moreover Delphi, even later, was more concerned with promoting the interests of its own worship, or of its protégés, than in teaching systematic theology to Greece. Delphi failing us, we are tempted to fall back on the familiar statement of Herodotus that Homer and Hesiod made the gods of Greece. If we could believe this, it would be a pleasant solution to imagine the Greek Pantheon springing full-grown from the head of a great poet, like Athena from the head of Zeus. But this is clearly impossible, for Homer's gods are evidently familiar to his audience, and need no introduction or description from him. Herodotus, therefore, if he had thought the matter out, can only mean that Homer and Hesiod had fixed and made more definite the figures of the gods, or perhaps merely that the later Greeks drew their ideas of the gods from them. The real difficulty is to discover where Homer found his Pantheon. It is not a fully organized or consistent system: Zeus, for instance, is sometimes an absolute monarch, sometimes maintains his authority with difficulty. But there is far more of a definite system than could have been gathered from studying the cults of any single state. All the greater gods are present, and their spheres and functions have been fixed.

This is the crux of the whole matter. Somewhere and somehow before Homer the discrepant local cults had been to this extent reduced to an intelligible system. This can hardly have come about by accident. If we could imagine a state in which all the gods of the Homeric Pantheon were actually, by some curious chance, worshipped under the aspects they respectively wear in Homer, the rest would be easy. The conception of the Olympian hierarchy would have followed not unnaturally. But the existence of such a state is barely possible. Even in later times, when, under the influence of Homer, all the great gods receive some sort of recognition, they never in

any given state correspond with the Homeric scheme.
Only a few are of real importance, and some or all of them
wear aspects unfamiliar in Homer.

The habit of tracing religion to the speculations of early
philosophers or priests, once common, is now rightly discredited; but in this case the facts are very hard to explain
without something of the kind. It is generally admitted
that in the works attributed to Hesiod we have in part the
fruits of early speculation as well as popular beliefs. In the
case of Homer the speculation must lie behind the poet,
for since he assumes his gods as known, it must have
already permeated the circle for whom he sang. This is
the more possible as that circle in the first instance may
have been narrow. Who did the work of systematizing we
cannot tell, but it is easier to believe that it was done
consciously than that it arose spontaneously from the
jumble of cults and beliefs which we find preserved in
later Greece. The only alternative is to suppose that later
jumble to be the ruins of an earlier system; but that is
hardly a serious hypothesis.

Once Homer is established, the gradual diffusion of the
Olympian theology, if we may call it so, is easy to understand. It was, as we know, gradual, and it affected men's
ideas of the gods more than it affected actual cult. Homer
probably lent some impetus to the worship of Zeus, but
on the other hand deities subordinate in Homer, Dionysus
and Demeter, for example, grew more prominent in
actual cult just when a knowledge of the Homeric poems
was spreading. On the other hand his influence on ideas
was great, and if we add to it that of Hesiod and other
poets, and add again that of such prophetic figures as
Musaeus and Orpheus, who, though legendary, stand for
a real movement in religion, we shall see that the Greeks
even before the rise of philosophy, must have attached
very different ideas to the rites they preserved from those
that originally belonged to them.

How the rites were preserved it is easy to see. Ritual
being the essence of religion, and any change in its form

dangerous, the most primitive rite had a tenacious life. It was not, as happens with religions dependent on dogmatic belief, abolished when it was found inconsistent with a changed dogma. Some primitive rites, as we have seen, survived to take a new meaning in the Catholic Church.

That survival is characteristic. The Catholic Church is in many ways the heir of ancient paganism. The influence of paganism on its ritual and doctrines has been studied by many writers, orthodox and infidel, with results sometimes useful, sometimes fantastic. But the influence is perhaps deeper in less obvious ways. Again and again in describing the Greek attitude in religion one feels that the thing described is not yet dead, but is still alive, if one looks for it in the right place. This statement is inoffensive, for the things so preserved are of enduring value. There are of course recrudescences of earlier superstitions, as there were in Greek Religion itself; but such things are universal. They are found very conspicuously in Buddhist countries, for instance. It is more characteristic of the Church that it preserves the better part of the earlier religion of Europe.

Thus, in both, religion is corporate and traditional. Though the Church admits and even welcomes converts, while paganism did not, neither regards membership as optional, or leaves the individual to decide by his private taste or conviction to what body, if any, he will belong. Religion implies membership of a particular body, and is not, as some would say, a question which concerns only or chiefly the individual soul and God. Moreover in both cases the family rather than the individual is regarded as the natural unit. In both, again, performance of the rites of religion is not optional or subordinate, it is obligatory; and in morality tradition determines the laws to be followed. The individual must exercise his judgement in application of the rules, but he cannot plead that his conscience exempts him from this or that rule. In both, once more, family ties are important, and prayers for the dead are enjoined; in both all the more important acts of life are consecrated by appropriate ritual (though the Church is not quite so meticulous here as paganism); and the year is marked by an ordered succession of feasts or fasts.

In all this the ancient Greek would find himself in a familiar world in any Catholic country. The chief contrast he would notice is that the tie between religion and the state is in some cases broken. But that is a modern phenomenon and a breach in the tradition, not part of it. Doubtless our ancient Greek would in due time discover some other important differences between the religion round him and his own, but still he would not feel himself entirely lost. Should we transport him on the other hand to modern England, or still more, to the United States, he would find himself lost indeed. He would have to search for anything he could recognize as religion. He would not be surprised at the number of different cults, but most of those he saw would seem to lack nearly all the marks of religion, as he understood it.

At the Renaissance men believed that they were reviving antiquity; they did in fact revive their knowledge of ancient literature and art, chiefly of Greco-Roman Art; but in many ways they rather enlarged the breach between antiquity and the modern world than lessened it. The Renaissance, with the schism in religion which followed it, broke through the continuity of European life more thoroughly than anything which had preceded it. This may seem a paradox, but the illustration already given proves it. An ancient Greek would have found himself even more at home in Medieval Europe than in Catholic countries at the present day. The familiar elements mentioned before would be more manifest, and the tie between religion and the state would be unbroken. He would be still at home.

This statement may arouse protest, for we are accustomed to think of the Greeks as happy in possessing freedom of thought, and of the Middle Ages as a time when thought was not free, and so are apt to make the two into opposites. Whether the Middle Ages were unfree is not our present business, but it is vital to note that the Greek freedom of thought was little like what we commonly understand by the phrase. A Greek, for reasons already given, had a wide freedom of speculation in matters of theology, and *a fortiori* in matters of science and metaphysics. Of that freedom he made good use, and thanks to it enriched the thought of the world for ever. But the Classical Greek did not claim an unrestricted right to challenge the fundamental moral ideas of his countrymen as embodied in law and custom. Such a challenge was indeed issued by some of the Sophists, and later by the Cynics, but both these were rightly regarded by most Greeks as subversive. The idea that the conscience of the individual was of more authority than the νόμος πόλεως was foreign to the earlier Greeks. Far from making conscience supreme, they had not discovered that 'conscience', as the word is sometimes used, existed. The common man derived his ideas of right from law and tradition, and the philosopher from right reason (λόγος); and neither would have had any sympathy for what we call 'conscientious objections'. To the common man the 'conscientious objector' would have been simply a law-breaker, to the philosopher a fool. For reason, he would say, is one. To suppose that each man can have a private Right Reason or *logos* of his own is sheer absurdity. Hence individualism in such forms as this seemed to the Classical Greek immorality or folly, and the Reformation and the Renaissance, to which jointly such individualism owes its origin, revived in this, as in some other things, not the spirit of Classical Greece, but that of its decadence.

These remarks may seem to range somewhat far afield, but they are not irrelevant, if they serve to bring home more forcibly the difference between the Greek point of view and the modern.

X

THE GODS IN HOMER

THE question of Homer's treatment of the gods is important for two reasons. First, that the value of Homer's evidence is impaired if it can be shown either that the passages offensive to modern feeling are later interpolations, or that the poems as a whole were written in a society which for some reason or other was exceptionally frivolous or irreligious. In either case it is clear that we cannot use Homer as typical of Greek feeling in general. And secondly, a right understanding of Homer in this regard throws light on later Greek Religion, and indeed on the attitude of paganism in general. If we misread Homer, we shall go astray in any study of Greek Religion.

For a modern reader to understand Homer's attitude to religion is not easy, and the difficulties felt are natural enough, but we cannot remove them in either of the ways suggested; for neither theory will bear examination. Interpolation is always possible, and it may well be that one or more of the offending passages is due to an interpolator. One such at least, the lay of Demodocus, might be removed without rending the structure of the poem, and bolder surgeons might contrive to excise others too. But many cannot be removed without violence. Nothing, for instance, is more repugnant to modern feeling than the gross deceit by which Athena in the twenty-second book of the *Iliad* lures Hector to his death. Yet the critic who would excise that on moral grounds is capable of anything. It would take a volume to examine the instances in detail, but any one who does so will find that many passages which offend or shock the modern reader are equally hard to remove on any sane principle of criticism. Thus the theory of interpolation does not help us, for it leaves us with some of the most troublesome passages still intact. That being so, it is safer not to assume interpolation unless there are other grounds for the assumption.

The other theory is even less tenable. Though the gods are sometimes treated with apparent irreverence, and though their actions are often, by our standards, highly immoral, the general tone of the poems is not sceptical or irreligious. It is abundantly clear that the poet and his audience believed in the gods and feared them and, after their fashion, honoured them. If they seem to us irreverent, it is not because they are sceptical.

We must therefore find some other explanation of the puzzle. It will clear the ground, if we state first of all what is and what is not to be regarded as irreverent or impious in Homer. And in this matter the first and most vital point to remember is that Homer's gods are not and are not meant to be moral, even by the standard of his day, and far less by ours. Moral perfection is as yet no essential attribute of divinity. All scholars know this, but the splendour of power and beauty with which Homer invests his deities so dazzles us that we find it hard to remember how far from perfect they really are. Homer's Olympus is drawn after the pattern of human society in an age still half barbaric. Zeus rules among the gods in much the same way as Agamemnon among the Greek chieftains.

This fact, once grasped and applied, removes many of our difficulties. Agamemnon is supreme in virtue of his power (ἐπεὶ πλεόνεσσιν ἀνάσσει), and even Achilles must yield to him, though sullenly and with disastrous consequences. Hera, and Poseidon, and other deities sometimes recalcitrant, must yield in the last resort to Zeus, because, as he tells them on one occasion, he is stronger than all the other gods and goddesses together. He is therefore more secure on his throne than Agamemnon, but none the less the other gods, like Achilles, do not yield without protest and even reviling, and they likewise thwart his will for a time and cause trouble. That was the kind of monarchy with which Homer and his hearers were familiar, and they thought it natural that heaven should be governed in the same fashion. If Homer makes his gods recal-

THE GODS IN HOMER

citrant, it is not to belittle Zeus or to hold him up to contempt. Again, if Homer's gods not only rebel against their ruler, but quarrel with one another, they are only doing what mortal chieftains, διογενεῖς βασιλῆες, habitually do; and when Homer describes their quarrels, he is not holding them up to reprobation.

So much as this most readers of Homer, when they consider the matter, will probably grant. But the gods of Homer offend much worse than this. They are guilty of deceit and treachery, of petty spite and jealousy, to say nothing of unabashed immorality. They persecute un-happy mortals for trifling reasons of pique. Hera pursues the Trojans relentlessly for the slight done to her beauty by the Judgement of Paris; Poseidon persecutes Odysseus for reasons little more substantial, and so on. No wonder that some critics have said that Homer's gods are worse than his human beings. This is perhaps to overstate the case, for the conduct of Homer's noblest heroes can be scandalous enough. Achilles and Odysseus can act like savages on occasion, and if Achilles hates a lie, Odysseus certainly does not. Homer therefore does not feel, or mean us to feel, that in the cases mentioned the gods are falling below the human standard. And indeed, even in the worst instances, they do not offend against his code as they offend against ours. Jealousy for personal honour, as then understood, and ruthless vengeance for a slight, are for him actually meritorious. Even the treachery of Athena is a stratagem, and that all is fair in war was an acknowledged principle then, as it has been later. It is often reiterated in later Greek Literature. For a god to act upon it in dealing with a mortal disturbs our modern feelings; but when gods and mortals met and fought on the field of battle, the case was different. And more than this, Athena by her treachery is helping her favoured Achilles, and Achilles is a Greek, and when the gods are helping men, the favoured side do not scan too narrowly the means by which the ruin of the enemy is brought about. He who weighs this, will see the action of Athena, and many other seemingly dubious actions of the gods, in a new light.

If the gods of Homer always helped his heroes, we should therefore, if we put ourselves in Homer's place, seldom wish to criticize their actions. But it must be confessed that they sometimes are unkind even to the heroes. In the *Iliad* certain deities are consistently pro-Trojan, and in the *Odyssey* Poseidon persecutes Odysseus. We therefore, if we see with the eyes of Homer, become more critical of their actions. But here another principle comes in. The society of heaven, like that of earth, is loosely organized, and gods, like men, have their local and personal ties: we might almost say their local patriotism. If some gods favour the Trojans and others the Greeks, their conduct is perfectly natural, and according to the rules of international, or so to say, of inter-deity morality. It is the same with Poseidon and Odysseus. We may think Polyphemus an unattractive child, but the fond parent has a perfect right to avenge him; as good a right as Athena has to protect her favourite, Odysseus.

In all these cases, when we are scandalized at the action of the gods, we are unconsciously making an unwarranted assumption. We are assuming that the gods are a sort of Supreme Court or glorified Hague Tribunal, and that it is their duty to do impartial justice between man and man, or nation and nation, without respect of persons. Homer and his contemporaries had no such idea. Far later in Greek history, as we have seen elsewhere, the gods still had their local sympathies and favoured this or that city. In fact the idea of the gods as impartial dispensers of justice never established itself firmly as long as paganism lasted. We find as early as Homer casual references to the gods as punishing the wicked and rewarding the good, just as we find casual statements that 'the gods know all things' or that 'a god can do all things'. But none of these ideas is consistently applied, and in practice we find that the gods are neither omniscient, nor omnipotent, nor impartial. And when we remember how hard later theologians have found it to work out these ideas consistently, and still more to square them with popular belief, we need not wonder that Homer does not attempt to do so. And to maintain the idea of divine impartiality consistently is especially difficult, because human weakness at all times craves and claims the special favour of the Deity. This happens, as we know, most of all in time of war, and for Homer and even for the later Greeks a state of war was almost normal.

Thus when we grasp that in Homer the divine polity reflects human society—and the human mind being what it is, must reflect it—we find that most of the defects which offend us can be explained more simply than by assuming that Homer is intentionally treating the gods with disrespect. And the same applies to another kind of offence which distresses some modern readers even more: the lax sexual morality of Olympus. Most of these offences would disturb Homer's hearers less than some of the actions already mentioned. It was not that there were no rules in such matters, but they were different, and what is more important, the breach of them did not excite any peculiar horror. In such matters, as we show elsewhere, Greek feeling even later was far less sensitive. To us rape seems peculiarly horrible; to any Greek it was a peccadillo when compared with perjury or filial impiety. And there was no ideal of purity against which such acts offend, for, as we have also tried to show elsewhere, 'purity' was for most later Greeks and certainly for Homer, merely physical and ceremonial.

Moreover the liaisons of the gods, which pervade mythology, had in Homer's time a special excuse. When every chieftain of note claimed divine descent, room must be found for a god somewhere in his pedigree. And as he was honoured by descent from a god, so his ancestress was honoured by that god's attentions. It was only in a more sophisticated age that such things became embarrassing and the propriety of the god's conduct was questioned.

In earlier times, when gods and mortals were so near to one another, such things seemed quite natural and did not create offence. After all the favour of mortal kings in more recent times has often been regarded as an honour.

Thus most of the scandals are no scandals, and no proof of disrespect. There remain some which are less easy to dispel. There are scandals in Olympus which Homer's code cannot condone. The Greek code never condoned adultery, incest, or parricide; and all these appear in Olympus. The explanation of these is quite different. They are parts of the traditional mythology, which Homer accepts but did not create. He obtrudes them less than Hesiod and some later writers, and probably he and his hearers, if they thought about them at all, would have said that these stories were strange. They certainly would not have created them, for they bear the stamp of very primitive and savage minds; but they probably accepted them without much scruple, as simple-minded people accept tranquilly some stories in the Old Testament which would startle them if they occurred elsewhere. These were the stories that men told about the gods, and that was enough. If a pious Greek of later times did not feel bound to maintain the truth of every legend, still less was Homer bound.

But to talk of truth is perhaps misleading. It is not easy for us to grasp the frame of mind in which such stories are told and received in an uncritical age. An imaginative child tells to itself or to others stories which to it are neither true nor false. To unimaginative elders they are falsehoods, but not to the child. Children do undoubtedly lie, but such stories are not lies. The child has not looked at them in that way, or tried to distinguish reality from imagination. It imagines the thing vividly and that is enough. This is, I believe, admitted by psychologists, and it is certainly proved by common experience.

Homer's hearers were not children, and in ordinary matters distinguished truth and falsehood as we do; but these stories of the gods, the stranger myths, like that of

Uranus and Cronos, belonged to a remote world in which anything may happen; a world like that of fairyland. In that world monsters and monstrous actions are taken as matters of course and no moral questions are raised. It was thus that Homer's hearers probably regarded these tales. Some may object that the gods do not belong to fairyland. They are real and intervene in human life. But the fairies also, when men told of them, were real, and they also intervened in human life. Yet when they return to fairyland, no man knows the laws of their being, or would dream of calling them to account. And so it is with the gods. They intervene for good or evil, when they will, but no man knows what laws they obey. At most he knows vaguely how they behave towards mortal men; that certain things please them, and others displease them.

Here perhaps some may object that we are rating Homer and his hearers too low. But to this objection there is a double answer. First we are not underrating the intelligence of Homer's audience or making them too primitive. For in fact this kind of belief, that the gods indubitably exist and indubitably intervene in the affairs of men, but that we know little or nothing of their real nature—this belief may be primitive, but it may also be intelligent. Few philosophers, if any, have advanced beyond it; excepting of course those who believe in a divine Revelation, and of that in Homer's day there is no thought.

The second answer to this objection is that, whatever difficulties we feel, this hypothesis explains the facts more naturally than the rival theories. It is easier to believe that this was Homer's frame of mind than to think that he deliberately treats the gods with disrespect. For to do that would be ὕβρις, and that was the very last offence of which any Greek would willingly be guilty. And the later Greeks, when they criticize Homer for imputing immoral actions to his gods, do not suggest that he did so in mockery, and they were better judges than we.

The later Greeks, like ourselves, were sometimes disturbed by the behaviour of the Homeric gods; for by the sixth century, and perhaps earlier, the idea that gods should be moral was already creeping in. Accordingly some bolder spirits, like Xenophanes, arraigned Homer for impiety, and the more orthodox defended him by means of allegory. Though the idea of divine holiness never established itself completely in popular thought, later ages had at least some scruples in the matter; and it may be useful to remind the reader how little such scruples are found in Homer. The belief that the gods are holy, that they are just and benignant, and better than men, is so much part of our idea of the divine that we forget sometimes how remote such ideas are from primitive religion. And though Homer is one stage beyond the primitive, in this respect he is still very near it; only the rudiments of higher beliefs are visible. Of the power of the gods Homer's heroes are conscious at every turn, but of any moral quality in them only in quite special and limited ways, as in their habit of punishing certain offences. Of holiness or purity as a necessary attribute of deity they have not even a suspicion.

And this state of mind, though strange to us, is natural. Modern theologians assume moral perfection as an attribute of God, and make that perfection the standard to which human beings must aspire. This, with the shallower kind of theologian, and indeed with most men, means that God is conceived as a perfectly virtuous man and that conduct improper in a man cannot without blasphemy be ascribed to God. But this assumption, though general now, is neither obvious nor easy to prove. It is in fact so hard to prove that many men, finding it impossible to believe in a just God, deny the existence of any god at all. The Homeric Greeks, like most primitive peoples, chose the other alternative. They took the existence of the gods for granted, but did not attempt to prove that they were moral.

This alternative, though strange to us, is to primitive minds quite natural. The savage who invented the myth of Uranus and Cronos, had no intention of holding up the conduct of Cronos to reprobation, still less of holding it up as a model for the guidance of human sons. It was probably reprehensible by his standard of filial duty. But that did not concern him. He was, according to his lights, explaining a natural phenomenon, and he had no more idea of criticizing its conduct than a scientist, when he explains the action of lightning, has the intention of criticizing it for setting light to a tree, or of suggesting that men should follow its example and set light to more trees.

Homer, of course, was no primitive savage, but he, and most Greeks much later than he, were probably nearer in this point to the savage than to the modern theologian. This does not mean that the Greeks had consciously passed a Dispensing Act freeing the gods from the obligations of human morality, but rather that it had not occurred to them at first that such rules applied to the gods. In Homer's day it had hardly begun to occur to them. Homer's gods, of course, are fully personal, and the theory which would see in all their qualities and acts an allegorical reference to natural phenomena is no longer in fashion. But, whatever their origin, they are morally nearer to natural forces than to men. In fact, though the Greeks are often cited as providing the typical instance of an anthropomorphic religion, they are in this point less anthropomorphic than many more modern theologians. If they give human forms and passions to their gods, they at least recognize in them something which makes human standards of morality inapplicable. In this there was a rudiment of philosophy, and the idea survived till later days, and even found a place in philosophy. The gods of Epicurus, who live a life of careless ease, indifferent to the fortunes of men, a life most reprehensible by human standards, are the lineal descendants of Homer's gods.

Thus we find that many things that offend in Homer are no proof of intentional irreverence. But there is yet another count in the indictment, which is less easy to

meet. Granting that Homer's gods are not moral by our
standards, and that we must not ask them to be so, surely,
we think, we may expect them to be dignified. And they
are not even this consistently. The domestic squabbles of
Zeus and Hera; the laughter of the gods at poor Hephaestus limping round with the wine-cup; Ares and Aphrodite caught in an embarrassing situation and exhibited to
the other gods; the same Ares bellowing with pain when
he is wounded, and the same Aphrodite running like a
child to be comforted when she receives a scratch; none of
these can be called dignified, and there are other episodes
of the kind.

It cannot be denied therefore that Homer, as it seems
to us, makes the gods undignified; and this is artistically
a worse offence than to make them immoral. For it is hard
to take undignified gods seriously, and if we cannot take
Homer's gods seriously, the interest of the poems is
destroyed, or at least gravely impaired. For the gods
intervene at every turn in the action, and the issue at
nearly every crucial point depends on their intervention.
It is bad enough if we merely find the gods absurd;
it is far worse if we cease to believe in them. For in a
poem where divine and human are so closely intertwined,
to doubt the reality of the gods is to doubt the reality
of the human actors too. If we cannot take the gods
seriously, we cannot take the fortunes of the mortal heroes
seriously either. But Homer presents the fortunes of his
heroes as real and serious enough, and he could never
have made so gross a blunder as to present the gods in
such a way as to throw doubt on their existence. To present them as unreal was far more destructive of interest
than to present them as immoral.

Burlesque, no doubt, is a recognized form of art, and a
burlesque epic was actually attributed in antiquity to
Homer. But the end of burlesque is laughter, and even
the maddest of critics would hardly call the *Iliad* and
Odyssey burlesques. Yet there is a grain of truth even in
the suggestion of burlesque; for burlesque is compatible

with faith, as is proved by the practice of Greek Comedy, and by the 'Mystery' Plays of the Middle Ages, which often treat sacred personages with levity. Though Homer is not writing burlesque, some passages, most notably the lay of Demodocus, do recall the spirit which permitted the gods to appear in undignified guise upon the comic stage. It would seem that Homer thinks it permissible to give rein here and there to something of the same spirit. If Homer was not writing a burlesque, yet to unbend occasionally was no real disrespect. The parallels of Greek Comedy and of the Middle Ages, as we have just seen, bear this out; and if that does not suffice to convince the reader, he should study for an hour or two the representations of gods on archaic Greek vases. There is no reason to suspect the vase-painters of deliberate impiety, and they do not scruple to make the gods undignified. We may say if we like that an age which could so treat the gods was not deeply religious, but the medieval parallel warns us against pressing that point too far.

If all this is not enough, we may even concede that Homer is not all of a piece, and that in some sections he treats the gods more lightly than in others. And we may explain this by saying either that the poet's mood varies with the occasion, as it well might, or else that the offending passages are the interpolations of a more frivolous age. This would seem at first sight the most obvious explanation, but, as we have seen, it involves serious difficulties. Not only are some of the offending sections hard to excise, but even our supposed more frivolous poet would have to take account of artistic propriety. He would be a very bad artist if he deliberately introduced a tone out of harmony with the rest of the poem. So that, even if he existed, he does not carry us very far. For if he thought such things admissible in a serious epic, he cannot have thought that they rendered the gods contemptible.

Whichever of these explanations we choose—and they may be variously combined or modified—we must further bear in mind that the sense of humour was still rudi-

mentary, and that what seems puerile or brutal to us
was to Homer's warriors a good jest. If the gods laugh at
the awkwardness of the lame Hephaestus, they are not
falling below the standard of human decency, as at first
sight we may think. The pains and discomforts of others
still form the basis of most schoolboy jests, and Homer's
auditors were like schoolboys. I remember in the East,
in Kurdistan, that when a bishop, a Nestorian, had the
misfortune to break a tooth on a specially hard lump of
sugar, the story was passed round the country as an ex-
quisite jest. The narrators of the story were devout
Nestorians, the bishop himself was much respected and
indeed considerably feared by backsliders. Those who
retailed the story had certainly no contempt for him. The
ways and thoughts of men in that part of the world daily
recall Homer, and if they were still pagan they would have
received the episode of Hephaestus with the same simple-
minded enjoyment as they did the story of the bishop.

Then again those who are disturbed by Homer's treatment of the gods sometimes forget that he is not alone.
Other writers of epics introduced the gods, and their use of
them sometimes presents difficulties. We are usually content to say that they took the 'divine machinery' from
Homer. He had used it, and as he was the accepted
model, they felt bound to follow his example. This may
be true, but even so they were bound, if they were artists,
to adjust this traditional machinery to their general
scheme, and avoid absurdity and incongruity. Whether
they believed in the gods or not, some adjustment was
obligatory. This adjustment could be secured in various
ways. One way was burlesque; another, stopping short of
actual burlesque, was to treat both gods and men as
characters in a fairy-tale whose actions are not to be
judged by ordinary standards. Another way was to treat
both seriously, but to avoid obtruding the ugly or ridicu-
lous aspects of the accepted mythology, and so save the
dignity of the gods. This was not easy, but it was possible.
It is noteworthy and significant that Homer's greatest

follower, Virgil, does not adopt exactly any of these ways, though he keeps nearest to the last. He banishes impropriety from his Olympus, but he does not avoid attributing to the gods unworthy passions, spite, and trickery. In fact he calls attention to them: *Tantaene animis caelestibus irae?* 'Can minds celestial such passions know?'

Now this in Virgil is almost as puzzling as what we find in Homer; for Virgil certainly means his gods to be taken seriously. This is even more necessary in him than in most poets, for not only do the gods influence the action, but the whole significance of the poem rests on the belief in the divine destiny of Rome. That belief is Virgil's inspiration. Yet our acquiescence in that belief is imperilled, if the divine beings whose actions prepare the destiny of Rome are made monstrous or incredible; and Virgil must have known it. It is not enough to say that Virgil believed in Rome's destiny as divine, but did not believe in the gods of mythology, and that he would have been puzzled to define the nature of the divine power in which he did believe. This answer evades the point; for he has chosen the gods of mythology as symbols of the divine power, and if the gods become incredible or repugnant, they defeat his purpose. Instead of rendering the idea of Rome's destiny more impressive, they make it less so. This in fact is what they do in the minds of many modern readers. It does not lend dignity to Aeneas or to Rome to feel that their fortunes depend on the caprices and passions of irresponsible divinities.

If Virgil, then, could make his gods behave as he did, gods whom he unmistakably meant the reader to respect, it is clear that we must not make too much of the peccadillos of Homer's gods. Virgil lived in a sophisticated age; he knew what the philosophers had said of the divine nature and how they had criticized Homer for his treatment of the gods; and yet he treated them not very differently himself. It is idle to say that he makes them a little less undignified and a little more respectable, for if we allow for the difference of time, his treatment of them is at least as shocking as Homer's. His gods and goddesses intrigue and bicker, take umbrage or show favour with no more self-reproach than in Homer, and to the Romans of his day such conduct on the part of beings divine must have been more questionable than the actions attributed by Homer to his gods were to his earlier audience. Yet Virgil chose to take this risk, and his motives for taking it are not hard to guess. The example of Homer doubtless was one motive, but he would not have followed it, if he had thought that by so doing he would impair the effect of his work. Everything that he does is deliberate and well thought out. He chose to follow Homer here because he saw that these anthropomorphic gods lent themselves to dramatic effect better than any more abstract and rarefied being or beings. Their very foibles helped. The rarefied deity would have been as hard to handle successfully as the virtuous hero in a modern novel. It would be hard to preserve him from priggishness or insipidity. Milton's attempt in *Paradise Lost* is a standing instance of that difficulty.

Virgil therefore preferred to use the anthropomorphic gods with their foibles. When he made that decision he must have been confident that he would not shock his readers' feelings in a way that would destroy the effect intended. They would be able to accept these gods, if not as strictly real, yet as worthy symbols of the power that governs the universe. Milton could not possibly have done anything of the kind. If he had deliberately represented the Deity as swayed by passions which are recognized among men as evil, his readers would cry out upon him and the effect of the poem would be destroyed. For he wrote for a public in whose minds moral perfection was an essential attribute of God. To impute to Him base passions would have seemed to them both blasphemous and manifestly false. If, as some think, his deity is still too anthropomorphic, the defect is involuntary; he certainly aimed at presenting a Perfect Being; and he so far succeeded that most readers are more likely to feel that

his Perfect Being has some of the weakness of the perfect
hero in a novel.

This contrast, I think, makes the issue clearer. In
Homer's day moral perfection was not yet imputed to the
gods in any definite and consistent way; there were at
best faint inklings of such an idea. By Virgil's day the
idea had been familiar to philosophers and to other
thoughtful persons for some centuries, but it had never
become universal, and it had never taken hold of the
imaginations of men. Whenever men thought of the
gods, whatever shadowy background of philosophy was
present, they still conceived them in the traditional way,
and the old stories came to their minds. The stories could
not be justified by strict reasoning or taken at their face
value, but they were vivid and endeared by association
with worship, which had a hold, as we have seen, even on
the sceptical. They could still be used as symbols and
their uglier aspects ignored or allegorized. Such stories
only become useless as symbols when they not only disturb the reason, but shock the feelings and imagination.
The ancient legends, as Virgil treated them, did not yet
do this. Men's minds in his day were not yet so sensitive,
or so jealous of the honour of their gods: a slur upon it did
not provoke instinctive revolt and indignation. That
feeling is a later growth, for paganism was tolerant in a
way we find it hard to grasp. There were a few exceptions:
Plato was shocked at Homer, and some of Virgil's readers
may have been shocked, but very few. If Virgil himself
thought the gods whom he depicts not unworthy of his
great theme, not many of his contemporaries would be more
scrupulous than 'the royalest of poets and the chastest'.

This being so, it is hard to escape the conclusion
that Homer, in his much less sophisticated age, may
have presented the gods as he does without any intention of satire or disrespect. This does not prove that all
the offending passages are parts of the original poem,
but it should deter us from excising on moral grounds
where the operation is dangerous to the structure of the

whole. Still less are we committed to the absurdity of saying that Homer's theology is always consistent, or that he reflects the spirit of a deeply religious age; we only maintain that the inconsistencies are not in themselves presumptive proof of composite authorship, or the seeming levity a proof of intentional irreverence or scepticism. Such levity, and even irreverence and careless sceptical utterances, are no proof of a settled scepticism; and scholars are sadly misled, who, on the strength of such things in Homer, have discovered an eighteenth-century France somewhere in Ionia, and turned Homer, or the poet who wrote the less respectful episodes in Homer, into its Voltaire. The instance of Virgil alone is enough to show how little ground there is for this engaging theory.

Some perhaps may try to escape from our conclusion by saying that Virgil was able to use the gods as he did just because neither he nor his readers had any belief in them, and it does not matter what conduct you impute to unreal beings. This will not do, for Virgil's gods are not wholly unreal. If they were, they would not serve his purpose. When Pope in *The Rape of the Lock* uses sylphs as his divine machinery, he does so just because neither he nor any of his readers believe even faintly in sylphs, and they therefore help to give the air of unreality to his theme; and that air is intentional. His whole purpose is mockery; if we took any part seriously, the effect would be lost. But had Pope, or any other, set out to write an epic on the History of England, he would be very ill-advised, if he used sylphs, or fairies, or the gods of pagan mythology for his divine framework, and made the fortunes and destiny of our island depend on the capricious intervention of Puck, or Titania, or of Jupiter and Juno. We should at once know that the poem was not meant seriously, for these beings are not real enough for us to make that voluntary suspension of disbelief which is necessary to poetic illusion. They are, in William James's phrase, 'dead hypotheses'. Poets can use them still, if kept in the mists of distance, but they have no contact with modern reality. A poet who used them seriously in a poem on the Great War would awaken ridicule or nausea. Virgil can still use his traditional deities in writing of the fortunes of Rome, and though he softens the shock by throwing his events into the far past, the Rome of his own day is always present in his own mind and in the reader's. His use of the gods of mythology therefore shows that they had still so much life in them that the reader could at least suspend his disbelief. They were not 'dead hypotheses'. And being so far real, they could not be treated preposterously without ruining the poem, and the argument we have drawn from his use of them holds good.

Whether the reader accepts this conclusion or not, the discussion at least helps to bring home once more how wide is the gap between ancient and modern conceptions of propriety and reverence. If we seem to have exaggerated the width of that gap, let him consider one point more. The belief in the moral perfection of God, as held by later theologians, does not rest upon experience, for observation of the world could never lead to it. It rests, in the minds of those who accept it, upon divine revelation, or upon an inward and mystical conviction, which is revelation in another form.

Now the ancient Greeks knew of no authoritative revelation, and though mysticism, individual and corporate, was not unknown, its pronouncements had no general authority either. Men found their ideas of the divine power chiefly from actual experience, and experience led them to think that such powers existed; but experience did not make it equally certain that they conformed to human standards of morality. We cannot wonder at this. The most orthodox of Christian theologians admit that the actual course of events in this world is not easy to reconcile with the belief in a beneficent and omnipotent God. And they admit that human attempts at reconciliation are tentative only, and not final. It was natural therefore that the Greeks, having no revelation to correct their inference from experience, were never quite convinced either that the gods were morally perfect or that they were omnipotent. Both these beliefs are affirmed quite early, as we have already seen, but both had only a precarious tenure. Both were clearly incompatible with much of the current mythology, and the divine omnipotence, side by side with a belief in Fate, presented a problem to the most orthodox philosopher, and whatever the philosopher might affirm, the views of the common man were at the best hazy. He might listen to the philosopher, but he remembered the legends, and the gods whom he really worshipped were, as in the legends, very like himself. Some will say that this is always so, and if in fact men who have been taught from childhood to believe in a perfect God still sometimes ascribe to him their own frailties, it follows that the Greek who had not been so taught, would slip all the more readily into the same pitfall, and slip deeper. When one weighs this, most of the difficulties we have been discussing disappear.

XI

THE DRAMATISTS

Wᴇ have noticed more than once that the study of popular ideas often throws light on Greek Literature and corrects errors into which, without its aid, we should naturally fall. Such cases are most frequent in the tragic drama. They are in fact so numerous that it would take a substantial volume to discuss them adequately, and merely to mention them without discussion would be of little use. Accordingly I have judged it better to deal at length with one typical case, the interpretation of the *Oedipus Rex* of Sophocles. But before doing so it will clear the ground to make some general remarks on the three great tragic dramatists. For to judge a particular case fairly one must have a general idea of the character of their work, so far as it concerns us. And having it, we shall better be able to decide in similar cases of difficulty, when they occur.

For our purpose the point of chief importance is the use made by the dramatist of his traditional material, and his attitude towards it.

In Aeschylus the theme is always either the exposition of a moral problem or the illustration of a moral law. This is plain, even though in several cases we possess only part of a connected trilogy and therefore cannot tell how the theme was worked out. This theme in itself is usually quite simple, as the punishment of ὕβρις in the *Persae*; and the characters have importance chiefly as illustrating it. The poet can draw character forcibly enough: no character in any play, ancient or modern, stands out more clearly than Clytaemnestra, or haunts the memory more. But his characters are always in the hands of powers outside themselves—even Prometheus is so, though not quite as the human characters are—and the poet is only at pains to show us that side of them with which they react towards these powers. In the same way the legend used only concerns him as it can be used to illustrate his theme. He

modifies it as he chooses, but he does not stay to criticize
it for its own sake, though he dismisses tersely with a
ὁ δ' οὐκ εὐσεβής an opinion of which he disapproves. His
thoughts move in regions supernal (or sometimes infernal)
where the correctness of this or that legend is of little
moment. In respect to tradition he is, strictly speaking,
neither conservative nor revolutionary. In themselves the
legends are not important; they are useful to illustrate his
ideas. If he thought fit, he would use the freedom of a poet
and correct them, as Pindar and others do occasionally.

Now Aeschylus, though so essentially independent and
to our eyes essentially a monotheist, yet did not shock
popular feeling. Aristophanes can use him as the type of
orthodoxy, or what served for orthodoxy with the Greeks.
He deepened, but he did not overtly challenge or ridicule
the traditional morality. By the standards of modern or
of medieval theology, which insist on correct belief,
he must be condemned as a heretic. That he was not condemned is another proof that Greek opinion allowed much
licence of speculation, provided that the existence of the
gods and the traditional worship and morality were not
directly attacked.

In Sophocles we have, from the Greek standpoint,
another 'orthodox' poet, though the reason of his orthodoxy is different. He too is little concerned with the
truth or falsehood of the legends he uses; but this is not
because his mind is occupied, like that of Aeschylus, with
superhuman problems. Much time has been wasted in
discussing Sophocles as a 'moral teacher'. He teaches
morality indeed—all dramatists worth the name do that
—but he is more interested in character than in abstract
laws, and in character less as a psychological study than as a
means to dramatic effect. He is the converse of Aeschylus.
He does not develop character in order to illustrate a
problem or a principle; the problem interests him chiefly
because it serves to exhibit character.

Needless to say this is not the whole of Sophocles. He
is possessed beyond any of the Greek poets by the spirit

of beauty, and in beauty of form lies half his significance. To Sophocles may be applied what Mr. March Phillips in his book *The Works of Man* says of Doric Architecture: that the perfection of form is carried to a point where it amounts to the creation of a new idea. It is in virtue of his manner more than of his matter that Sophocles is a moral teacher. It is not that he lacks moral ideas and the power of expressing them nobly, but the exalted beauty of his work leaves a deeper mark on the mind and character than any particular idea. The passage beginning ὦ φίλτατ᾽ Αἰγέως παῖ, to which we have already alluded, is a moral education, not in virtue of the ideas expressed, for they are familiar, but of the manner of expression. To Sophocles therefore the truth of the legend used and the question whether its moral is edifying are not the first considerations. What is important to him is that the story is such that the catastrophe can be made to follow naturally from the character of the actors. ἦθος ἀνθρώπῳ δαίμων (character is destiny) is the principle he seeks to illustrate, or rather does illustrate, for abstract principles are not his chief interest. To justify the ways of God to man is not his direct aim, though at times he seems to do so incidentally and with reserve, as in the end of the *Oedipus Coloneus*. Still less is it his aim to arraign the ways of God. Thus he, like Aeschylus, is strictly speaking neither a defender nor an impugner of traditional religion, but he treats it with respect, and thus he too passed as orthodox.

The reader may notice that in speaking of Sophocles we have not made the customary and expected statement that he 'was before all things an artist'. That phrase, though not exactly false, has misleading associations. We shall be much in error if we suppose that Sophocles pursued 'art for art's sake' in the sense current in the jargon of some years ago. No Greek poet or artist of the fifth century did that. Doubtless he, like every great artist, when he was at work, would care for nothing except getting the thing right; his genius would see to that, and it would tell him likewise when it was right. So far he worked for art's sake. But, if he were asked to define his object in writing, his function as a poet, he would probably not have quarrelled with the definition that Aristophanes puts in the mouth of Aeschylus, that the poet's function is 'to make his fellow-citizens better'. Nor could Euripides, the frank propagandist, have quarrelled with it either.

This definition of the poet's function may be inadequate, but it was usual, for theories of art were still undeveloped, as we perceive from Plato's somewhat crude theories at a later date. The fifth century had no serious theory of aesthetic, and Greek art is an example, perhaps the most striking, of the common paradox that art reaches its highest achievements when it does not know, theoretically, what it is doing, and when, according to some minds, it is in the bonds of some degrading servitude to morality or superstition.

To say that art does not know what it is doing does not, of course, imply that the artist is indifferent to technical knowledge. Though Plato by the mouth of Socrates tells us more than once that the poets and artists of his time could not explain how they achieved their success, and Socrates therefore attributed it to inspiration, nothing is more certain than that the technical problems of all the arts were studied with extreme precision and acumen. The artist made himself master of his tools ; it was the use he made of them that he was unable to explain clearly.

Euripides, who, as we know, definitely arraigns accepted tradition, is the only one of the three dramatists to whom the truth of particular legends and their morality is a matter of chief importance. In fact, though he attacks tradition, it may be said that he is the writer who takes tradition most seriously. Neither of the others has time to be angry with a legend or a convention. To ask Aeschylus his views on such matters would be much like asking the author of the Book of Job his views on verbal inspiration and its compatibility with Darwinianism.

Such things must wait till he has settled matters more important. Euripides on the other hand, though he is not unconscious of the larger problems, is interested in the opinions and beliefs of the common man, and when he finds them silly or immoral, he thinks them worth attacking and attacks them. By so doing he makes them important; and doubtless they were important, since they affected men's conduct.

There are always these two types of mind; the one which feels and resents the absurdities of popular theology and tries to correct them, the other which is occupied with problems prior to particular schemes of theology. Aeschylus belongs to the latter type, and it is probable that most thinking Greeks were nearer to him than to Euripides. For, as we have seen, theology was fluid, and they held it loosely, not much troubled by discrepancies. Euripides no doubt is concerned with more than the particular legends he attacks; he considers the current beliefs to be in many points foolish and pernicious, and uses the particular case only as an instance. He disapproves the common indifference. But the more acquiescent attitude was the commoner, and it too had a rational basis.

XII

THE GUILT OF OEDIPUS

OEDIPUS, according to the legend, had been guilty of parricide and incest. But both offences were committed unwittingly, for he did not know, when he killed his father and married his mother, that they were his parents. He was therefore by ordinary modern standards morally innocent, or at worst guilty of manslaughter, for he killed his father in a brawl. Yet in the *Oedipus Rex* of Sophocles the gods inflict appalling penalties upon him and his country, and the most natural inference is that the poet thought the offences real, and the penalty not unjust. For this Professor Murray accuses Sophocles of moral obtuseness, and Mr. Sheppard seeks to save his reputation by arguing [1] that the poet does not think the penalty deserved, but rather seeks to remind us that in this world such inexplicable things do happen.

In an earlier chapter we have maintained that the Oedipus of the play is not to be taken as wholly innocent, and we now give the grounds for that opinion more fully. First, we know that the Athenians long after the time of Sophocles still believed that the guilt of murder was like a physical infection that clung to the murderer whether morally guilty or not. Mr. Sheppard himself cites Antiphon in proof of this, and other orators show that the belief persisted much later. [2] We indeed assume as obvious the distinction between act and intention, with all its moral implications; but the history of Greek philosophy shows that this distinction is not obvious. Philosophy had not grasped it fully till a date much later than Sophocles, and Aristotle thinks it necessary to discuss it at length. Sophocles was not a philosopher and we are not accusing him of moral obtuseness, if we believe that the distinction was not so clear to his mind as to ours, or, it would be safer to say, did not present itself to him in the same way.

[1] *Oedipus Tyrannus*. Sheppard. Cambridge University Press. 1920.
[2] e.g. Demosthenes 1382 *c. Neaeram* 109; Lycurgus *c. Leocratem* 146.

Moreover this is only one more instance of the point we have seen illustrated so often, that the Greeks do not distinguish as we do between the 'inward' and the 'outward', form and substance. It is not that they cannot intellectually perceive the difference, but that they do not oppose them to one another, as we do. Plato, when he wishes to find a word for the essential nature of a thing, chooses a word (εἶδος) which means 'form' or 'shape'. Few modern philosophers, uninfluenced by him, would have struck on a corresponding word.

Men who think thus cannot easily or light-heartedly get rid of the guilt of an act by saying that it was merely an 'outward' act, that the 'inward' intention was guiltless. That to them was as difficult as saying that a man was pious who lived blamelessly but did not perform the rites of religion. We know what offence the Athenians found in the line which Euripides puts in the mouth of Hippolytus:

ἡ γλῶσσ' ὀμώμοχ', ἡ δὲ φρὴν ἀνώμοτος.

'It was my tongue, but not my mind that swore.'

To them the words seemed evident sophistry, for an oath was an oath, and no unforeseen circumstance could remove the obligation. Nor could any unforeseen circumstance remove entirely the guilt of an act. The act of murder, according to the original conception, in itself and apart from the intention of the doer, gives rise to the μύσος. A man can no more escape from it because his intention was innocent than a man who sets light to an explosive can escape the explosion because he did not know the explosive was there. Sophocles and his contemporaries had refined upon that view, as Athenian law shows, for it distinguishes accidental homicide from murder; but we can hardly doubt that he, and others much later, still felt that a μύσος of some sort attached to the act itself.[1]

[1] The Athenian procedure in cases of involuntary homicide is one proof of this. This and the conception underlying it are most clearly and curiously illustrated by Antiphon, *Tetralogy*, B.

Those who assume that Sophocles intends to present Oedipus as morally innocent are faced by another difficulty. The gods have sent the plague upon Thebes, and the natural inference from this is that the gods believe Oedipus to be guilty, or at least that his acts call for expiation so urgently that they take this terrible way of bringing it about. This is the natural inference and we can only escape from it by supposing either that the gods are represented as acting unrighteously, or that they have not sent the plague; that it arises from natural causes, and that Oedipus and the Thebans are mistaken in thinking that it has anything to do with the sins of himself or any other man. No student of Sophocles is likely to accept either of these alternatives. If Euripides were the writer of the play, the case would be different. The second alternative would then be plausible, and the late Dr. Verrall, if he were still with us, would have presented it most persuasively. It would be easy to show, for instance, that the Delphic oracle has been bribed for sinister purposes by Creon, and that Sophocles has taken pains to put us on our guard against him, and against prophets and oracles too. The herdsman and the messenger have naturally both been suborned; and other difficulties could be removed as easily. All now becomes clear, and we see that the moral of the play is simply the appalling effect of superstition. This in fact is to our minds one moral of the play, but few will maintain that it is the moral intended by Sophocles. It is pretty clear that the gods thought Oedipus guilty and that Sophocles agreed with the gods.

We cannot escape from the difficulty by saying that Sophocles meant Oedipus to be morally innocent, and was reminding us of the tragic truth that in this world the innocent often suffer. For this is no case of the inscrutability of the ways of heaven. What the gods are doing is quite clear. They are punishing Oedipus, and inflicting calamity on the whole land of Thebes; and they explicitly assert through oracle and prophet that they are doing so to exact expiation for an appalling offence. If there is no

moral offence, then the gods who act thus are something
much worse than inscrutable. Unless Sophocles intends to
represent the gods not merely as inscrutable, but as dia-
bolic, he must believe that the offence of Oedipus, in some
sense or other, is real and serious. However irrational this
belief may seem to us, it is easier to conceive that Sophocles
held it than to accept any of the other alternatives.

To judge the matter fairly, we have once more to fix
our minds not upon what seems rational to us, but on
what seemed rational to Sophocles. It is so easy to take
as self-evident the beliefs and views of one's own time and
circle; so hard to remember that they may not be self-
evident to the most intelligent man of another age. This
holds good even in matters of the intellect, where, if νοῦς
is the same, men's views of νοητά should likewise be the
same. Yet they notoriously are not, even in simple matters.
We know how the early Greek philosophers wrestle with
elementary principles of logic, how the interlocutors of
Socrates, and often he himself, are entangled by fallacies
which seem to us now incredibly puerile. Moral principles
are certainly not simpler than the laws of logic. How
many humane men not much more than a century ago
saw no evil in slavery; and how many later still accepted
without a qualm the doctrine of Predestination in forms
at least as shocking to the moral sense as anything we
impute to Sophocles, if we affirm that his Oedipus is not
meant to be innocent!

The truth is that though we talk of moral instincts, and
though we may even concede for the sake of argument
that a sense of right and wrong is instinctive, it is no
instinct that decides to what particular acts we affix the
ideas of right and wrong. That is decided by custom, by
convention, by precept and example, sometimes by personal experience; but never by pure instinct, and still less
by pure reason. Mr. Sheppard argues that because the
Greeks of the fifth century had grasped the distinction
between voluntary and involuntary actions, Sophocles
must have perceived that Oedipus, because his offences

were involuntary, was morally guiltless. This disregards the fact that, as Mr. Sheppard himself admits, the belief in a pollution attached to even involuntary homicide was general in Greece, and was still alive and predominant in the fourth century. Sophocles, no doubt, might have perceived the falsity of this belief, but it is easier to assume that he did not than to accept any of the alternatives. He ought, no doubt, to have rejected the belief, but it is to be feared that he did not.

This, however, we may concede. He felt that Oedipus was singularly unfortunate. If penalties so terrible are attached even to involuntary guilt, at least the offender is more deserving of sympathy than the ordinary criminal. Such a feeling would be natural enough, and there are signs of it in the play. The weaknesses which we note in Oedipus, arrogance, rash self-confidence and passionateness, are deliberately made prominent, and some ominous utterances of the chorus throw them into relief. These weaknesses are not the original cause of the catastrophe, but they contribute to it and partly determine the form it takes; and by so doing they soften the shock to the spectator. It would seem that Sophocles felt that without this the catastrophe would be shocking, μιαρόν in the sense meant by Aristotle.[1] If the blow had descended unprepared, if we had simply seen a blameless king struck down by the penalty of an involuntary offence in the far past, then, even if we believed that offence real and serious, the shock would have been too great and the catastrophe repugnant. But our minds have been prepared by noting in Oedipus those qualities which lead even noble men to disaster, and which to the Greek are always ominous. The man who announces himself as ὁ πᾶσι κλεινὸς Οἰδίπους καλούμενος is to the Greek in peril of a fall.

If we put the case in this way, we shall come nearer to the intention of Sophocles than if we assume either that Oedipus is meant to be innocent, or that Sophocles assumed for the purpose of the play beliefs which he did

[1] *Poetics*, XIII. 2.

not share. We have dealt with the matter at length because the varieties of explanation prove very clearly how difficult it is to see with the eyes of a Greek.

That we should ever see with the eyes of a Greek is doubtless too much to ask, but at least we can try to clear away some of the things that distort our vision. And the first step in this endeavour is to grasp that we have not only to cast off obvious prejudices, but to realize that our standards, our criteria of truth and justice, however self-evident they seem, are not always applicable. Nothing is quite the same; not even the eternal hills and the sea. If we think even of the epithets that the Greek applied to the sea, we perceive that it was not the same to his eyes or to his mind as it is to ours. A little of its beauty he sees, but only a little; it is grey, boundless, barren, to his eye, and to his mind unfriendly and treacherous, never friendly or loved, as we love it. He knows its uses, the Athenian especially, but he does not feel kindly towards it; it inspires terror rather than affection. And yet his sea was the Mediterranean, more peaceful and more obviously beautiful than our Northern seas.

If we were to take all the component parts of the external world in turn, we should find the same difference. Hills and plains and forest, the sky, the clouds, the sun and moon and stars, all these bring to the mind of the Greek feelings and associations quite different from ours; and the difference is not merely due to locality; it is due to the eye with which these things are seen. The difference between the Greek feeling for nature and the modern is a commonplace of literary criticism; and if things discerned by the physical eye looked so different, then *a fortiori* moral principles, which are discerned by the inward eye, must have looked different too. This is not to assert that the moral sense is either more or less trustworthy than the physical senses, but that the report given by sense, in either case, is coloured by the mind that receives it. And the influence of the mind is clearly stronger in the case of moral perception than of physical.

XIII

LANGUAGE

We have already seen that Greek Art and Literature of the Classical period are never afraid of the familiar, but repeat and develop the same themes from generation to generation. The same attitude of mind shows itself in another way less obvious, and equally worthy of study. Everyone who has read a page or two of Homer, even in translation, discovers that he abounds in stock epithets. Each one of the greater gods and of the chief heroes has his set of standing epithets, numerous in proportion to his importance. Men and beasts and things, concrete or abstract, death and war, no less than weapons and ships, have their epithets likewise. No common thing or idea but has at least one; most things have more than one. The use of such epithets is characteristic of early poetry; in our own literature we can trace it from the familiar ballads back to Early English verse. In both cases, too, these epithets—if we leave out of account some obscure archaic words of doubtful meaning—express some essential and striking quality of the thing described: ships are 'hollow', dogs are 'swift-footed', and so on. Homer has besides this adjectives and descriptive phrases in abundance to fit the case, as occasion arises, but on the whole the impression he leaves on the mind depends more on the standing epithets. They and the things they are attached to coalesce in the mind and are inseparable. To them, more than anything else, we owe the vividness and colour, the sense of a rich and variegated pattern, and the emotional tone, which fill the memory as we recall Homer.

In later literature this frank and abundant use of standing epithets is naturally pruned away, but even in the tragedians, and much more in the earlier poets, many a stock epithet, often Homer's own word, is found. Almost every choral ode will furnish more than one instance. But, though the stock epithet is restricted, the principle is not changed essentially. Greek surpasses all languages in its power of forming compounds, especially in adjectives. Even modern science has discovered this, and made use of it. Every fresh idea can find easy and clear expression in a new compound. The poets naturally availed themselves thankfully of this happy endowment, and they were far from restricting themselves to the vocabulary of Homer. The multiplicity of their coinage is the despair of every beginner in Greek.

But this multiplicity is in one way deceptive, it serves to hide from the casual eye the simplicity of many of the ideas conveyed. When Aeschylus describes fish as the 'voiceless children of the undefiled' (ἄναυδοι παῖδες τᾶς ἀμιάντου),[1] the reader, especially the delighted schoolboy, is more conscious of the oddness of the language than of the simplicity of the ideas. Yet they are simple. Fish as a race are dumb, and dumbness is the quality which most obviously distinguishes them from the inhabitants of the other elements.[2] And purity is a quality of water and of the sea, a quality more striking in the Mediterranean than in the shallower, sand-infested waters of our eastern coasts. It impressed itself upon the Greek imagination, as many customs and many epithets show. They even declare that 'the sea can purge away all human ills' (θάλασσα κλύζει πάντα τἀνθρώπων κακά);[3] a famous and beautiful line which the abhorred scum of oil has now rendered false. Thus the ideas contained in the phrase are essentially simple and to a Greek even more familiar than to us; the only strangeness is in the language. And this instance is thoroughly characteristic.

When we read Greek poetry, and above all when we read the lyrics of the Greek dramatists, we are struck and at first bewildered by the wealth of epithets and figures of language. The mind is sometimes overwhelmed by their complexity and variety, and is led to the feeling that the thought behind them is involved and strange. But this impression is delusive. If anyone will be at pains to read through, for example, some of the most elaborate and

[1] *Pers.* 578-9.   [2] Soph. *Aj.* 1297; Hes. *Sc.* 212.   [3] Eur. *I.T.* 1193.

extravagant passages from the choruses of Aeschylus and observe the ideas apart from the expression, he will find that this is so. He will find bold, and sometimes fantastic metaphors, he will find bold and novel compounds heaped on one another; but, when he examines these closely, he will see that they serve to throw into relief an idea originally simple. The metaphor or the adjective may be bold and unexpected, but it usually illuminates some familiar aspect or essential quality of the thing described. This point is difficult to illustrate by translation, for no natural English can reproduce the force of words and the form of expression, but a literal translation, if the reader will pardon the resulting abortion, will help to explain the point.

In the *Agamemnon* (ll. 151 ff.) we read (in reference to the sacrifice of Iphigenia) of Artemis: 'bent on another sort of sacrifice, lawless, feastless, close-cleaving artificer of feud, fearless of husband.' And then: 'for there abideth wrath, fearful, inveterate, house-keeping, crafty, unforgiving, child-avenging.' Here we have adjectives heaped on one another, simple and compound, metaphor, 'transferred epithet' (for σύμφυτον belongs in thought rather to νεικέων than to τέκτονα), in the first extract; in the next, adjectives even more deeply piled and bold personification. More than that, each epithet adds a separate touch to the picture, and our first impression is of confusion and verbosity. But when we look again we see that the ideas expressed are all clear enough and germane to the subject. What Aeschylus has done is to remind us in two or three lines of all the essential points of the story; he uses a word where he might have used a sentence. The sacrifice of Iphigenia, a human sacrifice, and that of the king's daughter, is 'lawless' and offends the code of Greece. It causes strife between the husband and the wife, and Clytaemnestra in her anger ceases to regard her husband with awe, as a wife should. That is the meaning of the first two lines, drawn out. In the last line she is identified with the avenging wrath that haunts the house unforgiving and takes vengeance for her child by craft.

That is one use of these heaped-up epithets and figures.
They condense an episode into a word and remind the
reader of aspects of the story which the poet does not
choose to relate at length. The method is somewhat like
that of the vase-painter who tells his story in a kind of
shorthand; a scrap of tree telling us that we have the
story of Sinis, or a necklace that the figures are Amphia-
raus and Eriphyle.

The power of suggesting much by a word is common to
all great poets, but the distinctive quality of Classical
Greek poetry is that it uses the power rather to bring out
and emphasize ideas already implicit in the act or thing
described than to show it in new and unexpected aspects.
Macbeth says:

> and wither'd murder,
> Alarum'd by his sentinel, the wolf,
> Whose howl's his watch, thus with his stealthy pace,
> With Tarquin's ravishing strides, towards his design
> Moves like a ghost.   (II. i. 52–6)

Here we cannot say that Shakespeare is developing ideas
familiar or implicit in the subject. He calls up one image
or association after another, all contributing to the effect
designed, and therefore appropriate, but he is not drawing
out what is implicit; he is throwing upon the theme a
light, in this case a ghastly light, which comes from his
own mind. And when he creates phrases like 'the primrose
way to the everlasting bonfire', one cannot rightly say
what he does. It is in its place, but it comes there by no
process calculable to man. It is as unforeseen as a flash of
lightning in the dark, and the light it casts has the same
mingling of beauty and terror.

With the Greek poet, however bold the language, the
ideas have not this unexpectedness. The figures and
epithets illuminate the object, but they show us the
qualities which we already know to be there. This at least
is the typical Greek way. There are exceptions, such as the
lines:

'Αστέρας εἰσαθρεῖς, 'Αστὴρ ἐμός· εἴθε γενοίμην
οὐρανός, ὡς πολλοῖς ὄμμασιν εἰς σὲ βλέπω.

'Thou gazest on the stars; would I might be
The sky, with many eyes to gaze on thee.'

Here certainly the poet has done something more than
draw out what was implicit in the theme, or at least more
than any other eye would have seen there; there is a thrill
of surprise; but from Plato one expects surprises, and moreover we can see how the idea arises from the play upon
words. Simonides is more typical, and when he writes in
the epitaph of those who fell at Thermopylae

βωμὸς δ' ὁ τάφος πρὸ γόων δὲ
μνᾶστις ὁ δ' οἶκτος ἔπαινος

there is again a sense of surprise and even of illumination,
as we see the tomb of the fallen sanctified as an altar. But
after all the ideas of tomb and altar lie very near together
for the Greek, who habitually made offerings at tombs;
and though the word casts a new light on the theme, it
still shows us something that intrinsically belongs to it,
even if unperceived before. The method is quite distinct
from that of some modern poets who find interest and
beauty less in things themselves (if metaphysicians will
permit the phrase) than in some accidental aspect of them;
therein resembling modern painters.

In fact the difference can best be explained by the
analogy of painting. Greek poetry differs from modern,
the poetry for instance of Mr. de la Mare, much as a portrait by Van Eyck or Holbein differs from a Whistler.
The early painter, like the Greek poet, is concerned to
show us the beauty and significance of the subject painted.
His skill, no doubt, enhances both the beauty and the
significance, but his purpose is to show us what is there.
His colouring and drawing, however delicate or elaborate,
are employed to that end. Most modern painters since
the Impressionists seek to show us not the thing as it is
essentially, but at most some accidental aspect of it. Light

and colour are their theme and the object depicted is
relatively insignificant; the more thorough-going indeed
prefer not to let us know exactly what it is. Members of
still later schools present us not with effects of light or
colour, but with patterns representing the reactions of
their minds to the object discerned; much as one might
represent a storm at sea by depicting a basin. These later
schools vary in detail, and indeed quarrel, but they agree
at least in this that all regard the object depicted as
negligible.

Modern poets have not succeeded quite in keeping pace
with painters. A few have almost done so; but the
majority have not passed beyond the stage of the Impressionists, the stage at which the momentary aspect of
the thing presented is more important than its essential
nature. Greek poetry did not, in spite of occasional
timid excursions, reach even this stage before Alexan-
drine times. Then we find something like it here and there
in the Anthology and the fragments of poets. It would
carry us beyond our scope, however, to consider these.
The typical Greek procedure may better be illustrated by
another passage of Aeschylus, in which the use of language
is slightly different.

In the *Persae* (ll. 610 ff.) Atossa describes the offerings
she has made at the tomb of Darius—we must again
inflict on the reader the horrors of a literal translation—
in these terms: 'milk white and potable of an unsullied
cow, the distillation of the flower-worker, shining honey,
with watery drops from a virgin spring, and the unpol-
luted drink from the wild mother, this brightness of an
aged vine. . .' There is more, but this is enough. At
first sight such a passage seems mere fustian, as indeed the
translation makes it; it provides scope for the parodist and
reminds us of the style of Bottom and his compeers. But
it is all the more instructive for that, because it forces us
to inquire what Aeschylus is doing. For if we know
Aeschylus at all, we can be sure that he has a purpose.
And the purpose is plain enough. In this and similar

passages he is not calling on the innermost strength of his imagination; he is not illuminating the moral or emotional significance of the things described; he merely emphasizes some of their most obvious qualities. And he does this with a frankness that seems naïve, and an elaboration that seems a little absurd. He tells us that milk is white and pleasant to drink, that honey is shiny and is made by bees from flowers, that water is wet, and so on. And these simple truths he clothes in somewhat strained and grandiloquent language, as in the two lines which remind us that wine comes from vines and is wet and bright (γάνος carries both these ideas).

The explanation of this odd procedure is that Aeschylus here is employing the same method as Homer, when he uses standing epithets. He does this not in mere imitation, but because his purpose is the same; to suggest with each object its most salient qualities, no matter how familiar. And he wishes to do this for the same reason; that he is still unsophisticated enough to take delight in the obvious qualities of things. He likes the whiteness and softness of milk, for instance, for its own sake.

This spontaneous delight in things is typical and very significant. Such delight we associate with early poetry; it gives a charm to many things that have little else to recommend them, as to many lyrics and other poems in what is now known as 'Middle English'. We hardly look for that charm in the poetry of epochs more mature; and in modern poetry we seldom find it. It is found in Aeschylus and in other Greek poets of the fifth century, who both in thought and style are mature. We cannot think of Aeschylus and the great Greeks of the fifth century as children; rather we still go to school to them, and wonder at times to find how little of vital importance was hidden from them.

It is this combination of maturity and freshness that makes Greek Literature and Art unique and restorative beyond any other. They have many eminent qualities, but this is perhaps the greatest. It is this that enables us at all times and in all moods to find refreshment in Greek Literature. It refreshes and strengthens by reviving in us the power of seeing the world with uncorrupted eyes, and recognizing again its interest and beauty.

Modern poetry and art stimulate by casting strange lights upon familiar things, or by showing us beauty in unfamiliar places, but the Greeks show us familiar things in clear, diffused light, with no trickery or enchantment of strange tones and shadows, and we perceive them to be beautiful and interesting. By so doing they impart to the mind a clarity and a calm exhilaration which we seldom attain by other means. It is for this most of all that we turn to them.

That Greek Literature and Art have this quality is a familiar experience. The use of language described is, of course, not the only thing which gives it this quality, but it is certainly one cause of it.

In the passages quoted from Aeschylus there are other characteristics less important, but not insignificant. The grandiloquence which amuses the schoolboy is partly personal to Aeschylus, but in part it is characteristic of the tragic dramatists in general and of some other forms of Greek poetry. Pindar, for instance, no less than Aeschylus, is oddly reluctant to call a spade a spade. Even in prose literature we discern a little of the same reluctance. Both Greeks and Romans, as we know from the critics of later times, drew a clearer line than we do between the language of poetry and prose, and the topics appropriate to each. Even in prose some innocent-seeming words are ruled out as undignified because they designate things base and mechanical. The criticisms made on this score are sometimes surprising. *A fortiori* both the language and the topics of verse must be duly elevated, especially in the drama and other forms of poetry associated with religion. The language of tragedy therefore is, like the costume of the actors, in part hieratic. To strip off the trappings in either case would be irreverent. By the aid of them it is possible to introduce, when occasion arises, such common necessary things as spades and shovels, boots and shoes, without loss of dignity.

But this apparently stilted language serves another purpose. It helps to enhance the significance of those common qualities of common things to which it directs attention. When we have read the last-quoted passage of Aeschylus in the Greek, not tortured into unnatural English, our ideas of milk and honey, of wine and olive oil have in fact been enriched and raised. We do not think of them as things that one buys and gets out of a jar or bottle. To be reminded that they are more than that is a real service, and a service greater and more necessary now than ever before. A man who could turn into Aeschylean Greek the catalogue of one of the great Stores would be a benefactor of mankind, or rather of that fraction of mankind that could translate him.

All poets, you may say, have this power. Their business is to show us the significance of things. This is true, but nevertheless the difference is important. It is much more than a difference of technique; it springs from a different attitude towards life. Greek Literature is often sad, but it is with the sadness that springs from love of life, not from distrust of it or weariness. Life is short and beset with dangers, men are feeble and foolish, and their prosperity insecure: these are the grounds of sadness. That life itself was good and the world rich in pleasant things to be enjoyed, if fate were not unkind, few Greeks doubted in the days before the disasters of the Peloponnesian War and of the following century brought disillusion. Even when the poet writes

ἀνθρώπων ὀλίγον μὲν κάρτος ἄπρακτοι δὲ μεληδόνες

'Little is the strength of man and vain are all his pains',

he is not condemning life itself, for in the next line he goes on to say not that it is worthless but that it is full of trouble, πόνος ἀμφὶ πόνῳ.

Even when Aeschylus through the lips of the chorus (if it be the chorus and not Cassandra) in the *Agamemnon* says that human life at the best is but a shadow, and that, when misfortune comes, it is blotted out clean as writing by a sponge (1327–9)—

ἰὼ βρότεια πράγματ'· εὐτυχοῦντα μὲν
σκιά τις ἂν πρέψειεν·[1] εἰ δὲ δυστυχῇ,
βολαῖς ὑγρώσσων σπόγγος ὤλεσεν γραφήν—

it is still the insecurity and brevity of life rather than its intrinsic worthlessness that he has in mind. Life may be insecure and brief and yet worth having. The Greeks as a rule found in its brevity an incentive to use it to the full, and to defeat fate by leaving a μνήμη ἀείμνηστος.

So long as the Greeks retained this conviction that life was good, they found no need to enhance it in art or literature by any search for novelty. Things were good, that is, interesting and beautiful in themselves, and it was enough to show each clearly with the goodness proper to its kind. The 'ideal' character of Greek Art, on which all critics insist, means just this. The dignity of Zeus, the rhythmical grace of an athlete in motion, are qualities proper to the subject, which the artist must express as completely as he can. He idealizes, as we call it, to make his work more truthful, not to make it prettier. If he fails to give the dignity or grace, he has not shown us the thing truly.

The search for novelty of treatment and subject begins in Greek Art and Literature, when the belief in life and the zest of living began to fail, as it did during the fourth century and later. The cause of the change was more than anything else a failure of courage. Some mystics and philosophers long before Plato had taught that the body was a prison and that things material and temporal were only to be valued as a symbol and expression of the eternal. But their followers were an isolated minority. The earlier Greeks knew well enough the perils and pains of life, but they thought life worth the risk. Later on, when they had lost their delight in life, they listened more willingly to

[1] I give Boissonade's reading.

philosophers, Stoic or Epicurean, whose systems were based on mistrust of life, and who taught men that happiness could only be found by detaching themselves from it; not by living, but by arming themselves against the evils of life, as best they could.

In Hellenistic Art we see the change everywhere and in many ways; the changes there, being more concrete, are easier to follow than in literature. We have exaggeration, both of treatment and feeling, sentimentality and theatricality, violent realism; these to some extent are general. In particular schools we have other variations, impressionist treatment of sculpture at Alexandria, anatomical over-emphasis at Rhodes, affectation and archaism at Athens. The search for novelty of subject is equally plain.

These adventitious aids became necessary when life lost its zest; and no art or literature in Western Europe since then has regained the special quality of Greek Art because the combination of maturity and zest has not returned, and hardly can return. Modern poets still show us the beauty or significance of common things; but in a different way. Wordsworth of modern ‘poets most persistently sought to show the beauty and significance of common things, and was at pains to describe them faithfully and in simple language. At times we feel that he delights in them for their own sake, for what they present to the sense. But he values them, we nearly always feel, for what they suggest more than for what they are. When he says that the meanest flower that blows can give him thoughts that lie too deep for tears he is plainly not thinking only of the sensuous qualities of the meanest flower. He, and in their various ways all modern poets, value the outer world not only for itself, but for the ideas it suggests, and colour it with their own thoughts.

By this change modern poetry and modern art have gained much. They can move us more variously and perhaps more profoundly than the Greeks. They see perhaps deeper into the truth, and at times make the simple delight in outward things seem shallow, but for the same reason they are not so tonic and tranquillizing, so independent of our moods. J. S. Mill and others have recorded that Wordsworth had this tranquillizing effect for them; but Wordsworth is not a poet for all readers or for all moods. His mysticism seems to many readers just moonshine, to nearly all readers it seems so in their more cynical moments. The Greek poet escapes this danger: he can hold us in all moods, if we have the power of appreciating him at all. And all can appreciate him whose natural taste has not been corrupted by excess of literary stimulants.

These characteristics of Greek language have more than a literary interest, for in them we see once more the power of tradition. Not only are the poet's themes and the forms and metres appropriate to each kind of poetry controlled by custom more completely than in the literature of modern nations, but even the language is prescribed too. Every scholar knows that particular dialects are appropriated to particular kinds of verse, and though the rules in prose are not so definite, the diction and in some cases the dialect were also more closely regulated by custom than with us. (An amusing instance of this is that Cookery Books must be written in Doric Greek.) We have now seen that the influence of custom goes deeper still. Not only is the dialect and diction prescribed, but the use made of it is in part prescribed, or at least modified, by custom.

Such differences, no doubt, are not quite without parallel even in English literature, to say nothing of French. A difference between the language of prose and verse, for instance, is natural and almost universal. And even in prose the diction naturally varies with the subject. Such differences are prescribed by common sense. But with us such difference stops far short of what we find in Greek; that is in the authors of the classical period. A scholar, faced by a fragment of prose or verse, can scarcely be in doubt for a moment to what kind it belongs. Even in prose there are characteristic differences not only in diction, but in the order of words, in the structure of sentences, and in the rhythm, which distinguish, for example, the historian from the orator. In poetry the differences are more obvious, but in both cases they are worked out more minutely and consistently than such distinctions (when they still existed) were ever worked out in English. In the iambic metre, for example, every scholar can distinguish at once a comic from a tragic line by the rhythm alone, and almost as easily by the diction. The distinction in the latter is so clear that it is a recognized principle of criticism that we cannot take any word or form in the comic poet Aristophanes as necessarily pure Attic until we have examined the context. He normally uses Attic, but if there is any suspicion of parody or mock-heroic in the passage, the word or form may be old Attic, Ionic, Homeric, or what not. It is obvious that his audience followed these distinctions, or the point would be lost.

Parody and mock-heroic are not unknown in our literature and drama, but when they are intended to please the multitude, they are, and must be, of a much cruder and more obvious kind. Our populace can recognize sheer absurdity and extravagance, but it cannot recognize mere departure from a recognized standard of propriety, for it has no standard. Such a standard in literature or drama implies a definite tradition and cannot exist without it. The audience of Aristophanes evidently possessed such a tradition, or they would have missed the fun. Again we are reminded of Greek architecture. Everything there is calculated to a nicety, and to appreciate it fully you must understand those niceties. And the reason in both cases is the same. It is that the artist is guided by tradition not less in the details than in the general plan. The presence of tradition is a commonplace, but we do not recognize its influence fully till we examine the details. Everyone knows that the general plan of a Greek temple follows usually one or other of certain simple types, and can be classified accordingly. It is Doric, or Ionic, 'peripteral', 'dipteral', 'prostyle', 'in antis', and so on, as the case may be.

The student soon discovers that the details and proportions are regulated by tradition even more than the general plan. Certain mouldings, for instance, are felt to be appropriate to one style, or to one part of the building, others to another; and these are usually adhered to. The architect, like the sculptor or the writer of drama, obtains his effects by small modifications of traditional forms, and we must grasp these forms before we can fully understand and enjoy his work.

XIV

EMOTION IN ART AND LITERATURE

THOSE who dislike Greek Art and Literature are accustomed to condemn them with such words as 'lifeless', 'cold', 'conventional', 'unemotional'; those who admire, praise them as 'restrained', 'impersonal', 'ideal', and so on. There must be some ground for these judgements, some real quality which both admirers and detractors have in view; but it is harder to say what this quality is. The very number of the epithets applied—and the list might easily be multiplied—suggests that the matter is not quite simple, that either the critics have not all the same thing in mind, or have not defined it clearly to themselves. More than this a moment's reflection shows that we cannot without reserve apply such epithets to Greek Art and Literature as a whole. In literature especially this is very obvious. The man who finds a lack of emotion in the *Troades* of Euripides, for instance, must be hard to please. And he who is not moved by the Cassandra scene in the *Agamemnon* of Aeschylus as profoundly as by any scene of any drama, must simply be insensitive to such forms of art. Such idiosyncrasy proves nothing. All critics have insensitive spots: Samuel Butler could see nothing in Aeschylus and preferred Handel to Beethoven. The normal and competent reader will admit that in some parts of Greek Literature there is emotion enough, and that it is powerfully expressed. In Art, it is true, emotion is less prominent, but even here there are instances enough to forbid us describing Greek Art universally as unemotional. Even in the metopes of the Parthenon there is at least an attempt to portray emotion in the faces of some of the centaurs.

There is manifestly a real difficulty here. We are all in fact inclined to apply to Greek Art and Literature words which imply a lack of emotion; yet we find that in some forms of both emotion is unmistakably present. We cannot escape from the difficulty by saying that our first impression was wrong, and that when we spoke of Greek Art and Literature as cold and unemotional we overlooked the exceptions; that we ought to have said merely that some forms of both were unemotional. This will not serve, for in fact we feel that the quality we are trying to describe is somehow present even in the works where emotion is strongly expressed. It is in fact a quality of classical Greek work in general.

It might seem best, this being the case, to amend our form of expression and seek for a word which does not so obviously imply absence of emotion. But this will not help us either; for any word we choose will lead to similar contradictions. 'Restrained', for instance is a tempting word, and seems to express the quality we have in mind better than most. But, if we turn again to Greek Tragedy, we perceive that it sets no restraint upon the expression of emotion. If we call Tragedy 'restrained' therefore, we shall be using it in a special and not obvious sense. There is in fact no word for the quality, and it matters little which of the words mentioned is chosen.

Here, as often, the shortest way to clear our minds is to begin by drawing distinctions. First of all we must distinguish between the artist and the spectator. The emotion felt by the artist is clearly distinct from that felt by the spectator, even if the two are connected, which some would deny. Emotion of some kind is always felt by the fitting spectator, for art which does not arouse emotion has failed of its purpose. The nature of the spectator's emotion is one of the most thorny points of aesthetics, and the question must be reserved for the present. All will agree that an emotion of some kind is felt. On the other hand, it is not so obvious that the work of art always expresses emotion, though here again we must distinguish. Many would say that every work of art necessarily expresses an emotion felt by the artist. That again is a difficult point, and must be reserved. It is at least clear that the artist's emotion is distinct from the emotions which

he portrays as inherent in his subject. It would perhaps
be better always to call this last the 'portrayal' of emotion,
not the expression of it, as is often done.

It is further clear that emotion is not equally inherent
in all subjects, in a peaceful landscape and in a battle-
scene; in the Parthenon frieze and in a Gigantomachia; in
a tragedy and in a hymn to Apollo. Of this at least there
is no question. Yet even here there is a caution necessary.
One artist may treat a quiet scene emotionally; another
may treat an emotional theme quietly. We must distinguish between what belongs to the theme and what to the
temperament of the artist.

Having drawn these distinctions, I hope not too tedi-
ously, we are better able to see what is meant by calling
Greek Art and Literature by the various names we have
mentioned. When we call them by these names we are
thinking sometimes of the emotion portrayed, sometimes
of the impression made on the reader or spectator; not so
often of the emotion felt by the artist, though, as we shall
see, that must be considered too.

If we begin with the portrayal of emotion, we must
admit at once that the Greeks in some forms of literature
at any rate portrayed emotion to the utmost limits of
which their skill was capable. We have cited instances
from Aeschylus and Sophocles, but others as pertinent
abound, and Euripides goes even farther. The *Troades*
from beginning to end is an almost unrelieved portrayal of
intense and agonized emotion. We know too that the
Greeks in Tragedy do not shrink from the expression of
grief or physical pain by inarticulate cries. The multitude
and variety of such, οἴμοι, αἰαῖ, ἆ ἆ, ἐή, ὀτοτοτοῖ, and
so on, quite outrun the powers of the English trans-
lator. They perplex and amuse the beginner in Greek, and
they certainly do not suggest to him that Greek Literature
is impassive. The portrayal of emotion is not restricted to
Tragedy. Greek Epic, whenever there is occasion, depicts
it as freely. Homer has scenes of heart-rending pathos, too
familiar to need mention, and his heroes set no limits to

the expression of their grief. Achilles in his anguish at the death of Patroclus tears his hair and grovels on the ground (*Il.* xviii. 26), and Priam does likewise in his mourning for Hector (*Il.* xxii. 414, and xxiv. 165). The poet omits nothing which can lend vividness to his portrayal of emotion. The only restriction is that he refrains from comment. Only very rarely, and then briefly, does he betray his own feelings.

The other forms of poetry offer less scope for the portrayal of emotion. The personal lyric of course *expresses* emotion, but that is a different thing, and must be dealt with separately. In the gnomic poets, too, when emotion is expressed, it is, as in lyric, the poet's own. In the impersonal form of lyric, such as Pindar's Epinikia, there are sometimes opportunities for dramatic portrayal of emotion, and the poet does not shrink from using them, but they are with him a subordinate resource of his art.

When we turn to prose, we find emotion portrayed not infrequently when the subject permits or demands it, as it does in history. Herodótus portrays emotion, when opportunity occurs, vividly enough, if not with the intensity of Homer or the tragedians. He enjoys a dramatic scene, and seizes or invents opportunities for introducing them. He comments, too, without scruple, but rather to point a moral than to indicate his sympathies. He is curious and interested in everything that happens, but, if he feels deeply, he does not show it. Thucydides is more reserved. As a rule he avoids drama, but here and there he gives us a dramatic scene, and can paint intense emotion most effectively, as in the famous picture of the crowd watching the fight in the Great Harbour of Syracuse. But he never betrays his own emotion by a word. He comments, indeed, as a historian must, to explain the motives of his characters, or the significance of their actions. He ever occasionally, as in his note apropos of events in Corcyra or the demoralization produced by the war, implies a moral judgement indirectly, but he never passes judgement directly. Still less does he tell us where his sympathies lie;

though the attentive reader can divine them clearly
enough at times, and perceives that he is in reality anything but indifferent.

Xenophon, on the other hand, though his portrayal of
feeling is less vivid, stands less aloof. His practice varies;
in the *Hellenica* and in the *Anabasis* he is more detached
than in his other works; in the *Memorabilia* he is openly
a partisan. The chief point to notice is that where he is
narrating his own experiences his attitude is usually detached; in things more remote from himself he has less
scruple in displaying emotion.

Of the early philosophers we have so little that it would
be rash to speak positively, but their fragments do not
suggest portrayal of emotion, and they do not write in a
form which would give scope for it. Plato, in adopting the
dramatic form, gave himself more scope, but he uses it
very sparingly. This is consistent with his purpose and
principles. The man who condemned Homer and the
drama for depicting violent emotion, because the contem-
plation of such pictures tends to unmanliness, could hardly
depict violent emotion in his own works. He can consistently and legitimately depict emotion as a warning, or
with a touch of humour, and so he shows us a defeated
Sophist sulking at his defeat, or the unrestrained grief of
Apollodorus in the *Phaedo*; but he never betrays violent
emotion himself or allows his nobler characters to do so.
All his readers have wondered at the divine restraint of
the *Phaedo*.

The orators stand, for our purpose, in a special and
peculiar class. Nominally, and prima facie, they do not
portray emotion, except in an occasional description, but
express it. For the emotions they express are professedly
their own. But on the other hand most of the forensic
speeches extant were written to order. The composer of
the speech is not himself a party to the suit; he composes
it for the man concerned to deliver, since Athenian law
did not usually allow the employment of hired advocates.
So far the composer is playing the part of a dramatist.

He is putting into the mouth of another man the words and the emotions appropriate to his part. But inasmuch as the speaker is supposed to feel the emotions expressed, such a speech counts not as the dramatic portrayal, but as the expression of emotion. It comes between the two; and all the more so, because the emotion itself is sometimes partly fictitious. We can discern from various hints that the Athenian jury expected some display of emotion, and felt slighted if this were not made.

The orators then furnish evidence what degree of emotion an Athenian audience thought it fitting for a man to display in a case where his own interests were at stake. Looking at the matter thus, we notice several things. First we see that Greek taste permitted and encouraged some appeals to emotion, which we should condemn; the production of a man's children to weep for him when his own appeals were insufficient; tears and other displays of emotion on his own part, and a freer use of oaths and adjurations and exclamations than modern English custom sanctions. On the other hand such things are naturally used with more restraint there than in drama, and the practice of individual orators varies. This variety is partly a matter of temperament—Demosthenes is obviously more emotional than Antiphon or Lysias—but it depends also on the period. The more manly and dignified orators at all periods deprecate humiliating displays of emotion, but the standard of restraint was stricter in the fifth century than in the fourth. We can see this by comparing the extant speeches, but the fact is also confirmed by the statements of ancient writers in regard to the style and delivery of orators at different periods. In the fifth century, as one could guess from Antiphon, and—when all allowances for the historian's peculiarities are made—from the speeches of Pericles reported by Thucydides, the style of the orators was restrained and, to our thinking, formal, and the delivery statuesque. Later, as in Demosthenes, the style was obviously less restrained, and we are told that the delivery too was more impassioned and animated.

One reason of this change undoubtedly is social. In the fifth century, till near the close, Athens, in spite of political democracy, was socially aristocratic. Her leading statesmen, before the Peloponnesian War, were aristocrats, and the canons of taste were aristocratic. In the fourth century, as in the present day, public men, and with them orators, if they wished to be influential, must suit their speeches to the taste of the multitude, and the multitude dislikes reticence. On the other hand, it is pertinent to observe that the statuesque and restrained oratory was not ineffective. Pericles, we hear (Ar. *Ach.* 531),

ἤστραπτ᾽, ἐβρόντα, ξυνεκύκα τὴν Ἑλλάδα,

thundered and lightened and turned Greece upside down. He 'beat all other orators by yards', and unlike the rest:

τὸ κέντρον ἐγκατέλιπε τοῖς ἀκροωμένοις,

'he left his sting behind', one of the finest compliments ever paid to an orator (Eupol.: T. Kock, *Comicorum Attic. Fragg.* 94. 7).

These comments are significant, for they show that the older style of oratory, though restrained in form and delivery, was not felt as cold or uninspiring by the audience to which it was addressed. And even if explicit statements were lacking, the influence wielded by Pericles is presumptive evidence that he knew how to hold and move an audience.

The evidence of art does not wholly coincide with that of literature. We have noticed that art occasionally portrays emotion, but the instances are not very numerous or important before the end of the fifth century. Art from early times had displayed violent physical exertion in scenes of combat and in athletic subjects; but physical exertion is hardly emotion, though it may provoke it, and the earlier artists do not often attempt to express it. Indeed the placid faces of figures engaged in deadly combat often produce a grotesque effect in early art. The fifth-century sculptors do not go beyond an effort to remove this grotesqueness by imparting a modicum of appropriate expression to the face, and they often stop short of that. If the works of the great painters survived, our impression would probably be different, for the literary evidence shows that they acquired the power of imparting expression to the face earlier than the sculptors, and made use of it more freely; though it was not till the fourth century that the portrayal of emotion became a leading motive even in painting.

The difference in this point between art and literature is instructive. The popular notion that Greek Art is 'cold' or 'reserved' because the Greeks disapproved of the display of emotion in itself will not hold water. If that were so, they would have banned the portrayal of emotion in literature too. Students of art usually suggest two explanations of the difference. The first is that Greek artists avoided the portrayal of intense emotion not because they disapproved of it, but because they were unable to render it adequately. Sculpture, at any rate, in the fifth century was technically incomplete. The devices by which expression can be imparted to the face had not been explored. The second explanation of the difference which is offered by students of art is that the portrayal of emotion was thought unsuitable to sculpture, though permissible in some forms of literature.

Both these explanations are true, so far as they go, but they are incomplete. It is true that the art of the fifth century had not fully developed its methods of portraying emotion. But art achieves the tasks on which it is most bent. If the Greeks of the fifth century failed to portray emotion, it was because they were chiefly bent on other things. Gothic art even as early as the thirteenth century A.D. succeeds, with technical resources far inferior to those of the Greeks, in imparting emotional life to its figures. In looking at them it is at once apparent that the sculptor has set out to portray, not the outward appearance, but the character and feelings of the person he represents. This aim determines every form and movement of his figures, and in spite of defective anatomy and crudely conventional drapery, he succeeds. His figures are moving and expressive, and the life of them comes unmistakably from within. It is inconceivable that the Greeks, had they desired to achieve the like as earnestly, would have been prevented by technical defects.

There remains the explanation that the Greeks thought emotion unfitting in art, or at least in sculpture. This explanation is expanded in various ways, as by saying that sculpture should be 'monumental' in character; that it should not express what is transient in emotion or movement, because the transient is felt to be in conflict with the solidity and permanence of the material. This again is true, but incomplete. Sculpture at various periods has overstepped these limits, and Greek Art did so occasionally even in the fifth century, and frequently in later days. If it did not do so oftener in the fifth century, there must have been a definite reason. It is shirking the issue to say that they were guided by some heaven-sent instinct. It is even begging the question, for many critics would not admit that their taste in this was sound.

If we seek for further reasons, some obvious ones occur. Greek Art in the fifth century was usually 'monumental' because it was destined for monumental uses, for the adornment of temples or for public monuments. And though it is fantastic to suggest that some instinct told the Greeks that sculpture should be monumental, it is not fantastic to assume that they could perceive that a monument should be monumental. The image of a god erected in his temple, the statue of a priest or priestess or even of a statesman or soldier, dedicated to a god within the temple precincts, naturally did not present violent movement or emotion. Even now, when art has no scruples about depicting emotion, we do not look to find it depicted in a portrait statue. In the statue of an athletic victor on the other hand movement, if not emotion, was natural and permissible, for its purpose was to record the feat rather than the man.

So far, then, the character of art is explained by its purpose, and there is no need to look for reasons more recondite. In the more decorative forms of sculpture, in temple metopes and friezes, even in pediments, violent motion is freely admitted. Scenes of combat are a favourite subject. Though Phidias perhaps was conscious, when he designed the Parthenon sculptures, that quieter subjects were better fitted for a pediment, Greek sculptors in general show no such scruple.

It seems therefore safe to say that the severity of Greek sculpture was due to the nature of its subjects more than to any theoretical objection to the display of emotion. This is not to say that it was accidental. It was no accident that art was chiefly employed in public monuments. Such a use of art was prescribed by the nature of Greek ideas. First, the πόλις overshadowed the individual so far that art, in its more imposing forms, was naturally devoted not to the pleasure or honour of the individual but to the glorification of the state, or of the gods on whom its prosperity depended. Even funeral monuments are restricted during the classical period to modest dimensions, and apparently are not intended as actual portraits of the dead. The glorification of individuals by elaborate tombs, or even the private possession of great works of art, would have suggested ὕβρις and in Athens at least offended democratic sentiment. It is significant that the only Greek recorded to have decorated his house with paintings in the fifth century is Alcibiades, who characteristically caught the painter Agatharchus and confined him in his house till the work was finished; or would have done so, if the painter had not escaped. (Andocides, *c. Alcibiadem* 17.) It is equally significant that pretentious monuments began to appear in the fourth century, though even then they were condemned by public opinion.

This brings us back by another route to the subject of emotion. The same cause which restricted art to public uses affected the character of art. The πόλις was all-important; the virtue or excellence of a man was to be a good citizen. His character, apart from that, was less important, his private feelings and emotions less important still. We have seen, for instance, how in the case of marriage the feelings of the parties to the contract were not considered, but merely the duty to state and family. If we contrast this view of things with that of Medieval Europe, we can understand the difference between Greek and Gothic Art. In Medieval Europe the individual soul and its relation to God is more important than any state. The kings of this world exist to serve the Kingdom of God, and the Pope himself is 'servus servorum Dei'. More than that, the body in comparison with the soul is insignificant. To men who believe such things the soul and its emotions is the supreme interest. It overshadows the state, and the body apart from it is insignificant. If the artist did not portray the soul, he did nothing.

The case of the Greek artist was quite different. As we have seen, he did not oppose body and spirit, and for him the body itself was interesting and beautiful enough. For centuries he was absorbed in its study. This was not merely because of his delight in the visible world. He not only admired the body as beautiful, but felt it to be significant. Not opposing soul to body, and conceiving physical perfection as a necessary part of human excellence, he could express his ideals and aspirations through it better than through anything else. And he could be understood. As Sophocles could express his inmost mind best by perfection of language, so the sculptor by beauty of form.

For a long time this power sufficed him, and he did not turn to other means of expression. It was natural that poetry from the beginning should portray emotion, for the poet can only show the thoughts and feelings of men, not their outward form. That he can only suggest or describe, and the greatest poets are sparing of such descriptions. Moreover the origin and nature of Greek Tragedy demanded and justified the portrayal of strong emotion, for in its earliest forms the action was subordinate to expression of emotion. The business of the chorus was to lament the sorrows of Dionysus, or, if

Professor Ridgeway is right, of the hero at whose tomb they performed. In either case they lament, and enact a mournful theme.

It is, then, clear enough why the expression and portrayal of emotion, while rare and subordinate in the formative arts, is familiar and important in some forms of literature. The cause was in the nature of the two arts themselves, and did not spring from any general ban on such expression.

But this does not exhaust the matter. The impression that Greek Art and Literature are both somehow 'cold' or 'impassive', or whatever the phrase used may be, is not a mere error based on a confusion between art and literature. There really is in both a quality which makes them seem cold to some modern observers. This is the quality we have noticed elsewhere, in speaking of literature, that Greek Art presents things under their normal aspects and in the clear light of day, and does not cast upon them, as modern art so often does, the colours of a mood or fancy which springs from the artist's mind. To many readers and spectators the absence of such colouring seems coldness and lack of feeling. They are wrong, though, as we shall see shortly, not quite wholly wrong. The reader who has followed us so far will know that the Greek did express real feeling in this way. Though content to show things as they normally are, he was not indifferent to their significance; he was an artist, not a scientist.

Some students, again, are disappointed because they do not find in Greek Art and Literature the stimuli to which they are accustomed. They miss sentimentality, if not sensation. To the taste for sentimentality neither art nor literature in the classical period make much concession. They do not hug and cherish emotion as something desirable, but rather regard it as something painful and disturbing. They regard it as Aristotle did when he defined the function of tragedy as the purging away of emotion. And neither art nor literature presents us with what is now known as 'sob-stuff', a name worthy of the thing;

C C

dying children and dear old mothers irrelevantly introduced to draw the automatic tear.

Such devices are unknown to literature before Euripides. He sometimes resorts to both, but uses them,
especially the child motive, a little stiffly. His children
in the *Alcestis*, for instance, are as unnatural as the rare
children of fifth-century sculpture. The child became
a popular subject in later sculpture, when it and literature
both began to exploit the field of sentiment. The modern
who requires sentiment will find it there, though not in
such abundance or so undiluted as he may desire. A spirit
of reserve clung somehow to Greek Art and Literature long
after the classical period. Even Oriental influences could
not quite eradicate it.

We have said that those who still feel in Greek Art and
Literature something cold are not wholly wrong. There is
something lacking beside sentimentality; and the comparison with Gothic art already made suggests what this
is. In activity and subtlety of intellect, in observation and
appreciation of the outer world as well as in artistic gifts,
the Greeks were probably superior to us; but their inner
life was less developed. The simple primary emotions they
felt strongly enough, but their range of feeling, like their
conception of duty, was narrow, and their understanding
so far narrow too. We have seen instances of this in the
case of Greek ideas of love and marriage. The indifference
to many aspects of nature is another.

Again, the Greeks were not interested till late in the
processes of their own minds. The primitive psychology
of Plato and even Aristotle illustrates this. Literature from
quite early times abounds in penetrating observations;
one sometimes feels in reading Homer that he knew some
things that escape our analytic novelists; but when we
analyse these observations, we find that they do not cover
a wide field. The Greeks observed in human nature what
it was of practical importance to know: how a man would
behave as a father, as a friend, as a citizen, and so on. On
such things they had stores of observations and shrewd

maxims. But the inner springs and motives less immediately connected with action, half-conscious instincts and secret dreams, these excited their curiosity less. And they had not discovered the delight of anatomizing the hidden parts of the mind in themselves or others. And not doing this, they were less conscious that such things existed, when they did exist, and attached less importance to them.

And in fact it is probable that these feelings were not present in the same strength and variety as in our minds. The physical instincts must have existed, but the Greeks had not learned to 'sublimate' them so ingeniously. Their conception of love before Plato illustrates this; and to take another instance, the mind of the ordinary Greek was not often disturbed by 'fallings from us, vanishings of sense and outward things'. Such things as these we do not often find in classical Greek Art or Literature; and so far as their presence is a gain, an art without them is the poorer, and moves us less. How much we feel the loss depends on our taste and judgement.

The compensation for this loss is the unclouded view of the world, and the delight in it, and in the powers of man, which we have so often mentioned. That unclouded vision, with the mood of tranquil insight which it induces, is worth much. It also in its kind is an illumination, and when we contrast it only with the wilful phantasmagoria presented by many of the lesser modern artists, we are tempted to think that the Greeks were wholly right; that they had seen the truth and held to it, and that we have given ourselves up to dreams. But, when we compare them with the greatest of the moderns, we perceive that we were wrong; that some things the Greeks neglected are real and will not be ignored. Even in studying an artist so fantastic and arbitrary as Blake we feel that he has here and there pierced deeper into the truth than any Greek could do.

Such things as this justify in part the feeling that

Greek Art is cold. There is another thing that contributes to the impression. We have distinguished from the emotion inherent in the subject the artist's own emotion in regard to it. Part of the artist's emotion, the most unimportant part, the afflatus, the vision of a necessary, predetermined end, a τέλος, which inspires him and guides his hand, this neither he nor anyone else can analyse; as Plato long since discovered. But his feelings about the subject he can, if he chooses, show; for they are simpler and more conscious. He can, if he be moral or pious, emphasize the moral or edifying elements of the subject depicted; he can in various ways underline pathos or prettiness; he can, as some portrait painters and biographers do, indicate his liking or dislike, his admiration or contempt, for his subject; or as other painters do, he can transform everything to his own likeness, or rather to the likeness of his mind and thoughts. All artists, of course, do this in some degree, but if the reader will think of Rubens or of Rembrandt, he will see what is meant. In their works we see the painter as much as the subject.

The Greeks of the classical period did none of these things, or did them no more than they could help. The difference is most easily discovered in literature. We have seen there how the Greek authors in various degrees hold themselves detached from their subject, and how little, compared with most later writers, they betray their sympathies. That Greek Art followed the same method is a commonplace of criticism and needs no illustration. This aloofness, as we saw clearly in the authors mentioned, does not spring from indifference; it is quite distinct from the limitation of feeling last discussed; it is a difference in method. But it also contributes to the disappointment of some modern minds, though it delights others.

There is yet one other cause of the impression of coldness produced by Greek Art, though it is only present in some forms of it. We have seen that neither art nor literature laid any general ban on the expression or portrayal of emotion. But Greek feeling at some times and places did regard unbridled emotion, and still more the outward expression of it in gesture, as undignified and servile. There is no such feeling in Homer, but later it was common, and in the Athens of the fifth century it was very strong. And it is reflected in art. Its presence is more clearly seen then than in the archaic period, to say nothing of later times. Some admirers of Greek Art therefore find the art of the fifth century formal and constrained, and actually prefer to it the more naïve art of the later archaic period. This therefore must be added to the causes of the popular view of Greek Art, for it is not identical with any of the others. On the other hand we must beware of exaggerating its influence. It is not universal, but peculiar to the art of one period, and to later imitations of that. The other causes mentioned are of wider range.

After this somewhat complicated statement a short summary will be useful. Greek Literature and Art in some of their forms both portrayed emotion freely; literature more freely than art. This difference is due in the main to causes inherent in the nature of art itself, not to a greater dislike of emotion on the part of artists. Dislike of strong emotion in itself is limited to a definite period; but the familiarity and greatness of some works of this period has created the false impression that a dislike of emotion is typical of all Greek Art. This impression is strengthened by the fact that the emotions of the Greeks, if intense, were in some respects more limited in scope and less profound than those of some later ages. (It is necessary to add the word 'some', for the statement would not be true of all later ages; hardly of the present age, for instance.)

On the other hand, the Greeks were in general more reserved than we in expressing emotion personal to the writer or artist; and this again helps to create and partly to justify the popular view. They did, however, admit the free expression of personal emotion in one form of literature, and the exception helps to make plainer the principles by which they were guided. The lyric poets, especially those of the Aeolic school which includes Sappho and Alcaeus, express personal emotion quite freely. It is customary in histories of literature to explain this by alluding to the freer life and standards of aristocratic society in Lesbos. This explanation is not false, but it is not the whole reason. Such a society was doubtless favourable to lyric poetry; but, given lyric poetry, the expression of personal emotion follows naturally. For personal emotion is the *raison d'être* of lyric poetry in the proper sense. For convenience, and for want of a better word, we class as lyric poetry the elaborate and relatively impersonal odes of Pindar and Simonides. But these are essentially different, and should in strictness have another name.

The real lyric exists to express personal emotion, and the Greeks permitted it to do so. To have banned emotion in lyric would have been absurd. They did not ban it, and this brings us to a point of some importance. We are accustomed to lay down rules with an absolute 'yes' or 'no'. 'Emotion is dangerous; let us ban it,' we might say; as some say: 'wine is dangerous: let us ban it.' Greek morality, as we have seen, does not rest thus on unqualified imperatives, but on the principles of measure and fitness. Most things are good or bad as time, place, manner, and degree make them so. Personal emotion is appropriate in lyric, less so in other forms of poetry and art.

We can see this principle at work clearly enough. The portrayal of emotion is legitimate in drama, for you can hardly have drama without it. In Greek drama it is doubly legitimate, because tragedy springs from rites of which lamentation was an essential part. This explains why Greek Tragedy in certain points even exceeds the limits usual in modern drama; for instance in the use of κομμοί, formal lamentations in which both actors and chorus take part. Such lamentations were a part of the original rite, and their use is sanctioned and even required by custom ; as lamentation over the dead was required in ordinary funeral rites. In such cases the most extreme expression of emotion is not a breach of the rule of measure, for the occasion calls for it. It is not indecorous. The indecorum would rather be to omit it. Neither the expression of emotion nor anything else is in Greek eyes indecorous, when it is appropriate to the occasion and prescribed by custom. Greek Religion on certain fixed occasions sanctioned words and acts which at other times would have been counted indecent. The actor in tragedy, when he exceeds the ordinary bounds of decorum in the expression of grief, has the same sanction. Where there is not this sanction, emotion except in the Epic is less freely portrayed. The Epic is an exception, for as already noticed, the standard of propriety in Homer is different. In other forms of literature the rule holds good that emotion is portrayed where the subject or the occasion calls for it. We have already noticed instances from the historians and other writers. In them we saw that emotion was portrayed where necessary, but a little more sparingly than by the corresponding modern authors. We now see that this is because the Greeks followed their principles consistently. The historian's business was to narrate events; the portrayal of emotion was incidental. The practice of historians naturally varies with their temperament, but on the whole the proportion of plain and colourless narrative is far larger than in most modern historians. The latter usually try to add some colour and picturesqueness where the Greek is content with a plain and even a dull statement of fact. All beginners are familiar with Xenophon and his parasangs; but the tradition persists later than this. Even the later, rhetorical school of historians admits passages of unadorned narration. Another reason for this practice is the ever-present principle of the mean. The highly-wrought passages are more effective by contrast, when they are reserved for great occasions. This principle is neglected by some modern historians, and other writers. Even the professional purveyors of thrills might remember it with advantage. Even a writer so competent as Mr. Masefield sometimes piles thrill on thrill so closely that the reader's power of sensation is exhausted, and he goes to sleep, as men are said to have gone to sleep on the rack.

It is the same regard for what is appropriate that restricts the display of personal emotion in nearly all forms of literature and art. It helps to explain the aloofness of the historian, for instance. The historian's business is not to tell us his private views and emotions, but to record, among other things, those of other men. Modern historians as a rule display their personal feelings more frankly, and they may be right. Many critics maintain that a frank and sturdy prejudice is a good quality in a historian; that, as all men are really prejudiced, the best historian is he who shows us plainly what his prejudices are. However this may be, the Greeks were consistent with their principles in aiming at impersonal narration.

It would be tedious to show at length how the same principles are manifested in art. We have already noticed some of their results, and the reader can easily trace the connexion for himself. But one point may be noticed, which has only been suggested, and not illustrated; namely that an artist may deal with a quiet subject emotionally, or vice versa. Such a treatment is of course clean contrary to the normal Greek principles. It is not what the occasion demands. Accordingly we can hardly find an example of it in the classical period. But we find it sometimes in the fourth century, and very frequently in the Hellenistic period. The typical Scopasian treatment of the face is a clear instance of it. It is true that Scopas prefers themes which give scope for the expression of emotion, but so far as we can tell, he and his followers appear to have imported emotion into all subjects. In the later period such treatment invaded even the temple statues of the gods, as we see, for instance, in the work of Damophon at Lycosura. A similar treatment of the gods is probable in the fourth century, but the evidence is hardly sufficient to show that it extended to cult statues, and though such treatment is in any case noteworthy, it is less significant in statues not intended for cult. The general prevalence of such emotional treatment is yet one more proof that the breach with earlier Greek ideas was clearly marked by the beginning of the third century. Wherever we turn, we find evidence of that.

XV

MEANING OF WORDS

WE have often had occasion to notice that the words used by the Greeks to denote moral qualities seldom coincide exactly with their nearest equivalents in English. In such cases the difference of meaning is instructive, and it is therefore worth while to consider some of the most important words more fully.

First among such words comes naturally, as having the widest scope, δίκη (*dike*) and its derivatives δίκαιος, δικαιοσύνη, &c. The origin and force of the word *dike* has recently been discussed at length by Professor J. L. Myres in his work on *The Political Ideas of the Greeks*, and we may therefore deal lightly with those political and legal applications of the term, with which he is there chiefly concerned. Our concern is rather with the relation of *dike* to morality; with δικαιοσύνη in fact more than with δίκη.

Every beginner in Greek soon discovers that no single term will cover the various meanings of δίκη, δίκαιος, &c. He finds that *dike* means not only justice, but a trial or lawsuit, and then the result of the trial, the sentence or penalty. Here however the development of ideas is simple, and some English uses, such as 'Courts of Justice', and the phrase 'to exact justice', offer a partial analogy. If he went further, the student would discover other uses of *dike* in Greek which are more puzzling, but the adjective *dikaios* presents the difficulty in a more obvious form. For it is very soon apparent that 'just' and 'unjust' cannot be stretched to cover all the meanings of δίκαιος and ἄδικος. If he sticks to that translation, our student finds that he must call a horse 'just', when it is docile, or a parricide 'unjust', when he kills his father; which seems inadequate. And when Homer talks of wooing 'justly' or says that the Cyclopes were 'unjust', we again feel the words to be unsatisfying. And the case is still plainer when we come to the statement that all virtue (or excellence) is comprised in justice (ἐν δὲ δικαιοσύνῃ συλλήβδην πᾶσ' ἀρετή 'στι, Theogn. 147). Manifestly that maxim would be absurd if *dikaiosune* meant no more than the English 'justice'. We feel this once more when Plato in the *Republic*, desiring to exhibit a pattern of justice, proceeds to develop a system which covers nearly the whole of life, embracing many things which we should not think of as falling within the sphere of justice.

Such instances make it clear that *dikaios* is a word of wider meaning than the English 'just'. *Dike*, in fact, is nearer to 'right' than to 'justice', and justice is only one form of rightness. Unfortunately the word 'right' does not carry us far. It will occasionally serve to translate *dike*, but not often; and we can call an act which is *dikaios* 'right', but English idiom forbids us to call a man who is *dikaios* 'right'. If only we could call a man 'right' as we call his action 'right', that would be the best translation for *dikaios*. We must not do it, but if we wish we could, we have some idea of the meaning of *dikaios*. 'Righteous' and 'righteousness', which suggest themselves as substitutes, unluckily have acquired a theological flavour which is alien to the Greek words.

The origin of these various meanings (various to us, if not to the Greek) is simple enough. All come from the root idea of *dike*, and *dike*, as already noticed, means originally 'the way', and then by an easy transition 'the right way'. How natural the transition is, the English use of the same word shows; we talk of showing a man 'the way' to do this or that. This use implies that there is a recognized way of doing everything, and that this way is right. There is a right way of doing everything and the man who keeps to that way is *dikaios*.

The fundamental and characteristic Greek belief is that there are rules, 'right ways', for everything. The rules, as we have seen elsewhere, are determined by custom, and custom again by various things; by nature, by experience, by the object in view, and so on, as the case may be. In the case of animals δίκη is obviously very near to 'nature'. 'Let dogs delight to bark and bite, for 'tis their *dike* to', an early Greek would have said, though he would not have meant to deny that animals had rules of their own. When an animal is tamed, its *dike* is partly imposed by man with a view to the use required: the *dike* of a horse is to be tractable. And when we come to man and human actions, the end in view is still more important. The *dike* of a builder is to build a good house, and the *dike* of a *polites* is to be a good citizen, because a *polis* is found by experience to be the best way of securing safety and happiness.

But however the forms of δίκη may differ in nature and origin, the essential point is that they are originally conceived as similar and designated by the same word. This was of real importance. If the Greek conception of morality was in one respect narrow, because it rested on isolated rules, on the other hand it was wide, for these rules covered nearly the whole of life. And if it was a defect to regard as similar the rules of an art or profession and the rules which we call moral, it was also a gain. For, if it lowered morality to a kind of art or craft, it raised arts and crafts to the level of a kind of morality. And the fact that all operations were under divine protection and connected with religious rites increased the likeness.

Here many readers will protest that the Greeks cannot have thus confounded morality with mechanics, and that they knew the difference between them as well as we do. This is partly true, but not wholly. The Greeks did not regard a murderer and a bad workman as equally culpable, but they did not distinguish them as sharply as we distinguish between a moral offence and incompetence. Murder, however, is an offence which stands in a special class, for it creates, as we have seen, a μύσος or μίασμα. It will be safer therefore to take something less formidable, say fraud or assault. These to the Greek are breaches of rules and definitely wrong, against the rules, but they are not felt quite as we feel them. They are not so definitely *moral* offences. In a sense they could not be so, for the

Greeks had no word for moral. They had nothing better than δίκαιος and ἄδικος, the words we are discussing. True, they had also καλός and αἰσχρός, 'beautiful' and 'ugly', but these words rather increase the confusion than not. For they are obviously quite as appropriate to works of art and craft as to morality. It is at least probable that the Greeks had no clear conception of a distinction for which they had no word.

This fact may perhaps throw light on some problems which we have discussed elsewhere, such for instance as the unscrupulousness, especially in money matters, betrayed by otherwise decent Greeks. Apart from the conspicuous instances of eminent men, one feels often in reading the orators that some of the actions described are not easy to account for. It is not that they cannot be paralleled in modern law courts, and law courts notoriously exhibit the worst of man; it is that the actors do not always seem to fit the acts. In the extant speeches we seldom meet with the criminal classes. The persons concerned are ordinary citizens; not the best of them doubtless, but still not what we should call criminals; and we get the impression that the average, more or less decent man in Greece was capable of a brutality and unscrupulousness which we should hardly find in the corresponding type to-day.

This difference, as we have already seen, is explained in part by what we have called the tribal nature of morality, the absence of obligation where no special tie exists. But even where there are ties, the respectable Greek can still be unscrupulous or callous in a way that surprises us; and that too in matters that are covered by his code.

In such matters doubtless judgement is difficult, and we cannot rely on isolated instances. When we find, for example, in the orators, frequent instances of dishonest trustees and guardians, we cannot at once conclude that the Greeks were more unscrupulous than we in such matters, for men accounted respectable are sometimes guilty of such offences now. But nevertheless, when we look into the evidence, the conclusion that they were more unscrupulous is justified. For not only are such cases frequent, but we notice the care which the testator takes to remove temptation from the guardian and to secure his honesty. It is evident that the possibility of his proving a rogue was present to the testator's mind. Nowadays in making a will a man usually assumes that he can trust his relatives at least to prove honest as trustees or executors, even though they receive only a nominal recompense for their trouble. That fact is more significant than the number of such cases. And again, the dishonest trustee with us not only risks imprisonment, but, if convicted, he cannot hold up his head again. In the case of the Greeks he normally escapes at worst with restitution of the money misappropriated, and the offence does not appear to carry the same stigma. Doubtless it was not a nice thing to do, but the offender does not become an outcast. And the same holds good with other offences which with us would mean at least loss of caste.

Thus it is not fanciful to suppose that the habit of regarding all offences, except those which carried a definite μίασμα, as simply breaches of the rules at least helped to make the Greeks less scrupulous. Their consciences, if we may use the word, would prick them less. This is not to say that they felt no qualms, and made no distinction between dishonesty and lack of skill or breach of rule in a game;[1] or that no Greek could be trusted altogether. The case was rather that such offences being less odious than with us, the man who could be trusted utterly was the exception.

The same consideration obviously is applicable in other cases, such as the difference in Greek standards of propriety discussed under αἰδώς. An offence which is merely a breach of rules does not evoke the same repugnance or shame as one which is felt to be inherently bad. And, as we have seen, it was only by degrees that the Greeks reached this conception; when the philosophers, for in-

---

[1] ἀδικεῖς is the Greek for ' foul ! '.

stance, explained that wrongdoing (ἀδικία) was an offence against nature, an injury to one's own soul, or a
corruption of the divine in man.

This is one side of the picture. But there is the other,
that morality, if for the moment we may so call *dikaiosune*,
covers the whole of life. Plato, who here is typically
Greek, is seeking in his Ideal State not merely for what we
call justice, but for a right way of life and he finds it in
the principle that every man shall play the part in life for
which he is fitted by nature; and having found that principle he proceeds to regulate the whole of life in accordance with it. Being a Greek he assumes that a standard
of right conduct must cover the whole of life, and that
each part has its appropriate rule of rightness; and, being
a philosopher, he seeks for a rational principle on which to
base his rules. Commentators see, doubtless rightly,
reminiscences of Sparta in his regulations, but in fact
Sparta is only the most conspicuous example of a widespread belief. The idea that right conduct is concerned
with the whole of life, and that it can be reduced to rules
is general. Even at Athens the freer life (ἀνειμένη δίαιτα),
of which Pericles boasts, was regulated in a way which
would be irksome to most men now.

That there is a right way of doing all things is an idea
which has many applications in Greek life. It is common
form, even with scholars, when speaking of the Greeks, to
lay stress on their intellectual and artistic achievements,
but to speak with more diffidence of their moral qualities.
In England, especially, since the days of Matthew Arnold,
it has been customary to contrast the Greeks with the
Hebrews. 'Morality', 'righteousness', 'conduct', whichever name we prefer, is the especial distinction of the
Hebrews, and 'conduct', as Arnold is fond of saying, 'is
three-fourths of life'. The Greeks must be content to
claim the other fraction in which the Hebrews were less
pre-eminent, art and philosophy.

The Greek himself would have regarded the matter
quite differently. He would naturally have disputed the

Hebrew's claim to a moral superiority. He would have said, rightly or wrongly:

These people attach a fantastic importance to certain rules of conduct, but their code, good or bad—and some parts of it are arbitrary and grotesque—only covers a small part of life. They have minute rules of ceremonial, but they neglect things more vital, and lack half the qualities that go to make a civilized man. They lack αἰδώς, and therefore, like other barbarians, are cruel and treacherous. They lack the sense of measure and σωφροσύνη both in thought and act. They are sensual, inordinate in their desires, extravagant and fanatical even in their virtues. They are moreover servile, ἀνδραποδώδεις. They conceive their god as the arbitrary master of slaves, whose caprice is law; and in secular life they have not the qualities that make men free and capable of self-government; they must be governed by a despot, who, to be respected, must be tyrannical as well as benevolent. Accordingly they have no idea of a good life or of the proper excellence of man. They not only are indifferent to the free use of the mind, and enemies of higher arts, ἄμουσοι, but they have no idea of the physical perfection proper to man, and the delight that comes from the use of a well-trained and active body, as of a well-trained mind. Their conception of happiness is the slave's conception; abundance of food and drink and of fine clothing, with idleness and immunity from the rod. Naturally therefore their men are flabby and σκιατραφεῖς, and in women they admire the sensual forms of beauty.

The Greek who said this of the Hebrews would have been partly unjust, for he would have missed some important qualities, but his judgement would be quite clear and unfaltering. He would be clear in his own mind that the Hebrew was a worse man than himself. He would not say exactly that he was less moral, for he had not invented a corresponding word, but he would say without a doubt that the Hebrew fell short of him in ἀρετή, in the excellence proper to man. He would not say, with Matthew Arnold, that the Hebrew, though inferior in intelligence and love of beauty, was more 'righteous' than he, for to him righteousness included these things.

We are accustomed to say, in fact it is a truism, that the Greek aimed at an 'all-round' excellence, that his ideal included the excellence of the intellect and of the body, as well as of the moral faculties. But this is not the Greek way of regarding the matter. To the ordinary Greek the man who is merely 'moral', but with a stunted intellect and undeveloped body, devoid of grace and of the enjoyment of beauty, a type very common now and often admired, is not a good man who lacks certain graces; he is not a good man at all. No doubt good men are rare, he admits it:

ἀνδρ' ἀγαθὸν μὲν ἀλαθέως γενέσθαι
χαλεπόν,

the poet says;[1] but a man must at least aim at completeness. If he has one half of his faculties unused or distorted, he cannot be good, any more than he can be beautiful with a handsome face on a withered body.

Thus the ode of Simonides from which the line last-quoted comes is not base flattery. The Thessalian prince whom he honours, Hiero and the other 'tyrants' whom Pindar honours so often, were not perfect men—both poets indeed imply this—but they were men who had aspired to ἀρετή, to an all-round perfection. Therefore they were by Greek standards so far admirable, more admirable than any man who has specialized in some single form of excellence, even though it be in what we call 'righteousness'.

This point of view is very different from ours; an extreme instance may help to bring it home. When he reads the story of Florence the average man-now will feel that Savonarola, though narrow, is indubitably a good man, and that Lorenzo de' Medici, in spite of some fine and engaging qualities, is not what he would call 'good'. A Greek of the fifth century, and still more of earlier times, would have reversed our verdict. He would not think of calling Savonarola a good man; he would have said at best that his many defects were partly compensated by some good qualities, but that he lacked nearly all the qualities that go to make up the ἀνὴρ ἀγαθός. Above all, he would say, he lacked σωφροσύνη, for no fanatic can

[1] The passage is quoted and discussed in Plato, *Protagoras* 339B–344B.

be σώφρων (sophron). Lorenzo, on the other hand, possessed most of the qualities of the good man. Like Hiero and the other despots celebrated by the Greek poets he had aspired to an all-round excellence. If, like them, he had not wholly achieved it, if he was not 'four-square and without flaw', (τετράγωνος ἄνευ ψόγου τετυγμένος), it was because perfection is impossible to man except by special grace of heaven (θείᾳ μοίρᾳ), and θεία μοῖρα had not assigned to him a path free from overmastering temptations.

There is no doubt that Lorenzo to Greek eyes would seem the better man. And, to go further, if for Lorenzo we substitute Alexander Borgia and compare him with Savonarola, the comparison will not present itself to the Greek quite as it does to most modern readers of the story. To most of them the contrast is plain between the saint and the sinner, to use the mildest word for Alexander. The Greek would be less confident in his verdict. He would not acclaim Alexander as a good man, but he would allow him some admirable qualities; he would not be so much troubled as we are by his proved vices (if we except the more doubtful and darker imputations). Plato indeed might have placed him in Hell among the incurably wicked, but Simonides and Pindar would scarcely have found him worse than some of the tyrants they praised not altogether insincerely. ὕβρις, the besetting sin of tyrants, was not specially conspicuous in him.

The idea of ὕβρις (hubris), which we have just mentioned, is almost as important as *dike* itself, but it may be dismissed more briefly, for though, like *dike*, it has no precise equivalent in English, its meaning is not hard to grasp. We usually translate ὕβρις by 'insolence', and this in some cases is near enough, but the name is applied to many things for which 'insolence' is not the natural term. It covers assault and battery no less than arrogant self-confidence. A gross act of tyranny, for instance, or of impiety or sacrilege is often described as ὕβρις. In fact almost anything which is wrong (ἄδικος) may under cer-

tain circumstances become ὕβρις. Any breach of the
rules prescribed by custom or law is wrong or *adikos*; it
becomes ὕβρις when the breach proceeds from wanton
pride or arrogance. The motive changes the act from
mere ἀδικία to ὕβρις. Thus to knock a man down and
rob him is merely ἀδικία, if the motive is robbery. But
the same actions when due to malice and wantonness (as
in the case described in Demosthenes κατὰ Κόνωνος)
become ὕβρις. Similarly a man who steals from a temple
is guilty of sacrilege and impiety as well as *adikia*, but he
is not guilty of ὕβρις, if his motive is merely gain. On
the other hand a general who deliberately disregards the
omens, a tyrant who subverts, like Cleisthenes of Sicyon,
the established rites of religion, or a man who, like Alcibiades, travesties them in mockery, is guilty of ὕβρις as
well as impiety. It is the wanton and contemptuous
defiance of the rules that regulate a man's relations with
his fellows, or with the gods, that constitutes ὕβρις, whatever the particular rule may be.

In relation to the gods ὕβρις, as we have already seen,
comes very near to the sin of Pride. In that shape especially it is the standing theme of moralists. But it may
take many shapes, some of them strange to our eyes, as
when ascetic chastity or abstention from wine are counted
by popular morality as offences of ὕβρις against Aphrodite
or Dionysus, as the case may be, since the offender pre-
sumes to defy the power of a god. To us such things might
seem unwise, or we might call them a defiance of the
'laws of nature', but few if any of us would call them
mortal sins. And that is what the Greek virtually does
when he calls them ὕβρις. In this he acted reasonably
enough, for he did not distinguish between 'laws of nature'
and laws of God. To him any departure from the safe
middle path prescribed by his principles, whether it be in
the guise of μέτρον or καιρός, or of ὁσία, or what not, might
lead to ὕβρις. Extravagance of any kind was perilous. This
idea is latent in the stories of the giants Otus and Ephialtes
told by Hesiod. Growing, as they did, at super-natural

speed, they were violating the natural order: it was only
to be expected that they should seek accordingly to over-
throw the gods.

The statement that Greek morality is based not on
general principles but on particular rules is subject to
reservations, and the chief reservation is suggested by the
word αἰδώς (aidōs). When rules and custom fail, you can
appeal to this. It is rather a feeling than a principle, and
'a sense of decency' is as near as we can get in English to the
idea it conveys. As early as Homer the idea and the word
(with its derivatives) are firmly established and appear frequently. The ground it covers is familiar to all scholars,
but it is not easy to define, and does not coincide exactly
with that suggested by any English word. In part it
merely reinforces the rules of the accepted code; αἰδώς,
for instance, is due towards the gods, towards one's elders
or superiors. In these cases, and this is perhaps the commonest use, αἰδώς is 'respect' or 'reverence'. But common
too, and perhaps more primitive, is the use which occurs
in the line

αἰδέομαι Τρῶας καὶ Τρῳάδας ἑλκεσιπέπλους (Il. xxii. 105).

Here we can only say 'I feel shame before the men of Troy
and the women of Troy': αἰδώς is nearer to shame than
reverence. At other times it means 'shame' pure and
simple; but shame in a good sense, and therefore often
'modesty', though seldom modesty in the sense most
familiar in English. αἰδώς in fact is the sense of embarrass-
ment that a man feels when he is conscious of being at a
disadvantage, whether as a young man with his elders or
superiors, or because he is conscious that his acts are somehow discreditable. In the latter sense it is in fact the
rudiment of a conscience, and thus supplemented the
defects of the traditional code. Even though you had not
broken any particular rule, you might feel uncomfortable.
Αἰδώς then is closely akin to shame, but the occasions on
which a Greek would feel αἰδώς are often very different

from what the English translation would suggest. The difference comes into sight very clearly in the common word ἀναιδής, literally meaning 'shameless'. The stone which Sisyphus for ever pushes uphill is a λᾶας ἀναιδής; a ruthless and unreasonable stone. That is perhaps the commonest meaning of ἀναιδής, and its derivative ἀναίδεια. They are applied by Greek writers of all epochs not so much to what we should call shameful actions as to brutal or unreasonable conduct. Lack of shame, effrontery, is not ἀναίδεια, but ἀναισχυντία. The man who is ἀναιδής is not so much brazen, indifferent to the opinion of others, as lacking in a restraining sense of decency. He is especially brutal, or cruel, though any lack of such restraint is ἀναίδεια.

αἰδώς, as we have said, is different from 'modesty', though sometimes near to it; and one result of this difference is important for the understanding of Greek life and literature. There is a vulgar belief, already noted in another connexion, that the Greeks and Greek Literature were somewhat immoral. This belief is fundamentally false. The Greek code of morals differed from our own, as we have seen, but they observed it more strictly than we observe ours, and Greek Literature, as compared with modern, may be called almost puritanically austere. It is, in certain departments licensed by custom, indecent, very thoroughly and frankly indecent; but it is not, properly speaking, immoral.

The Old Comedy of Athens illustrates this distinction very clearly. In Comedy indecency is licensed, and indeed expected—it is in part a survival from various primitive practices and ideas—and Aristophanes takes full advantage of this license, and is therefore not always the most edifying reading for the young. But, far from being immoral, he is the champion of morality, as he understands it; the morality of the traditional Greek code. Once we eject from our minds the persistent notion that indecency implies moral laxity, we cannot be in any doubt of this. He persistently attacks immorality. He satirizes the real weaknesses of his countrymen, and the vices which in his opinion make a man a bad citizen; and as we have seen, virtue to the Greek is essentially that which makes men good citizens. He glorifies the virtues of the old code, and has no indulgence for any breach of it. He preaches concord and reasonableness among fellow-citizens, and justice for allies, and even has sympathy with the sufferings of enemies. We may say, if we like, that his code is narrow, we may even say that by our standards it is immoral, but we cannot without absurdity call him an immoral writer. If we do that, we must call all writers who ever lived immoral, for no man escapes the prejudices and errors of his time.

In the original sense of the word Aristophanes is peculiarly a moral writer, for he is the defender of customary morality, of the *mos maiorum*. His attack is nearly always directed against those whom he believes to be a danger to the state, or to be enemies of the received morality. In him the old order defends itself against novel and dangerous ideas. He is therefore quite logical in attacking Euripides and Socrates. Though the points chosen for attack are often frivolous and grotesquely unfair, such as his harping (in *Thesm.* 275–6, *Ra.* 1471–5) on ἡ γλῶσσ᾽ ὀμώμοχ᾽, ἡ δὲ φρὴν ἀνώμοτος (Eur. *Hipp.* 612), and τί δ᾽ αἰσχρόν, ἢν μὴ τοῖσι χρωμένοις δοκῇ; in the case of Euripides, and his travesty of Socrates' views in the *Clouds*, still the indignation is sincere, and even the choice of points has significance. To attack a dramatist for the sentiments he puts in the mouths of his characters is doubtless quite unfair, but it is clear that the phrases he parodies from Euripides shocked the Athenian audience, and this shows that far from being tolerant of immorality, as they conceived it, on the stage, they were shocked by the mere utterance of sentiments they thought immoral. And in the case of Socrates they showed that, however tolerant they were in some ways and however loose in their theology, they had no toleration for any man who was suspected of attacking the points they considered vital.

The severity and unfairness of Aristophanes in the *Clouds*, and still more the actual condemnation of Socrates, surprise those who have hastily ascribed to the Athenians modern ideas of tolerance. They are misled partly by the surprising freedom of Greek thought in some directions, and still more by the error we are now discussing. Because the Greeks were not shocked when we should be, they assume that they were never shocked at all. They impute to them, half unconsciously, an attitude of detached and humorous indifference. But in truth the Athenians of the fifth century—and it is hardly likely that in this they were behind their neighbours in any part of Greece Proper—were very easily shocked. Athens was as censorious as a Cathedral city, and as careful of the proprieties. The Athenian gossips—and Athenians of both sexes liked scandal—would not whisper that so-and-so had been seen with a young woman who is no better than she should be—that was not scandalous enough—but they would whisper with equal satisfaction that his mother was in the greengrocery line, and it is very doubtful if she is a true-born Athenian; or that he is mixed up with these disgusting foreign superstitions; that he associates with these atheistical philosophers, and as for his breeding, well, he does not know how to carry his *himation*; he hurries along the streets like a madman; he never goes to the gymnasia or hunts, to keep himself in condition as a gentleman should, but is flabby and pallid. 'And, my dear boy, what can you expect? He drinks water!'

This list of offences against morals and propriety is drawn from actual instances; any scholar will recognize them. All are mentioned with serious reprobation, and many more offences might be added to the list. The Greek demanded strict observance of those rules of morality and propriety which he recognized, and if he did not always secure observance of them in life, he insisted on it in literature. In modern literature and drama the current code permits a writer to question or attack all the fundamental rules of morality and the tenets of religion. No restriction is imposed except that if he wishes to be indecent in regard to matters of sex, he must place a veil of some sort, a very thin one will now suffice, over his indecency. The Greeks dispensed with this veil, but in return they imposed severer restrictions in other departments. And even impropriety was kept strictly within its accepted field; we find no indecency in Greek Tragedy, which was not licensed ground. In Tragedy there is occasional plainness of speech, but less than in the Old Testament. Compared with that of Shakespeare, Greek Tragedy is almost prudishly correct.

Αἰδώς, then, is not propriety, as we understand it. Even Plato, when he expels the poets from his Ideal State, does not do so because they are improper, but because they teach bad morality and bad theology; and the charge on which he lays most stress is that they make men cowards by depicting heroes as overcome by pain or grief and breaking into lamentation instead of bearing their fate stoically. Seeing how strictly he regulates the lives of his chosen guardians, this is noteworthy. Most modern legislators would expurgate the poets upon very different lines.

But if αἰδώς does not cover all the ground covered by our modern, or rather by nineteenth-century notions of propriety, it does, as suggested above, include correctness of deportment. Not all the offences mentioned above would be breaches of αἰδώς, some are rather breaches of τὸ πρέπον or of σωφροσύνη. A hurried gait, for instance, is an offence against both these, for it is unseemly and undignified, and at the same time the sign of an ill-regulated and excitable mind. In this sense, then, αἰδώς is reinforced and supplemented by kindred ideas, τὸ καλὸν, τὸ πρέπον, τὸ ἐλεύθερον; though the last most often is referred to by stigmatizing its contrary, the ἀνελεύθερον, or ἀνδραποδῶδες, the positive being more familiar in the literal sense. (A similar restriction is seen, and for the same reason, in the use of ἀεικές in Homer.) All of these words may apply either to manners and deportment or

to morality. Τὸ πρέπον naturally relates most often to the
external, but τὸ καλόν, when applied as a criterion is, in
spite of its origin, nearly always moral; and τὸ ἐλεύθεροι
is so more often than not. It, more definitely than the
other words, indicates conduct 'worthy of a gentleman'.
For to a Greek the opposite of a gentleman is a slave;
though in matters of outward deportment, if not in
morals, the rustic, or sometimes the artisan, may furnish
the contrast. But the use of βάναυσος in a disparaging sense
is somewhat late. The true opposite to the gentleman is
the slave, or if the offence be gross enough, the barbarian.
All these ideas help to define the sphere of αἰδώς. They
are distinct from it, but closely connected with it, because an offence against any one of them provokes αἰδώς
in the offender. The fact that both apply equally to
morality and to external deportment need not be discussed at length. The Greek habit of applying 'aesthetic'
standards to conduct has been mentioned by every writer
upon Greek life, and its importance has more often been
exaggerated than ignored.
    Another aspect of the matter, to which we have al-
luded already, though hardly novel, is somewhat less
trite: namely, that αἰδώς and these complementary ideas
help in the popular morality of Greece to fill in the gap
which is left by their somewhat confined circle of particular duties. In the moral sphere αἰδώς is supplemented
by other qualities not strictly included in the rigid list;
by οἶκτος and ἔλεος, compassion and mercy. These were
qualities on which the Greek, especially the Athenian,
prided himself, but, as already noticed, he did not always
live up to them. Like ἀνδραγαθία, when used in the
special sense of 'generosity', they were, so to speak, extras,
or works of supererogation. The verb ἀνδραγαθίζεσθαι can
be used disparagingly to convey a reproach something
like that conveyed by the offensive word 'high-brow', suggesting that a man claims to be governed by higher
motives than his fellows.
    One reason for this difference of attitude is that Greek

morality, originating as it did, was naturally self-regarding, and remains so to the end. Even when Socrates argues that it is better to suffer than to inflict wrong, it is because the wrongdoer injures his own soul. Even the Stoics, though they broke through the traditional limits and affirmed the natural equality of men, did not go beyond this. That happiness could be better attained by the disinterested love of one's neighbour than by the most enlightened love of self was a discovery the Greeks had not made. The idea that such a principle could be made the basis of morality was still more remote from them. They did more and more recognize that morality should include regard for the rights of others, but they never thought of using that principle as a foundation; it was rather the pinnacle of the building, easily impaired and not indispensable.

Hence there is no word in Greek for 'selfishness' or 'unselfishness'. And it is significant that while 'selfishness' can be partly expressed by πλεονεξία, for 'unselfishness' there is nothing at all. Unselfishness was not a virtue. Justice might forbid you, if you were scrupulous, from claiming more than your share, which is πλεονεξία, but not to assert your rights to the full was a sign of weakness, μαλακία, and want of spirit. ἀνδρεία, which is the opposite of μαλακία, is usually translated by 'courage' or 'fortitude', but it includes more than either of these words. It includes manly spirit and energy, and a man is not truly ἀνδρεῖος unless he shows such spirit in defence of his rights.

Finally we may notice another point in which the Greek αἰδώς differs from one of its English equivalents, 'honour'. We still speak sometimes of 'honour' in matters of business, and count the unscrupulous man as dishonourable. But αἰδώς with the Greek does not extend to business dealings. The dishonest or unscrupulous man is ἄδικος, but not ἀναιδής. He only becomes ἀναιδής if his greed for gain leads him into other offences, such as oppression, or the breach of natural ties. But then another principle is involved. The fact that the sense of shame, or as we should say, of honour, had not extended to such things, or at least not far enough to affect language, may help to explain the shortcomings of the Greeks in this point.

The two words ἱερός and ὅσιος present an anomaly in their use which is familiar to all scholars. When used separately ἱερός is normally 'sacred', and ὅσιος 'holy'. But when combined ἱερός and ὅσιος stand respectively for 'sacred' and 'profane'. The explanation of this apparent difference of meaning in the case of ὅσιος is not far to seek, and anthropology provides the clue. It is pretty clear that ἱερός originally applies to those things or persons which possess what anthropologists know as *mana*, a mysterious, undefined potency for good or evil which makes them dangerous to approach or handle. Such things according to primitive and widespread custom, are *tabu*. They must either be avoided, or approached with special precautions. In societies more advanced the things once *tabu* become what we call sacred. The *mana* in them becomes sanctity; and they now possess sanctity as belonging to some god. They still retain something of their dangerous quality. Some sacred objects may not be exhibited at all to the vulgar, and purification of some kind is usually required before acts of worship, or before entering a temple; and like things *tabu* certain temples and certain rites are definitely forbidden to certain classes of persons. That this was the history of the word ἱερός appears plainly enough from its use in Greek. In Homer all kinds of objects and living things (fish for instance) which we find it difficult to call sacred, and which do not appear to be under the protection of any particular god, are called ἱερός. If we think of them not as 'sacred', but as possessing *mana*, this use becomes quite intelligible. Needless to say the word in Homer is already taking on its later meaning of 'sacred', and the other use is a survival. If the conjecture which connects ἱερός with a root which means 'power' or 'force' is correct, this further supports our explanation. If ἱερός then denotes originally what is *tabu*, ὅσιος denotes those things which are not *tabu*, the things which it is safe to approach, the acts which it is safe to perform. As *tabu* develops into 'sacred', so that which is not *tabu* becomes 'clean' or lawful. It is generally supposed, for instance, that the animals which are marked as 'clean' or 'unclean' by the Mosaic and by the Mohammadan codes were originally distinguished for this reason. In their case the thing originally *tabu* sometimes becomes not sacred, but unclean. The reason for this is that some at least of such things were by the time of the law-giver associated with the worship of false gods, and so unclean to the monotheist. In a polytheistic society they more often became sacred, though some remained *tabu* to certain persons or on certain occasions. The thing which is not *tabu* becomes, as we have said, clean or lawful, and this character is expressed in Greek by ὅσιος. And the idea of ὅσιος, when applied to persons or acts, develops to something which we translate as 'righteous' or 'holy'. But it is important to notice that neither translation is strictly accurate, for the idea conveyed by ὅσιος to the Greek remains essentially negative. A thing is ὅσιος when it is safe and permissible, when it involves no danger of pollution or other evil. Even when Ὁσία is personified by a poet, as when she is made the subject of an ode by Euripides (*Bacchae*, 370), it is not the spirit of holiness that he celebrates, it is rather the spirit of prudence and sobriety that avoids offence, and keeps the safe path of the mean. The same sense appears in the phrase ὁσίας ἕνεκα, which means not 'for love of righteousness', but 'to avoid all possible risk', almost, though not quite, 'for form's sake'.

As in the case of δίκαιος, it would be foolish to press the point too far, and pretend that to the Greeks ὅσιος and its derivatives never suggested anything more than mere freedom from risk of pollution. Something of a higher sense is sometimes visible. But nevertheless it is not and never became a real equivalent of 'holy', and in studying Greek Religion it is often important to bear that in mind.

EPILOGUE

IT is probable that a reader who has followed us so far will have been tempted more than once to complain that the picture we have drawn of the ancient Greeks is out of perspective; that the objects in the background are too big and receive all the high lights while the foreground is left dim and insignificant. This criticism would be just, if this were meant as a picture of ancient Greece. But it is something much humbler than a picture; it is rather a handful of sketches of some objects, or aspects of them, which have been overlooked or neglected by the greater masters. The student who wishes for a complete and well-balanced picture must go to them.

Nevertheless it may be useful to notice one or two of the more obvious difficulties. Most readers will probably feel that we have throughout exaggerated the influence of tradition. Tradition, it may be said, is strong in all early societies; the distinction of the Greeks is that they were less cramped by tradition than any race before. This may be true, but none the less it is necessary to lay stress on the power of tradition. For unless this is done, the student, constantly told to admire the Greek for his freedom of thought and manners, usually, unless warned, pictures him as resembling a modern European, and goes astray accordingly in ways that we have seen.

Again the study of tradition in the case of ancient Greece brings to light another point worth noting. We habitually and instinctively speak and think of the Greeks or others, as the case may be, casting off the 'trammels' of tradition. It is therefore well worth noting that in the case of the Greeks these supposed trammels seem to have acted more often as an aid and support than as a hindrance. It is quite certain for instance that Greek Art and Literature, as we know them, would not have existed without tradition, and that when that tradition lost its hold, Greek art and literature lost their distinctive quality. Any one who looks with an unprejudiced eye on the Hellenistic sculpture of the third century B.C. or later, any one who reads Theocritus or Apollonius Rhodius, will find himself in the presence of a new thing. We are sometimes told that we must not call the work of the Hellenistic Greeks 'decadent', seeing the variety and brilliance of its achievements. That is a matter of opinion; but we may at least say that their work, whether decadent or not, is no longer Greek in spirit.

This difference is not always apparent, for there is often a close imitation of earlier forms, especially in some kinds of sculpture; but in many cases it is obvious. In looking at the most characteristic work of the Hellenistic period we are reminded, if we have eyes, of many schools and periods, of Renaissance Italy, of Japan, of modern 'Impressionism', of Rococo; but seldom, except in externals, of Classical Greece. And when the Hellenistic writer or artist imitates earlier work, as he often does, he imitates it as a modern artist might, or as the Romans did. He is not expressing his own life in the form natural to him, but borrowing a form ready-made. He is a little nearer to the tradition than we are, but he already stands outside it. If the reader wishes to convince himself of this, let him study the illustrations in any good work on Hellenistic or Greco-Roman art.

The mere fact that classical Greek work differs from Hellenistic does not in itself prove that it owes anything to tradition. Both might conceivably be as experimental and unfixed as modern European art. The proof is rather that classical work shows the definite and consistent character which marks a traditional art, while in the later work we see the fluidity and mixture of tendencies which belong to an art without a fixed tradition, or, what comes to the same thing, a tradition that is outworn.

There is another point which has hardly emerged so clearly as it should from these disjointed pages. We have seen the Greek doctrine of the 'Right Way' illustrated again and again in Greek life, but we have not dwelt on one important side of it. The Greek not only believed that there was a right way in all things, but he had a clear notion what that way was, and set himself to follow it consistently and intelligently. It was this not least which enabled him to perform what he did. Few nations, if any, and certainly none in modern Europe, have had aims so clearly defined, or pursued them so consistently. This clearness and consistency of aim is exhibited in many forms; of which the polity of Sparta is perhaps the most conspicuous. Sparta knew exactly what she wished her citizens to be and trained them accordingly. But the polity of democratic Athens, and of other states in Greece, was directed almost as consistently to a definite ideal, and such far-reaching schemes as the *Republic* of Plato exhibit the same turn of mind. The aim in all these cases, being human, was limited and defective, and when Sparta decayed and Greece decayed, the decay was due to these defects as well as to external causes. But, in spite of limitations, the Greeks had discovered a way which led to a modest happiness and to many shining virtues.

This clearness of aim, we may note, helps to explain the bitterness of party-spirit and of quarrels between states. Parties and states stood for different ideals and they were too clearly conscious of that to submit readily to compromise. This is one unfortunate result of thinking clearly. Yet, in spite of it the results of the Greek method show that it has some advantages over the modern English one of thinking confusedly and therefore compromising freely.

INDEX